intrigue of truly trusting God are inspiring for developing our own path of faith. Dr. Lee also presents effective questions in guiding us to seek and examine ways to grow our connection with Christ and to rest in His faithfulness."

Babs Rymer, Chair, Mid-South Teen Challenge, Chattanooga, Tenn.

❧

"This book, a dream of Jimmy Ray Lee, is a masterpiece. *Faithful, No Matter What* comes right out of his life, and Jimmy readily identifies this in others. When you pick up this book you will not be able to put it down. I was thrilled to read of these humble giants of God. May you be blessed as I have been. I am honored to endorse this great book."

Ken Johnson, Founder/President, Christian Network Team (CNT), Finlayson, Minn.

❧

"Have you ever wondered why so much of the Bible is biographical? It's obvious to even the casual reader that its pages are permeated with the stories of real people. It's clear the Holy Spirit loves to teach us from the lives of others. You see, the Word becomes flesh through people. This book you hold in your hands by my friend, Dr. Jimmy Lee, is a significant book. Read it, enjoy it, and be inspired by it. Then pass it along to a friend. They will thank you."

Dr. Tom Lindberg, Lead Pastor, First Assembly Memphis, Memphis, Tenn.

❧

"This book immediately brings to mind Revelation 2:11:'*Our brothers conquered him (Satan) by the blood of the lamb and by the word of their testimony, for they did not cling to their lives even in the face of death.*'A faithful life is possible only by the blood of the Lamb, and it is the testimony of lives that have made an enduring difference in this world that counters the devil's efforts to neutralize Christianity. Given the increasing indifference, and even hostility, to Jesus in our culture, this book will be a powerful weapon of the Holy Spirit. It will serve as an inspiring book of devotions to introduce Bible studies, bedtime stories for children, sermon illustrations, and daily testimonies that stir the heart to be more than a hearer of the Word."

Dr. Don Miles, Pastor, Psychologist, Denver, Colo.

"For 24 years I have seen the author live his life as a testimony as to how God is faithful to those who trust him. Jimmy Lee learned these principles from his father and now, through sharing his testimony and the testimonies of many faithful friends, we can be encouraged and inspired to trust God even more. Everyone should read this book."

Dan Strickland, President, Living Free, Chattanooga, Tenn.

FAITHFUL, NO MATTER WHAT

Amazing Stories of God's Presence in Any and Every Circumstance

Dr. Jimmy Ray Lee

ISBN: 153700610X
ISBN 13: 9781537006109
Library of Congress Control Number: 2016913289
CreateSpace Independent Publishing Platform
North Charleston, South Carolina

"The Lord is righteous in all his ways and faithful in all he does. The Lord is near to all who call on him, to all who call on him in truth."

(Psalm 145:17-18)

TABLE OF CONTENTS

INTRODUCTION

I am blessed to have had a great role model in my life. My father, Charles O. Lee (1915-2007), served as the inspiration for this book. Simply put, he was faithful – faithful to God, to his calling from God, to his family, and to the churches he served. As a child, I could see that he was a faithful man, and as I became an adult I could see that he had remained faithful throughout his life.

He never pastored a large congregation; generally they were 150 people or less. It seems he was never high or low, but consistent in his walk with Jesus. He spent much time studying the Bible and was often referred to as a "walking Bible." When I was a young minister, instead of going to a concordance or dictionary, I would often call Daddy to ask for his help in finding a verse and its meaning.

On one occasion as a child I went with Daddy to haul wood in a borrowed truck. We started home with the truck loaded with wood, but at the bottom of a hill we got stuck in mud. He could not get the truck to climb up the hill. I suggested that we pray. Daddy draped himself over the hood of the truck and prayed that God would move the truck. After he prayed, he started the engine, the truck came alive with a loud VROOM!, and it climbed right up the hill. He later quipped, "When I drove that truck, it drove like a Chevy. After we prayed, it climbed up that hill like a Ford."

I was so influenced by my father that I actually cried when he was not elected President of the U.S.A. in the 1952 election, which was won by Dwight D. Eisenhower. I didn't understand the election process, but just knew my father would have made a great President.

When my father went to guest preach at a small country church in Tennessee to possibly become their pastor, I (then a five-year-old child) stood by his side on the platform as he preached. Without words, I was saying, "This is a great man. Vote for him." He did become the pastor at that little Mt. Zion church.

Although he was not a well-known preacher, the central theme exhibited in Charles O. Lee's life was faithfulness. I remember walking a mile with my father, trekking through muddy conditions to visit and pray for a woman in the church who was dying. God healed her and she proceeded to live a fruitful life.

On another occasion I was with him as he was visiting another lady on her deathbed. I heard her say, "Brother Lee, the angels have come and left a beautiful bouquet of flowers over there in the corner. Aren't they beautiful?" I looked and did not see the flowers, but to this day, I believe the angels visited this lady. She died a short time after our visit. The Scripture says, "Do not forget to entertain strangers, for by so doing some people have entertained angels without knowing it" (Hebrews 13:2).

On his last day on this earth, we continued to see my father's faithfulness reflected by the influence he had on family members who had gathered around his bed. He seemed to be struggling to hold onto this life. The lady from hospice suggested that I talk to Mama, who was in the back part of the house at that time, about releasing Daddy to Jesus. Reluctantly she released him. She was ready to let him go to meet his Lord face to face.

I went back into Daddy's room, many family members assembled around the bed, and spoke to him. I said, "We the family love you and want you to know that it's okay for you to go on to heaven. I've just talked to Mama, and she said it was okay. I also want you to know that we will take care of Mama." We could see a sense of calmness come over him, and he died within 10 minutes.

As we listened to my father's final breath, my brother, Sammy, immediately declared with emotion and authority, "That's it, he's there!" We were claiming the promise from the Scriptures, "We are confident, I say, and willing rather to be absent from the body, and to be present with the Lord" (2 Corinthians 5:8, KJV). To the very end, Charles O. Lee, the most inspiring man I've ever known, was being faithful to his wife, our mother.

My father's entire life was a journey characterized by faithfulness. He was faithful to God – and God was faithful to him. I have seen over and over again, through my father's life, my own, and the lives of many other people I've had the privilege to know, God's faithfulness manifests itself through our journey. As we are assured in the Scriptures, even when "we are faithless, he will remain faithful" (2 Timothy 2:13).

In his commentary on Psalm 25, noted pastor James Montgomery Boice says, "Psalm 25 is great…. It is a thoughtful prayer by one who knows that the only adequate foundation for any worthwhile life is God" (*Psalms, Volume I*, page 222).

King David in Psalm 25 has written a prayer for instruction that provides a wonderful guide for a life of faithfulness. He says, "Show me Your ways, O Lord, teach me Your paths. Guide me in Your truth and teach me, for You are God, my Savior" (verses 4-5).

Notice the action verbs David uses: "show me…teach me…guide me," and then, "teach me" again. One of the main themes of God's faithfulness is His trustworthiness in any and every circumstance. As Mother Teresa said, "I do not pray for success, I ask for faithfulness." Pastor Maury Davis, one of the contributing authors in this book, says, "Faithfulness is the root of the fruit."

In a broadcast interview with Dr. Billy Graham, commentator Shawn Hannity asked him, "How do you want people to remember you?" The Rev. Graham said, "I want people to remember me that I was faithful – faithful to the gospel, faithful to the call that God gave me" (Foxnews.com, June 27, 2005).

"Every time you see a rainbow, remember that God is faithful – He keeps His promises. Every time you pick up a Bible, remember that He said, 'Heaven and earth shall pass away, but My words shall not pass away' (Matthew 24:35)" (https://www.barberville.net/sermon112.htm).

In his beautiful psalm, King David wrote, "My eyes are ever on the LORD, for only He will release my feet from the snare" (Psalm 25:15). Walking with our eyes focused on the Lord keeps us on the path He has planned for us. But it doesn't stop there. It helps us look to Him to free us from snares that threaten to entrap and entangle. He protects from the unknown. We can walk into the days to come with faith in our faithful God instead of freaking out. David admonishes us, "Fear the LORD, you His saints, for those who fear Him lack nothing" (Psalm 34:9).

We can move forward in full assurance that, "The faithfulness of the LORD endures forever" (Psalm 117:2). We can be comforted by Psalm 48:14, "For this God is our God forever and ever; He will be our guide even to the end." As Don Finto, another of this book's contributing authors, says, "Let us stay riveted to Jesus."

In this book we offer a diverse collection of inspiring, heartwarming and sometimes very unusual stories of people who share some of their experiences of God's faithfulness. The authors of these enriching accounts come from many walks of life. Some are pastors; some are missionaries, and some are people whose "full-time Christian service" has taken place in the so-called secular world. But regardless of their unique callings in life, they all point to a faithful, unfailing God whose desire for us is to strive to be faithful to Him. The Lord is not a respecter of persons, and as the old song, "It Is No Secret," reminds us, "what He has done for others He will do for you."

Dr. Jimmy Ray Lee
   Chattanooga, Tennessee
   July 2016

1

A MARRIAGE MADE IN HEAVEN

By Peter Herschend

ete Herschend has devoted his professional life to the family business, which includes owning and operating Silver Dollar City in Branson, Missouri, as well as Dollywood, a partnership with Dolly Parton in Pigeon Forge, Tennessee, and Stone Mountain, Georgia. He served the parent company, Herschend, as Executive Vice President of Marketing and Vice-Chairman. His innovative spirit and unselfish persistence contributed greatly to the businesses and communities and set a clear standard for today's leaders. He earned his business degree from the University of Missouri-Columbia and is active in numerous church, community and educational organizations, most notably serving three terms on the Missouri State Board of Education including two terms as board President.

Sometimes God is working in your life and you do not even know God. Sometimes His hand touches you long before you are ready to acknowledge that Jesus Christ lived and died and lives again – and that is my story. It is really the story of my brother, Jack, and of myself, as well as the story of our company. It is the story of our growth: Who we were, and who we are today, and who we will become. It is not a business story, but it definitely involves the business.

Jack and I were raised in a good home, but not a strong Christian home. When we talk about it today, we struggle to remember if God or Christ was an acknowledged part of our upbringing. That does not mean unacknowledged. That is not to say we were walking away from it, or that we were taught the things of God were not good. There was none of that. In our home God was neutral.

Our parents sent us to Sunday school. I can clearly remember one of the most miserable times in my life was Sunday school. I am not quite sure what brand of church we went to, but that is immaterial. But these doting old women (remember I was 10 at the time, so someone could be 30 and be an old woman to me), they would come and we would sit at little round tables with hard, hard chairs.

There would be five of us – the daughter of the old woman, who always had a hat on (I can remember the hat but not the names of many of them), and four guys. All I really wanted to do was get outside and play. I had zero interest, but Mom and Dad wanted us to be there. My brother, Jack, has the same memory. But I cannot tell you a thing that I learned. Maybe we did learn something, but I am just telling you from my standpoint.

Our life kind of proceeded along that line. I started attending church when we came to Missouri in 1950, going to the local Presbyterian church. There was a really, really good reason for that. Her name was DeeAnn, and I was enamored of her at that time. She was my age and we remain good friends today. But at that time nothing spiritual rubbed off on me while going to church.

I was there, you might say, because of the "fumes." Let me explain: One of my grandsons is in Boy Scouts right now, and his dad and I have been working hard to get him to be an Eagle Scout. One day the scoutmaster said, "Yes, that is really, really important and we need to do that before the 'fumes' set in." I said, "Fumes?" He replied, "Yes. There are two of them. There are gas fumes and perfumes." That applies to where I was in attending that church in Missouri – I was struck with perfume. I was perfectly happy to be in church when DeeAnn was there, and when she was not there, I definitely preferred not to be in church.

It continued that way for me, although I was not antagonistic. I was just neutral. Christ was not in my life. Nor was he in my brother's life. I went to the University of Missouri and graduated from there. While there I was elected president of the Presbyterian Student Center, which was an interesting situation because I was neither Presbyterian nor a Christian, but there I was. The "fumes" worked there too. They were coming from a different lady, but the fumes were effective none the less. And my brother, Jack, was riding roughly parallel with me in neutral, non-allegiance to the Lord. Not antagonistic, not against Him. But not for Him either.

Then two things happened about the same time. First, early in the days of Silver Dollar City, our first two years in operation in 1960 and 1961, Jack and I made a base decision that we wanted to run our company as though it were a publicly held corporation for business reasons. Second, in 1967 an Episcopal priest, Dennis Bennett, was in the neighboring town of Springfield, Missouri, and we were invited to a friend's house where Dennis was talking. If you have ever been around Dennis Bennett or listened to any of his recordings, he doesn't just talk – he brings the Spirit of our Lord into the room.

Both Jack and I made a commitment to Jesus that night. That changed our lives, both individually and as brothers and business partners. We effectively married Jesus Christ into our life and our company. That has become our story ever since, and it's important. Soon we decided that in addition to running a business – it's a big business now, we are up to 11,000 employees – Christ-centered would be in the stockholders' written objectives. To this day we only have three objectives: 1) profit, 2) being a great place for great people to work, and 3) operating the business in a Christ-centered way that is pleasing and honoring to the Lord Jesus Christ.

It is that last point that has become the umbrella of consideration for how we operate our business. And today we are not only in Missouri, but also Tennessee (Dollywood in Pigeon Forge) and Georgia (Stone Mountain, just outside of Atlanta). We are engaged in running a business to the best of our ability, and we sometimes make mistakes, but we always come back to the screening test. Are we operating our businesses in a way that pleases and honors the Lord?

Essentially with any new operation that we put in – whether it is a food service or a new attraction for kids – we have to put gas in the tank, and that is called making a profit. We have to know that it will enhance the overall revenue and continues to make Silver Dollar City, Dollywood, Stone Mountain or wherever we are a greater place for great people to work. Those are important statements. It has to pass that screening question: Would it be pleasing to Christ?

A lot of business people come to us and tell us we ought to serve beer. I suspect they are right, as far as making money. Except in our case, they are wrong. Not because I am against those who drink. But it would be unnecessarily offensive in the sense of disappointing too many people who want to bring their kids to a place where they know they are not going to have to deal with somebody who has had too much beer. Or people who come there just to have a beer and not to enjoy our facilities. So we don't do it.

We have over the years talked about putting in certain shows that ultimately we have decided no. We felt they were not right because they did not honor Christ in the way we think it should be done. Are we absolutely, always correct? No, I promise you that we are not. But we strive. Striving is a good word by the way. Always striving, trying to get there.

So, that decision in 1961 to run our family business as if it were publicly held, the change in our lives in 1967, and the marrying of those two decisions has become the genesis of hundreds and hundreds of people who come to Silver Dollar City, Dollywood or another of our properties, and in the process came to know the Lord. Each spring we do an event called "Young Christian's Weekend." As the name implies, it includes church youth groups from probably a 200-mile radius, with 14,000-16,000 kids over the weekend. They don't just come for the rides; they also come to seminars. We have some 5-6 seminars that require reservations to get in, but there is no charge. We do a mass celebration Saturday night and Sunday morning with about 5,000 kids at a time. Big stuff.

I cannot tell you how many youth leaders who have contacted us afterward, but it measures in dozens and dozens, who said they had kids in their group that came with the group for social and not spiritual reasons; young people who had never really accepted the Lord, but at Silver Dollar City or on the bus going home, they accepted Christ into their life.

We have been faithful to marrying Jesus into the business for 65 years. If you went into our corporate headquarters and spoke to our CEO, and asked what the corporate objectives were, I promise he would give you the three that I have already mentioned.

The three objectives really are simple and straight-forward: To be a Christ-centered, Christ-honoring business; a great place for great people to work; and financially experiencing a three-year rolling average rate of return on the invested dollars. We tell the company what kind of a profit to get – the rate of return. There is always a tension between those three, because all three are important if we are to succeed as a business that honors God, serves people, and remains fiscally sound.

If I were talking to a young pastor or a young businessperson just starting out that wants to make an impact in this culture today, I would say this: Learn to listen very carefully to what people are saying. Not just the surface stuff. Be a classic listener to your customer. Then inquire when you don't understand. You don't do this just in one-hour sessions with members of your church or business. Listen first, then formulate your program.

I would say, "It's your job, young pastor or young businessperson, to put it together. It is not the people's job to put it together. It is your job. But it isn't your program. You have to build a program that will be valuable to them, their program. Pay attention to where their heads and hearts are."

Bringing It Home

Peter Herschend is quick to point to his personal relationship with Jesus Christ. Building on that relationship, he and his brother, Jack, have built a business that consistently strives to glorify our Savior. Their success can be seen in their goal of remaining anchored to Jesus Christ, having Him as the foundation. As he says, although they haven't been perfect and haven't always been right, they have been faithful to marry Jesus into their business for 65 years.

In what ways have you married Jesus into your life goals? Have you ever made this a serious consideration in your planning, both personally and in your work and ministry? Explain what this means for you.

How do you see this marriage of Christ and business contributing to the Herschend's long-time success? Where does God's faithfulness fit into the equation, in your opinion?

2

SENDING A DEPUTY TO FEED THE HUNGRY

By Dr. Jimmy Ray Lee

*D*r. *Jimmy Ray Lee is the founder and president emeritus of Turning Point Ministries, Inc. (now known as Living Free). He is the founder and honorary chairman of Project 714 (now known as National Center for Youth Issues), a chemical prevention/intervention program for schools. Dr. Lee started the Chattanooga Teen Challenge and served as its president for three years. He also served as the Executive Director of Nashville Teen Challenge during its formative years.*

On February 16, 1915, a man was born who would go on to exhibit and walk in faithfulness to God for nearly a century. Born to unbelieving parents (they later became believers), Charles Ora Lee received Christ as his Savior as a young man at Berra Tabernacle in Detroit, Michigan. He was born again one night and started preaching shortly after his conversion. From that very first evening, Charles O. Lee experienced the transformational power of Christ. Years later he would explain that from the moment of his salvation, he could immediately identify with the promise of 2 Corinthians 5:17, "Therefore, if any one is in Christ, he is a new creation; the old is gone, the new has come!"

Even though he started preaching soon after coming to know his Savior, little did Charles O. Lee, affectionately known as Brother Lee, know that God was preparing him for a lifetime of faithful ministry of God's Word. At age 24 he received a dream one night that would go with him the rest of his life. The dream was Psalm 9:10, "Those who know your name will trust in you, for you, LORD, have never forsaken those who seek you."

Although my father, Brother Lee, had only a sixth-grade education, he became known as a "walking Bible." He had hundreds of verses committed to memory. I would often call Daddy wanting to know the whereabouts of a specific verse. He was usually my choice before going to a dictionary or concordance, because asking him was much faster.

In 1941, with just 50 cents in his pocket, he married Esther Myrl Malone, and the next day they were serving in revival services. Esther would play the guitar and sing, and Brother Lee would preach the gospel. Although he was a great preacher, Brother Lee's singing was definitely not his ministry gift. So he wisely chose to preach the Word rather than sing about it.

In the beginning of his ministry, Brother Lee learned quickly to trust God's faithfulness. One of his first revivals was in a rural area of north-central Tennessee, a little community named Windle, Tennessee. He led a very successful revival there, with a large number of people receiving Christ as Savior. It was during his time at Windle that he would experience God's faithfulness in a profound, heartfelt way. He, his wife, Esther, and their son, Jimmy (that's me), who was four years old at the time, lived in an upstairs apartment in nearby Livingston, Tennessee while he preached the tent revival in Windle.

One morning Jimmy began to cry for something to eat, but there was no food in the house and no money for purchasing any. When Esther told Brother Lee of the dilemma, he said, "There are a lot of things I can take in life, but I cannot take my child crying for food." So he immediately got on his knees and began to pray. In his prayer he said, "Lord, we have come here to do a work for you. You said You would supply our needs. I cannot take my child crying for food. We need You to help."

About five minutes after his prayer was concluded, we heard footsteps coming up the stairs to our second-floor apartment. There was a knock on the door and it was the deputy sheriff of Overton County. He sat down and wrote a check to my father for $5.00. Today that does not seem like much, but that was a lot of money in 1947. It definitely was enough to buy the groceries we so desperately needed.

As he was writing the check, the deputy had gone on to say, "When I got into my car a few minutes ago, God spoke to my heart and said that you had a need. Then he drew my attention to a verse in 1 John 3:17, 'If anyone has material possessions and sees his brother in need but has no pity on him, how can the love of God be in him?'" Although I was very young at the time, that experience of my father and mother's faith in God has served as a lifelong inspiration to me.

Bringing It Home

In the Scriptures, Jesus reminds us of our importance, His love for us, and His desire to come to our aid in everyday needs. Jesus says, "Therefore I tell you, do not worry about your life, what you will eat or drink; or about your body, what you will wear. Is not life more important than food, and the body more important than clothes? Look at the birds of the air; they do not sow or reap or store away in barns, and yet your heavenly Father feeds them" (Matthew 6:25-26).

Centuries earlier, King David wrote, "I was young and now I am old, yet I have never seen the righteous forsaken or their children begging bread" (Psalm 37:25).

What comes to your mind when you think about a time when God met a special need in your life? What did you think about that experience then? And how do you feel about it now? Has your perspective changed at all?

If you were to think of life as a journey, one that starts with birth and ends with death in this life, describe what comfort and encouragement you might receive from Psalm 37:25.

3

DEVELOPING A HISTORY OF FAITHFULNESS WITH GOD

By Don Wilkerson

*D*on Wilkerson is the founder and past President of Global Teen Challenge, a faith-based, Christ-centered program helping to reach and rehabilitate troubled youth and adults, particularly those with life-controlling problems such as drugs and alcohol. Don, along with a staff team, pioneered the development of Teen Challenge centers worldwide. He has been involved in working with troubled youth for 50 years, having served as the Executive Director of the first and original Teen Challenge established in Brooklyn, New York in the late 1950s. Teen Challenge was founded by Don's brother, David Wilkerson, author of the best-selling book, The Cross and the Switchblade. From 1987 to 1995, Don also served as a co-pastor of Times Square Church on Broadway in Manhattan, New York.

In light of what is happening in our country right now, I think back about God's faithfulness and protection while I was working in New York City – working with gangs in an urban environment. I remember Nicky Cruz and I used to go into a neighborhood and bring Hell

Burner's gang to our center. We would drive two different vehicles. Nicky would pick up some guys by prearrangement, and I would pick up some other guys.

In those days I was too naive to be scared. If I had of known then what I know now, I might have been scared because we would come in the back parking lot to the back door of the center and require them to check their weapons. We had a big closet as they entered the chapel, so if they wanted their weapon back as they left, they knew they were sure to get them. Sometimes one of the guys would not want his weapon back, but most of the time they did.

We would have riots break out on our street and gunshots would come into our apartment building at times, so we experienced the faithfulness of the Lord in providing protection for us over the years. We used to go in neighborhoods and the police would try to chase us out. We would have open-air meetings. Today the protocol is more sophisticated and you have to get permits, but in those days we could just go out with sound equipment and set up anywhere. The police used to try to discourage us and tell us to leave, but when we explained why we were there, what we were doing and who we were trying to help, then they would do the opposite and say, "Oh, we admire you people." They then would station a police car in the area, telling us they would be nearby in case we needed them, but not too near because that would scare off the people we wanted to help. Thankfully we never did need them, another example of the faithfulness of the Lord.

In this kind of ministry, another way the faithfulness of the Lord is seen is in His providing the needed finances. We seemed to get tested again and again and again on finances. My brother, David Wilkerson, used to say the hardest part of faith is the last half hour. When Jesus came to the disciples when they were out on the sea in the life-threatening storm, He came in the fourth watch of the night (Matthew 14:25). That is why my brother would say the last half hour is the hardest – testing us by allowing us to wait so that when the answer came, we knew it was from Him.

There was no question about it. We knew God would hear and respond. But even though we knew the answer would come from Him, it was never easy to wait until the last minute of the last half hour. It never is. It is hard to go through that, the waiting and trusting, but it makes you stronger and emboldens your faith for the next trial that you go through. And we go through many of them.

God brought Teen Challenge from its small beginnings through faithfulness. People have asked me, "Did you ever envision the Teen Challenge ministry spreading around the world?" No, I didn't, and Mike Zello reminded me that one time in those early days my brother Dave said, "There are only five other cities in America that need Teen Challenge." David was known for his prophetic words, but he was not prophetic on that situation.

In a ministry enterprise like that, you just do what God sets before you, striving to be faithful day by day. Then God begins to use what you plant. There is never overnight success. There is no such thing as overnight success in any field of endeavor, but especially in the work of the Lord. So you plant and you water, and God definitely gives the increase (1 Corinthians 3:6) in His own way and in His own time.

When I was in Bible college, we had to have a verse that went with our picture when they printed the yearbook. The verse I would choose was 1 Thessalonians 5:24, "Faithful is he who called you, who will also do it." The "who" is the Lord. I chose that verse at the time not knowing what it would take. I had no idea about the cost of faithfulness, what it would take to fulfill that verse even before coming into the Teen Challenge ministry.

In time God gave me vision to do other things, but at the beginning it was just to be faithful in what we were doing. My father was a pastor and often told me, "Son, there will always be a place for somebody who will be faithful in the Word, faithful in prayer, faithful in doing what God called you to do. Do little things in a big way, and one day God will give you bigger things to do." And that's the way it has been. I would have never believed I would be flying all over the world helping to plant Teen Challenge centers, especially in former

Soviet Union countries that were behind the Iron Curtain. But that has been the fruit of being faithful in the early days.

I think a lot of people miss certain things because they do not want to pay the price of faithfulness. They want to jump from first base to home plate without going through second and third. Or, to shift the analogy to football, they don't want to grind it out ten yards at a time. And maybe, when they get near the goal line, they find they will not score the touchdown until the fourth down.

In my generation, I think faithfulness was a part of our DNA. Another thing my father used to emphasize comes from Psalms, where it says, "promotion comes from the LORD. It does not come from the east or west but from the north. It comes from above" (Psalm 75:6). When I went to work with my brother, I ended up working in an office. I was a "gofer." I had graduated from Bible college and had already been preaching, and it was humbling to me to just be a gofer. I complained to the Lord, but it did not help. Then my upbringing and training through my father and mother kicked in. That was the admonition, "whatever thy hand finds to do, do it with all your might" (Ecclesiastes 9:10).

I think it is a great thing to get out stories of people's faithfulness, because nowadays even kids want to go into immediate success. They don't want to pay the price of going through the steps of a righteous man. It is not taking a jet plane from one place to the other; it is "the steps of a righteous man." I would even say, the steps and the stops, the times of waiting we talked about earlier.

Talking about faithfulness resurrects many memories of serving faithfully, and even to this day continuing to do just what God has assigned me to do one day at a time. When you do that, eventually you develop, as my brother used to say, "a history with God." The only way you can have a history with God is to be able to point back to those faithful steps of doing what God wanted you to do.

Being faithful is not very glamorous sometimes, not very glamorous at all. It is like planting a seed and waiting until eventually, wow! Something comes up and God, in His faithfulness, rewards. I have been blessed by the rewards of faithfulness. If you go into whatever God asks you to do looking for the rewards, that is not good. You cannot be thinking about the rewards, whether it be financial rewards, rewards of a position, or whatever. You can't think about it; you just do what God has called you to do, and then those things happen as a result.

I think the other thing is remaining faithful to people – commitment to see them through. Any ministry that is successful understands that. It is what you do, and what we have done. It involves faithfulness to stick with people who have shown every sign of not making it, yet remaining faithful to give them the Word and pray for them. Then you see the reward of being faithful to people. So many times I have seen people come into our program and I would say, "They are going to make it," but they don't. Then there are others you think are not going to make it, but they do because you were faithful in giving the Word to them. In working with people with life-controlling problems, there is no overnight success.

Sometimes I would represent Teen Challenge in churches and introduce a few converts who gave their testimonies. I would get up afterward and say, "Folks, the half has not been told." By that I would mean the struggles the students have been through, along with the struggles we had with them to bring them to the point where they are deserving to stand up in church and give a testimony. That is the other aspect of it – being faithful to people, and I really think that is being faithful to your calling.

Bringing It Home

Every day we are writing a history lesson with our life. Don and his late brother, Dave, continue to write a history lesson through the numerous Teen Challenge ministries around the world. A history with God requires faithfulness. The Scripture says, "The steps of a good man are ordered by the LORD, and He delighteth in his way" (Psalm 37:23, KJV). Paul writes, "You yourselves are our letter, written on our hearts, known and read by everyone" (2 Corinthians 3:2).

How would you describe your "history with God?"

Would you say this history is consistently marked with faithfulness?

If not, do you think there is a need of a fresh start?

What inspired you most about Don Wilkerson's "history with God?"

4

WHEN GOD SPEAKS, WE REALLY NEED TO LISTEN

By Mike Chapman

*D*r. *Mike Chapman has been the senior pastor of City Church of Chattanooga, Tennessee, since September 1976. City Church has become known as a thriving, innovative and cutting-edge church. Pastor Chapman, a gifted communicator and visionary, came to the congregation after serving as pastor of churches in Fremont, California, and Honolulu, Hawaii. He is the author of* Authentic Living in an Artificial World *and* A Passionate Pursuit of God.

This is a story of our son, Shannon. We only have one son, but he has blessed us with now six grandchildren. He and his wife, Mandy, have four children and they're adopting a little boy from Congo – and in the process of adoption, low and behold, Mandy became pregnant again. So before the end of 2016, we will have six grandchildren.

Already they've got enough for their own basketball team, their own rock band, or whatever other kind of assembly they want – they've got it! But Shannon is an only son, and my wife, Trudy, and I were married seven years before he was born. When he was seven years old, in 1985, we were coming off a tremendous season of blessing in our church. We had just built our new worship center, the biggest project our church had ever undertaken. Our church had doubled in attendance in a year, and things were just going phenomenally.

However, about six months after we had dedicated the building and with our attendance continuing to grow, Trudy and I had gone to a prayer conference, leaving Shannon with a lady at church and her family while we were gone. After we picked him up, we noticed as we came to our house that he could barely walk up the three or four steps to the front door. I asked him, "Did you hurt yourself?" I thought maybe he had injured his leg, but he said, "No, my legs aren't hurt." It was on a Friday when we got back, but we noticed on Saturday there seemed to be something about his legs that if he was lying on the floor, Shannon could hardly get up unless he was able to use a chair to pull himself up.

It happened that we had tickets to a University of Tennessee-Chattanooga basketball game, and Shannon loved basketball, so we were all going to the game. Our tickets were located in one of the higher sections and he could not walk up the steps. I had to lift him up. Trudy and I wondered, "What is this?" We fretted about this the remainder of the weekend, and when he was not getting any better, we decided to take him to the doctor on Monday. We thought maybe it was some strange virus, they would give him a shot, and he would soon be okay.

After examining Shannon, the doctor was showing a great deal of concern. He walked out of the room, then he called me into another room where he had a huge medical dictionary opened to a word that we had never heard before and could barely pronounce. The doctor told us he thought Shannon had something called dermatomyositis, an autoimmune disease. It is very rare for children to have this disease, in which the immune system attacks muscle tissue and skin.

Shannon had a rash that had appeared, but we hadn't connected the rash with his problem. We thought it was carpet burn or something, but it was a rash. The doctor said Shannon needed to have some blood tests, and we were immediately sent to a hospital at Chattanooga where they said, "Yes, he does have dermatomyositis." Next we spent a week at the Emory University Children's Hospital in Atlanta, and they agreed that Shannon had dermatomyositis. We learned there's no cure for dermatomyositis and the prognosis is very grim. It can leave a person crippled, can kill the person, or result in an early death.

Just when things were going so well at the church, it was a trying time for our family, one of those times when I was crying out to God. I was trying to be strong when I was with Shannon, as well as when I was with Trudy, but that first day when I got in a car by myself to drive somewhere, I found myself crying uncontrollably, saying out loud, "God, I'm not ready for this. I can't take this. I'm not ready."

Then I heard God scream in my car. It truly was a very loud voice, so loud that I actually looked in the back seat to see if someone was there, because it startled me so much. What I heard God shout was, "My grace is sufficient for you!" In mid-sentence I thought, "Oh, wow!" I'm sure His voice wasn't audible; no one else could have heard it but me, but it sounded loud – and like it was coming from inside the car. When I got home, I told Trudy, "God spoke to me today," and she replied, "That's good." But I said, "No, God spoke to me today!" And I explained that I had heard him through my ears and my heart. I'd had that happen only one other time, a long time ago, and that was more of a whisper. But this was a loud voice.

Even with that, I didn't know whether our son was going to live or die; Shannon was in a wheelchair for most of that time. His doctor in Atlanta was a pediatric rheumatologist. We learned she also was an agnostic. She was kind in acknowledging that we were Christians and that we were praying, but basically told us that she didn't really believe in all that. I said, "Well, we do – and we're praying." And that's what we did, we prayed and prayed. Shannon was getting blood tests every week and was getting worse, even being on medication like steroids along with other drugs. But we were told the steroids would be only temporary; you can only take steroids for so long.

That was in February. Our church was praying, and I remember our elders calling a special church-wide prayer meeting on a Sunday night. The sanctuary was packed and we all did nothing but pray for our son. Then Mother's Day was coming and we were continuing to pray for Shannon. I believe intercession is an amazing thing. I believe it is not just praying through a prayer list. That's good; we should do that. I have a prayer list that I use regularly. But I believe real Biblical intercession is when God lays a burden on somebody and they know it. They feel, "This is my burden."

I learned later there were several people who had received this powerful burden. There was one lady in our church I did not know who would find herself periodically fasting for my son and praying for him. One day, she told us, "I was painting in the living room in our house and I was thinking about Shannon. I heard the Lord say to me, 'I'm healing Shannon starting this Sunday' (that Sunday was Mother's Day)." She didn't tell anybody. She later said, "This is what the Lord told me, that the choir was going to sing a song, and the song was, 'We Are Standing in His Presence on Holy Ground.'"

This came after everyone had been praying from February to May, with Shannon's not getting any better but getting worse. He was confined to a wheelchair, because if he got the slightest bit off balance he'd fall. He didn't have the muscle strength to hold himself up or catch himself if he stumbled. So he was getting worse, but we were continuing to pray. I was still holding onto the promise I had heard from God, "My grace is sufficient," and we felt the strength of God, even though we didn't know what was going to happen to Shannon.

Anyway, this woman I had not met before continued to explain. She didn't know if the choir was going to sing that song God told her about or not. It was just what the Lord had told her. "When it does," she had heard God say, "you are supposed to stand in the middle of the service." This would take a lot of courage for her to stand up like that, get the pastor's attention, and tell him that God had spoken to her, telling her that the choir was going to sing this song. God had also given her the names of three specific men that were going to call

Shannon up. They were going to come and lay their hands on him, with the rest of the congregation agreeing with them in prayer. She said God had assured her, "Healing is starting today."

So when she came to church that Sunday morning, the woman had her spiritual antennae up. Nobody else knew anything about it. But we didn't sing that song Sunday morning. That's the crazy thing – we didn't sing that song, and suddenly the lady had a spiritual crisis to face. Silently she prayed, "Now God, You told me we were going to sing that song." Well, it just so happened that we had a Sunday night service and had invited the Lee Singers from Lee University to be there that night.

The woman also came to that service, expectantly. She had already looked around for those three men, and she only found two of them at church in the sanctuary. Because she didn't see the third man, she continued on in a crisis of faith. But included in the Lee University Singers' repertoire that evening was, "We Are Standing in His Presence on Holy Ground." There was the song! Then she realized, "That's the song, and it is Sunday." As she explained after the service, it also occurred to her, "The Lord didn't say Sunday morning. He just said Sunday."

As that song was being sung she continued looking around and saw man number one, and man number two, but she did not see man number three. She prayed, "Lord, You told me these three men." While the choir is singing, the side door of our sanctuary opened, man number three slipped into the service and sat down on the back row.

We learned afterward that he had been in Cincinnati for a business trip and drove back to Chattanooga that Sunday, but had no plans to come to church Sunday night because, he thought, "I'm tired and I've been driving a long time." But his route home took him straight past our church. As he was driving by, he saw the cars and decided, "Well, I'll just pull in and get the last part of the service since I didn't get to go this morning." So he slipped into the service, with no further intentions. But the woman got up as soon as the song was over and said, "Pastor, I've got to say something." Everybody looked at her, wondering what she had in mind.

She proceeded, "God told me we were going to sing this song this Sunday, and He also told me He wanted to bring healing to your son today, that it is going to begin today." Then she said, "And there are three men. The two are here and the third man just slipped in the door right over there."

As God had told the woman, the three men brought Shannon up. He sat on the wooden altar at the front and we prayed for him, with all the people gathered around. We all had a tremendous sense of God's expectancy, trusting that what she had said was true.

Shannon went for his blood test the next week – he had one every week – but for the first time the report said it had actually stopped getting worse. The next week showed he was starting to get a little better and that continued until when we went back to his agnostic pediatric rheumatologist in Atlanta in January, which would have been almost a year after he was diagnosed.

She said, "Well, I've never seen this happen. He doesn't have dermatomyositis. There's no sign of it." Then she added, "That doesn't happen." I just smiled and said, "But you know, God can make things happen." This time she didn't say, "I don't believe in that." After I told her that story of what had happened at the church, and how God had spoken to the woman, she replied, "Well, all I can say is that he is well."

It took Shannon another six months for all the strength in his legs to come back because they had atrophied some, but that June he played baseball again. He's now 37 years old, and I remember just three or four years ago he got into bike riding, something that at one point in his life seemed an impossibility. I'll never forget the day while he was sick when he called me to his bedroom and said, "Dad, I'm scared." I asked, "What are you scared of, son?" He said, "The devil's talking to me." I said, "What's the devil saying?" Shannon answered, "He's telling me I'll never ride my bike again." I replied, "Well, son, I believe the devil is a liar, so we're going to see what God's going to do."

So Shannon got into biking, I think they call it street biking. In Chattanooga each year they have a three-stage, three-mountains bike ride, a 100-mile course. Riders go up Lookout Mountain, Sand Mountain, and Signal Mountain. Shannon, the guy doctors said would never get better, rode in that, finishing it in a little less than 5 hours, covering that 100-mile distance up and down those mountains, all over the place. I remember after taking his picture when he got off, Trudy turned, looked at me and said, "This is a miracle, because there was a day when he said, 'I'll never ride my bike again.'"

Just this year, Shannon went riding for the Chattanooga prison ministry, raising money for them. He was one of six guys who rode the Natchez Trace from Mississippi to Nashville, 500 miles in five days. Back in 1985, that would have seemed unimaginable. But we didn't know what the Lord was going to do.

So we see the miracle, look back on it and say, "Wow, God!" We see how faithful God is, and then we wonder, "Well, what about people who didn't get a miracle?" But God is faithful. I know our miracle was a phenomenal thing: I heard God speak, a lady heard God's voice, we saw God do a miracle, and I believe in miracles.

This is my theology, that God still does miracles, just as He did in Biblical times. I hear people say, "We ought to have a lot more miracles," and I respond, "Well, maybe so, but miracles are designed first of all to capture our attention and make us look up and say, 'Wow, something happened here that is not normal.'" If miracles happened every day, they'd be normal and not miraculous. Miracles have to be infrequent enough to still be miracles. God gives us enough miracles to say, "See, I'm with you, I'm faithful, trust Me no matter what happens, and I'll never leave you."

Bringing It Home

As Pastor Chapman writes, seeing a miracle or experiencing one involves the "Wow!" factor. It is a phenomenal thing designed to capture our attention and make us look up. The writer of the book of Hebrews says, "God also testified to it by signs, wonders and various miracles, and gifts of the Holy Spirit distributed according to His will" (Hebrews 2:4).

Have you ever witnessed or experienced a miracle (in addition to your salvation) that was an unexplainable act of God? If so, what were the circumstances – and what impact did it have on your life, or the lives of the people affected by it?

What touched you the most about the story of Shannon's healing?

5

WELCOMING HOME A 'PRODIGAL DAUGHTER'

By Ruth Graham

R uth Graham, third child of famed evangelist Dr. Billy Graham and Ruth Graham, is an experienced conference speaker, author and Bible teacher. Ruth is known for her honesty and authenticity as she shares her journey of faith, which has been painful at times. Her story is a testament to the faithfulness of God in the face of painful choices as presented in the Living Free Video Training.

Throughout my own life, I have struggled with life-controlling issues. And I would just like to share with you that there was a time in my life when I was being very stubborn, very willful, and made a choice that went against all advice. A very painful choice. But through it, a loving, forgiving God demonstrated the depth and breadth of His faithfulness, perhaps in ways I couldn't have experienced in any other way.

The advisors that I trusted told me not to do it, but I thought I knew what was best for my life. It wasn't long before I realized I had made a terrible mistake, and had to admit that I had fallen victim to life-controlling issues. Where was I to go? I was away from my home and I had to make the humbling, heartbroken drive home to see my father.

My father had been one of those that had advised me not to make this decision, one that had taken me a two-day drive from home. As I drove homeward, my fears and apprehensions grew with every mile. I had failed so miserably – myself, my children, my family. Questions swirled in my mind. "What was my life going to be like?" "What was I going to say to them?" "What were they going to say to me?"

Despite my fears, I kept my foot on the gas. Adrenaline tightened my grip on the steering wheel. As I rounded the last bend to turn into my father's driveway, I saw that he was standing there. And as I got out of my car, he wrapped his arms around me and he said, "Welcome home."

That's what God does for us when we come with our brokenness, when we come with our life-controlling issues. He welcomes us. He doesn't look for ways to keep us away. He opens his arms wide and He says, "Welcome home." As God had shown me through my earthly father, He is faithful even when we're not faithful. He is faithful *especially* when we are not faithful.

Let me encourage you so you can hear that "Welcome home." May God bless you and give you the joy of experiencing His limitless, unending faithfulness, no matter what your circumstances might be.

Bringing It Home

We can always go to Jesus to find comfort, love and peace even in the midst of poor choices we have made or the choices of others that have hurt us. The "Parable of the Lost Son" in Luke 15:11-32 shows us the love of a father and a picture of our heavenly father. "So he got up and went to his father. But while he was still a long way off, his father saw him and was filled with compassion for him;

he ran to his son, threw his arms around him and kissed him" (Luke 15:20).

How do you relate to Ruth Graham's story – and the parable of the prodigal son?

What in the parable stands out most for you?

6

DID IT MAKE ANY DIFFERENCE?

By Roger Helle

*R*oger Helle *serves as Executive Director of Teen Challenge of the Mid-South. He experienced firsthand the horrors of the Vietnam War, serving three tours of combat duty there. During those deployments Roger was wounded three times, the last time nearly taking his life. Understandably, Vietnam was one place he had no desire to see ever again – but God had a different idea.*

The third time, they say, is "the charm," but I can attest it's anything but that. Between 1965 and 1970 I served three tours of duty of Vietnam in the Marine Corps. Even though I had been wounded twice during my first two tours, in 1970 I willingly was deployed to Vietnam for a third time. While leading my platoon on a search and destroy mission, I sustained critical injuries when a grenade went off at my feet, I was hit twice by bullets, was bayoneted as I lay on the ground, and suffered burns from phosphorus.

I was left to die out there on a field of battle in Southeast Asia, only twenty-two years old, and felt certain my life already was over. I didn't welcome the thought of dying on that field, but there was

FAITHFUL, NO MATTER WHAT

nothing I could do about it. Through God's grace, another Marine and a Navy corpsman came out and pulled me to safety. They medevaced me to an Army hospital in DaNang, which we referred to as "China Beach."

Lying in that hospital six days later, I heard the doctor tell my twin brother, Ron, that I was going to die. He explained the medical team had done everything they could. Earlier my brother had walked right past my bed without knowing it; I was not recognizable because of my injuries. As a boy I had attended church a little bit, but did not grow up with a Christian background, so lying alone in that hospital bed I experienced a fear greater than anything I have ever felt before. Thinking maybe it was time to try and strike a bargain, I said, "God, if you let me live, I will do anything you want." He did – but I didn't.

Nine months later and twenty-seven operations, including four plastic surgery procedures, I miraculously walked out of the hospital. But you know, I quickly forgot that promise I had made in the hospital bed. I remember thinking I was pretty tough because I was a Marine. When I was discharged from the hospital, they also medically discharged me from the Marine Corps. As they say, once a Marine always a Marine, but once I "retired" from the Corps in 1971, if you had asked me, "What are the top ten places in the world you would never want to go to?", Vietnam would have been right at the top of the list.

Vietnam to me, was three tours of horror and painful memories. I'd seen death and destruction, and had lost many friends. It was a place I definitely never wanted to see again. Over months and years afterward, like a lot of veterans, I struggled with post-traumatic stress, not even knowing what that was back then. My sleep was riddled with wartime nightmares, and I became an alcoholic trying to forget Vietnam.

I married my wife, Shirley, but two years after we were married we separated. This was no trial separation; we were going to get a divorce. However, then God stepped in. Ten days after we separated, Shirley and I both gave our hearts to Jesus Christ and accepted Him as our Lord and Savior. I can't explain it, other than the grace and mercy of God, but my nightmares stopped, along with the drinking. I mean God literally turned my life upside down. That was December 1974, and the crazy thing was that in 1975 something in my heart said, "You're going to go back to Vietnam." Almost immediately I had thought, "Why would I want to go back to Vietnam?" Finally I mentioned it to Shirley. I said, "Honey, I wonder what it would be like to return to Vietnam, now that I'm a Christian?"

A month or two later, Vietnam fell, on April 30, 1975. The North Vietnamese armies overran the entire country. Vietnam fell behind the bamboo curtain and was shut off from the outside world. And yet, for years I would run into people, missionaries in different parts of Asia, and ask them, "What's going on in Vietnam?" Their typical reply was, "Nothing's going on in Vietnam. Why?" Then I would explain to them my interest in knowing.

In August of 1988, I had the opportunity to go on the "Focus on the Family" radio program with Dr. James Dobson. There was another man on the panel that we were talking with about Vietnam – how it affected men and how that also had affected the families. Dr. Dobson had invited this other gentleman named Bill Kimball. I looked at him and said, "Bill, I understand you just came back from Vietnam on a fact-finding trip." He answered, "Yes, I did." I kind of let the subject drop, but my interest was definitely cued up. After we were finished with the radio interview I said, "Bill, can Shirley and I take you and your wife, Rose, out to dinner?"

At dinner I asked him, "Tell me about this, your trip to Vietnam." He said, "Roger, I believe the answer for Vietnam is that God wants to take Christians who had served there, people that are now Christians, back to Vietnam with a ministry of reconciliation." Wow, what a thought! We all know 2 Corinthians 5:17, "If any person is in Christ, he is a new creation," but the next verse says, "God has given us this ministry of reconciliation" This, Bill said, he felt was the answer for Vietnam. Then he looked at me and said simply, "Do you wanna go?" And I said, "Yes."

Seated next to me, Shirley about fell off her chair when she heard me say that. But we prayed about it and God confirmed my decision. In January of '89, I made what I thought was just going to be a one-time trip down memory lane, an opportunity to go back to the country that had impacted my life so much. We took 10,000 Bibles with us that the government allowed in, even though afterward they'd probably wonder, "What did we do that for?" But they did let us bring in 10,000 Bibles, the first time the Word of God had been openly brought in since the fall of the country fourteen years earlier.

That was amazing enough, but that was not the end of it. What I thought was going to be a one-time deal turned into repeated visits. God broke my heart for the people of Vietnam. While over there I spent most of my time living in the villages with the people. At the end of each tour of duty, it was like I had left Vietnam, but Vietnam never left me. As a non-Christian, I realized that I had sympathy for the living conditions of the people of Vietnam. When I became a Christian, God gave me more than sympathy. He gave me compassion, and compassion requires you to do something. Only I had no idea what that meant or what that looked like.

One of the things that had happened during the "one-time" trip to Vietnam in January 1989 was that we wanted a project. So we were introduced to a Vietnamese Catholic nun, Sister Jean Marie, who had run a Catholic orphanage until the country fell and Communists took over everything. She still worked there, but they ran it. These people were probably great soldiers, but they were lousy administrators, and after a number of years they had just run the orphanage into the ground, so they had asked Sister Jean Marie to take it back over. She'd only been running it for a couple of years when we arrived.

Sister Jean Marie was like Mother Teresa to Vietnam, especially to orphans. There were 400-450 kids in this polio orphanage when we first came into the gates, and when we saw these little kids in their homemade braces and twisted limbs, along with the conditions they lived in, it just broke our hearts. I mean all of us veterans stood there and just wept for these little kids. So we began taking on projects, aiming at improving the lives of these unfortunate children. Every six months for six years we would take on one project after another, and then another, each lasting for six months. All these kids were so happy to see us, and we'd take them toys and clothes, as well as medicines and other things they needed. I passed out happy-face stickers, which they loved. We would stick them on the kids, and they'd put them on their faces, or balloons we gave them. It seemed like so little, but it brought them so much joy. We were privileged to do that for six years.

Sadly, Sister Jean Marie was killed in a motorbike accident and the government put somebody else in charge, so we moved on to other projects. We always marveled because we couldn't openly tell the people why we were there. We couldn't publically evangelize, but sometimes people would ask, "Why are you doing this? Why are you coming here?" We could certainly tell them that the love of Jesus Christ was compelling us to do this. At the same time we still wondered, "Did it make any difference?" Was what we were doing, our various projects, able to make any difference? We had branched out to working with the underground church, although on the surface we were building medical clinics, taking doctors and dental teams with us. Still the question always remained, "Did it make any difference?"

In 2009, while on our 20th anniversary trip, Shirley and I were up in the mountains of what was formerly South Vietnam, near a place called the A Shau Valley, a place where the army had fought a very serious battle called Hamburger Hill. Only now in this area we had set up a medical clinic to help the poor tribal people living there. A couple of the doctors who were with us had laptops with satellite reception, and we had been watching a typhoon that had actually hit the Philippines as a tropical storm, proceeded past the Philippines, moved over the South China Sea, and was growing to become a Category Five typhoon. It was bearing right down on us, and we were watching its progress on the computer screen.

One morning the government called us and said, "You need to get out of the mountains right now." So we made our way down to the coast and got into a hotel. The typhoon turned just slightly south, so we missed the direct hit, but it was still a pretty crazy night. The next day we went back to Saigon, wrapping up our trip. We had a house-church pastor that was working for us, kind of an administrator-coordinator on the ground. But he also was pastoring a church in Saigon that our organization supported. We had to go by his house because a couple was expected – a veteran they had met previously had wanted to send some money. It was about $100 or $150, a lot of money for the average Vietnamese.

This couple was coming to receive a gift sent by an American serviceman. When they showed up, they were a husband and a wife and two little children, all riding on a little motorbike As they pulled up and were getting off the motorbike, it was obvious the wife and husband – the mom and dad – both had polio. The father's polio was more pronounced; he had to have leg braces and crutches to be able to walk. The wife could walk more easily with braces. The children were fine. Thankfully, now polio has pretty much been wiped out there.

While this family was standing there, I felt prompted to ask, "So, how did you guys meet?" And they said, "Well, we met as children. We grew up in the same orphanage together. But at eighteen we had to leave the orphanage. The government kicks you out, and so we met again later and fell in love, got married and now we have children."

Somehow they had been directed to this church, and after starting to attend they met Christ and were now members of that home church. About that time I just got a curious feeling, so I said, "Can you remember the orphanage?" because I knew there was more than one polio orphanage in Saigon. I said, "Do you remember, when you were growing up, Americans coming to the orphanage to visit, doing projects and bringing toys and balloons and candy?" Then I pulled out a little happy face sticker that I always carried and added, "and giving you happy face stickers?"

The husband and wife, their mouths fell open, their eyes got big, and the husband had such a beautiful smile. Shirley and I were both staring at him. It was like déjà vu, and we both began wondering, "Why does this guy look so familiar?" Suddenly we knew why. When I asked about their orphanage and showed them the happy face sticker, they both just started crying and said, "Yes. We remember." So you know, sometimes you wonder, "Did that do any good?" And sometimes in His faithfulness, God shows you, "Yes, yes it did."

Amazing, isn't it? It was twenty years later, in the city of Saigon with more than eleven million people, and the Lord not only brought these two children – to whom we had expressed the love of Christ to the only way that we could – but He also brought them as adults with children of their own, back across our path. Not only that, but we also learned they had gotten saved and met Jesus, and were being discipled in the very church that our ministry had started supporting only a few years earlier. It was like the still, small voice of the Holy Spirit assuring us, "Nothing you do in my name will be in vain."

What an incredible blessing, twenty years later, to have God telling us, "It was not in vain. You were faithful." At the time we didn't feel like we were doing much. But it didn't matter. If we simply do what we can, His faithfulness will then do what we are not able to do.

Bringing It Home

Over and over, the Scriptures assure us that God works in our lives even when we cannot always see the immediate fruit of our labor. "A man scatters seed on the ground. Night and day, whether he sleeps or gets up, the seed sprouts and grows, though he does not know how. All by itself the soil produces grain – first the stalk, then the head, then the full kernel in the head" (Mark 4:26-28). Our work for the Lord is not forgotten. As Paul writes, "Therefore, my dear brothers, always give yourselves fully to the work of the Lord, because you know that your labor in the Lord is not in vain" (1 Corinthians 15:58).

How have you seen the process of spiritual growth God has built into your life through people and ways you did not recognize or understand at the time?

What comfort do you receive knowing that your labor for the Lord is not in vain, that in His faithfulness, God uses even our imperfect efforts to accomplish His perfect, divine purposes?

7

GOD'S REASSURANCE - IN A GLOVE COMPARTMENT

By Mike and Kay Zello

*K*ay Zello and her husband, Mike, served as pioneers in the Teen Challenge ministry, working closely with young people struggling with addictions and life-controlling issues. They also devoted a number of years to pastoring congregations in New Jersey and Maryland. Kay's story is a stirring example of the reality that faithful service to the Lord does not make us exempt from real, serious problems. But, no matter how dire our circumstances, God is faithful and He promises to remain with us always and guide us through all of our struggles and difficulties.

As children of God, we are unique, and He works in each of our lives in unique ways. Thinking about how He has ministered to us individually during times of adversity, it's sometimes hard to explain ways the Lord used to touch our lives, knowing He might have led someone else down a different path. For instance, in times of disease, some have received complete healing, while for others the healing they prayed for did not come – or has yet to come. So, I do not offer my story as a "template" of how God works. At the same time, I feel responsible before God to share my life and what happened to me, along with what I perceive to be the fruitfulness from my suffering and God's healing power.

During our early years of ministry, one of the greatest times of adversity for Mike and me happened while we were pastoring a small church in Bayonne, New Jersey. We were still in touch with Dave Wilkerson, founder of Teen Challenge and helped pioneer Teen Challenge centers in several cities. But, it was God's time to teach us what it means to be in the same church, in the same pulpit, year after year, ministering to the same small group of people and being faithful in doing so.

At the time we had three small children. Our oldest daughter was four, our son was almost three, and our baby girl was six months old. We lived in a small apartment in the back of the church. When you walked out the door of our apartment you were immediately in the sanctuary. There was no buffer between the two. Being so close had one advantage: On Sunday nights, when Mike and I were both involved in church, I could put our little ones to bed and crack the door to our apartment, so I could hear them if they needed me. And during the wintertime, we did not have to take them outside to go to church. However, this did not make us immune to illness.

I got sick with a bad cold. Nothing seemed to be helping me get over the cold, so eventually I went to the doctor. He put me on an antibiotic and stronger medications but I continued getting progressively worse. When my husband called the doctor, he said to bring me into his office. He listened to my lungs and said, "I am going to send you for a chest x-ray." I thought that maybe I had low-grade pneumonia.

I had x-rays taken and Mike and I returned to the doctor's office to wait for the results. When we went in and sat down, the doctor came to us and said, "I don't have good news for you." He told us he could see signs that I had tuberculosis, so he referred me to another physician in our city who specialized in lung diseases.

We went to see the specialist and he looked at the x-rays. Moments later he said, "You have tuberculosis. It is very active in both of your lungs and I am going to have to put you in the hospital." When I asked how long I would be there, he said it would be at least several months. Mike and I were in shock!

"How had this happened so quickly?" we asked. The doctor explained, "Sometimes it happens rather suddenly, and that is what has happened to you." In other words, he was saying it did not build up year after year; it just hit and it had already done some damage to one of my lungs. I had not been sleeping well because of a terrible cough that would not quit, and also had developed some night fever and sweats. So I understood that I was pretty sick. Finally he said, "It is late in the day now, so you go home for the night and check into the hospital for chest and lung diseases tomorrow morning."

We went out of the doctor's office and got into our car. We were hugging each other and weeping. We kept a Bible in the glove compartment of the car. By this time, neither of us was in very good shape emotionally. Mike took the Bible out and prayed, asking God to direct us and speak to us. He opened the Bible to Romans 8, and tearfully read it from the first verse to the last verse. By the time he had finished reading that chapter, my faith was as solid as it had ever been in my life. Today, years later, I recommend that everyone commit this chapter to memory. Because it is about a God who is faithful, unmoving in His love toward us, able to do all things, a God who assures us that we are more than conquerors through Him who loves us.

As we read, we felt God's message just soared from one verse to the next. His presence filled the car! By the time we came to the ending of the chapter, "for I am convinced that nothing shall ever be able to separate us from the love of God...neither the present nor the future...," we had experienced such a moving encounter with God through His Word. In spite of the dreadful diagnosis, and despite my extreme illness, chronic coughing and weakness, I knew how deeply I was loved by God – forever! I was only 27 years old at the time. I knew at that moment no matter what happened to me, no matter how long I had to stay in the hospital, and no matter what we went through as a couple and as a family, I would not be shaken. No matter what happened, I was in the safest place I could be – in the hands of a very loving, faithful God. I said, "I gave my life to you, Lord, and whatever I am going to go through, I am still yours and I choose to believe that it is for my good and for your glory." My faith was strong, even though I had no idea what the future would bring.

We drove home. Our apartment had only two bedrooms, and all three of our children in one, Mike and I in the other. That night, after Mike had dropped off to sleep, I got up and I went to the children's room. I started to pray over them. I remember crying and saying. "Oh, God, I know I am in your hands, but how am I going to be able to leave my children? How am I going to be able to walk away, not knowing when I am going to be able to hold them again and take care of them?"

After I prayed over my children, I became very quiet. Stillness filled the room, and I heard God speak to me. I have often been asked, "How do you know the voice of God?" The answer is that God will say to you what no one else will. God said, "Kay, I will take better care of your children than if you were here." No one else would ever dare say that to me! No one, not even my husband, would say that to me! "I'll take better care of them than if you were here." Who says that to a mother? No one could say such a thing except God. I knew that I could fully trust Him when He said it.

The next morning Mike took me to the Pollack Hospital for chest diseases in Jersey City, New Jersey. As I was standing at the desk checking in, the lady had a chart the doctor had sent over with my x-rays and exam information. I realized just how sick I was when I saw classifications printed on my chart – *minimal, moderate,* and *far advanced.* My doctor had checked "far advanced." I knew then that I was very sick, and that a lot of damage must have already been done to my lungs. I spent the first few nights in the hospital fighting for my life. My fever had gone up to 104 and 105 degrees. Those were dark nights. My life was hanging in the balance.

Since giving my life to Jesus Christ at the age of 14 years old, one of my favorite hymns to sing was, "He's All I Need." When I was a teenager, I would kneel at the altar of my little Pentecostal church in Covington, Indiana and sing over and over, "He's all I need. He's all I need. Jesus is all I need." At that time, I was the only Christian in my family. My father owned the tavern on the town square. Everyone was worried about me, thinking I had gone off the deep end or joined a cult. My friends and teachers were worried about me, too. They brought me in for counseling because my life changed so much. So when I sang that song at the altar, I was thinking, "Jesus, You are all I've got. My walk with You has cost me my friends at school, and my family thinks I am fanatical, so you are all I've got."

During those long nights in the hospital when I was so ill, that old hymn came back to me. The Holy Spirit just seemed to sing it into my soul. After experiencing the joy of having a wonderful husband, three beautiful children, and pastoring a loving church, I was all alone in that hospital. I was high up on the 13th floor, in room 13. There were bars on the window. I wondered, why would there be bars on the 13th floor? Later I found out that the entire floor had been a TB sanatorium at the turn of the century, and those bars had been put there to keep people from jumping out. It was such a stark, clinical environment, and I was all alone when the Holy Spirit came like a breath from heaven. I sang over and over, "He's all I need. He's all I need. Jesus is all I need."

After several nights, I made it through the acute crisis stage. There were visitations from pastors and friends who came to pray for me. There was another young woman about my age two doors down from my room. She had been in the hospital for nine months with TB and her condition was moderate. She heard the prayer meetings going on in my room and was so touched. She told me later that she called her Catholic priest in and asked why the woman in the room down the hall seemed to have faith. "People are praying for her. I can hear the prayers and faith that's going up," she told him.

She asked her priest, "Why am I so depressed and suffering so much? I'm a Catholic, I'm of the true faith, and this woman is a

Protestant." Later she told me her priest had patted her on the hand and said, "Don't you worry about those spiritual things. I will take care of them. You just get well." But she was not satisfied. She heard prayer meetings going on in my room, and she saw that I was improving. She told God, "If something happens and that woman gets healed or some miracle takes place, I am going to go talk to her and find out what she has that I don't."

Tuberculosis patients were hospitalized back then for two reasons. The first reason is that patients were extremely sick, especially in cases as bad as mine. The second reason is because TB is a highly communicable disease. State law required patients to be sequestered. In order to be released, a patient had to have three consecutive negative sputum tests, with one month between each test. After a month there was no change in my test results. None whatsoever. So the doctor said, "I am going to send you down for some tests and x-rays to see how your lungs are doing."

The first time I went down for x-rays, it was a standard front and back of the lungs-type of x-ray. The next day the doctor said, "Your x-rays were not conclusive, so I am sending you down again today for a more detailed one." I went back down to the x-ray room that day, and they had me lean both forward and sideways. On the third day the doctor came to my room again and said, "We still need more information, so I am sending you down today for a more extensive x-ray." This time I was on a table and the machine passed over me and took pictures of my lungs by sections. That was in 1968, long before advanced technology like the MRI.

When I got back from the test, I saw my doctor was in his office, which was located across from my room. My Catholic friend, Marilyn, who had made her deal with God, was still in her room two doors down. The door to the doctor's office was open, so she could hear when he told me, "I don't know how to explain this, but we can't seem to find the cavity *(the size of a half dollar coin)* that was in your lung." He could not get himself to say it wasn't there any longer. I remember exactly what he said: "We can't seem to find it."

After I came back to my room, Marilyn made a beeline to my room. She told me about how she had talked with her priest and made an "arrangement" with God. Then she said, "I heard what the doctor said to you, and I want to know what you have because I want it." Heaven came down in that room as I prayed with her and led her to the Lord Jesus. She was so ready and received Him as her Savior so beautifully.

Marilyn became a wonderful, vibrant Christian, and she became my best friend during the time I was in the hospital. Every year after my hospital stay, I received a Christmas card from her. One year she wrote, "I never told you this, and I need to share it with you. If you were only in that hospital because of me and what God has done in my life, I want you to know it was worth it."

I have experienced many other trials in my life, like quadruple by-pass surgery and six-hour brain surgery, but the one lesson I have learned is that the fruit of our suffering sometimes comes in ways we can't begin to anticipate or fully understand. When I gave my life to the Lord I prayed, "God, please use me. That is all I ask – that You put me some place where You can use me." He heard and answered my prayers many, many times over, and He has done it through my suffering and subsequent healing.

While still in that hospital, I experienced such beautiful visitations from the Lord. Sometimes I would walk down to the solarium where it was all windows, and on my way down the hall I would hum the hymn, "Blessed Quietness, Holy Quietness...What assurance in my soul! On the stormy seas, He speaks peace to me, how the billows cease to roll!"

Even though the medical staff could not find the cavity in my lung that reflected the damage caused by tuberculosis, only two of my tests came back negative. So, the doctor would not release me from the hospital. Finally, after three months Mike asked the doctor if he could sign me out and take full responsibility for me. The doctor replied, "I am hesitant to do that because she will wind up right back in here again." When tuberculosis infiltrates and ravages your lungs, it takes away your strength. I remember days when I prayed that I would just be able to push a broom again. I had never imagined praying for anything as simple as that. Mike reassured him that even though I was extremely weak, I would be well taken care of. And, I was well taken care of by my good husband, by church members, by family and friends, but most of all, by God, my eternal, loving, heavenly Father.

That was in 1968, almost 50 years ago. Today, I remain free of tuberculosis without a trace. And the doctors never could explain why the cavity caused by the disease had disappeared. This proved to be just one step in a process God used to take us through as the years went by.

Bringing It Home

The apostle Paul writes, "All Scripture is God-breathed" (2 Timothy 3:16). Through His Word, God offers to sustain us, comfort us and guide us through challenges and difficulties. Often His Word is the very thing we need at the right time, giving us the needed assurance, "...in all these things we are more than conquerors through him that loved us" (Romans 8:37).

Kay Zello writes about how powerfully God spoke to her and her husband in a critical moment in her life. How important is the Bible in your life?

She recounts a time when God spoke to her directly and personally, but He also communicated to her very clearly through His written Word. In what ways have you experienced the Bible speaking to your heart?

8

FAITHFUL TO THE CALL, AND FAITHFUL
TO FULFILL THE CALL

By Robert Webb

*T*he late Robert Webb and his wife, Dorothy, were veteran missionaries. Robert was an ordained minister for more than 60 years. He and "Dot" served more than 40 years on mission fields around the world, with much of their ministry being concentrated in Africa. Over those years, their ministry became known for their strong commitment, integrity and amazing faithfulness and fruitfulness.

We have sometimes heard people say, "God is good – all the time. All the time, God is good." To this wonderful sentiment I would like to add, God is faithful – all the time. All the time, God is faithful. Throughout my life and more than four decades of ministry in different parts of the world, I have yet to see a single exception.

From the moment my wife, Dot, and I met, our story has been one of God's faithfulness. After He drew us together and we were married, we knew we were going to serve Him in Africa. We had no idea how it would happen, but as circumstances came together, God let us know in a very definite way that it was Africa that He had in mind for us.

God called me when I was a pastor of a home missions church in Bowling Green, Kentucky. I attended Southwestern Bible College in Texas, but certainly had no interest in going to Africa. But in Bowling Green, while still a single young man, a day came when I said, "Yes, God, if it is Africa, then that's okay. I am ready to do what you want me to do." Then I added, "You have got to confirm this."

I went to the church on that very cold day. At that time of day it was very unusual for a visitor to stop by and pay me a visit. But Waymond Rogers, who was the pastor of a great church in Kentucky, came by to visit me. He had asked me, "What are you going to do with your future?" He had asked this many times, but this day I replied, "Waymond, I am going to Africa." I never had been willing to make that statement before. In reply he said, "You go and we will stand behind you with our prayers and our support." That was the encouragement I needed to even think about going to Africa.

God faithfully confirmed His call through a fellow minister. I know to some people that might seem like a very small thing, but I was not willing in any way to go to Africa until that day when a man I trusted and loved, who was a little older than me, came by and confirmed that he knew God had indeed spoken to me.

He is faithful all the time or we would not be where we are now, but to me the faithfulness of God includes confirming in a definite way the conviction in your heart for what He has called you to do. I need to have confirmation from God, and to me this is one of the greatest signs of His faithfulness. I can have people encouraging me, but when God comes through in a definite way and confirms it, you know you have not missed it. You are on the right track, and not a step ahead.

Time after time, whether it initially was going to Africa, preparing to move to another place in Africa, ministering in some big city – whatever it was – to have God to confirm that I was not making a mistake was evidence of His faithfulness. It is good to have friends encourage you as you do something, but that is not enough. You must have a direct confirmation from God. He has been faithful in many,

many crises we have experienced, but for Him to let me know that I am in the will of God and have not been misled demonstrates His faithfulness.

I can recall many times when I had to stand on God's faithfulness, but I think the biggest thing after we got to Liberia was when we were told we could not get land for a church because the people held it to be sacred. To me that seemed like a huge hurdle, because after all, the other missionaries had been in Africa for a long time and we had just gotten there. Certainly they knew better than we did.

We had an established congregation for which we were thankful. So I told my missionary friends, "Well, I am going to try anyway because I believe God wants a church in this place." Back then I was a very young man, but the locals still called me "Reverend" because that was their practice. I approached the very first African man I knew who owned land and said, "I am looking for land and I see you have an empty lot." He replied, "Reverend, of course I will sell you that land." As it turned out it is was a long-term, 99-year lease, but in effect it was the same thing.

Then, of course, there was the matter of erecting a church building. I told everybody we did not have the money to build, so they naturally asked, "Well, how are you going to do it?" I told them if the money came in from the Africans, we would use that, and if it came in through my missionary account, we would use that. But we would not go into debt.

We started building the church. I am not a builder or a bricklayer, but as the building went up I would reward the workers. By the time we got to the roof level, everything had been paid for – but there was no roof on the building. That was a special crisis for us, so we prayed; I had the congregation pray and others were praying.

Not long afterward the senator's son came knocking on our door in the night. If a high-ranking man like a senator is willing to contact you, you never know what that means. You may have been charged with something. Unknowingly you might have done something illegal, or maybe you didn't do something right. We knew this well because on one occasion Dot had been charged for not flying the national flag correctly. She had not put the flag up in the first place, but she still got the blame for it. So you never knew what government officials were going to say.

The senator's son's name was James, and I welcomed him. Finally he got around to asking, "I am wondering about the roof. What are you going to use for a roof for that church building?" I told him we were going to use zinc roofing, the type they used there at the time. He said, "Well, do you know where it is coming from?" I replied, "No, I don't."

I explained, "So far, James, as the money has come in we have built. Money came in for the bricks, money came in for the windows, and we built. We did not build unless we had the money. We are not going to put the place in debt." Then James said, "That is why I am asking. If you will go down to a certain builder, my father, the senator, has already paid for the whole load of roofing for your church. All you have to do is go there and pick it up."

You talk about the faithfulness of God! God knows ten times more about our needs than we do. He has already seen ahead. Of course, this had seemed like a crisis for us, but it was not a crisis for God.

There are so many ways God came through for us during our years in Africa. There have been heartbreaks, but God knew how to straighten out the situations so that our family could continue living for God. This is what many people somewhere along the line fail to understand. Missionaries are extremely human – I am talking about myself. It is not claiming to be something special or unique, or being sanctimonious. All it is, actually, is having the right attitude. That is what we discovered. If anybody gets the wrong attitude in their spirit, no matter what they call themselves – a preacher, missionary or whatever – the bad attitude is wrong.

A little incident stands out for me: We had a raging war in Nigeria, a horrible war where thousands and thousands were killed. It was a civil war known as the Biafran War. Because people prayed, we did not have a single one of our preachers killed. Many other people were killed, but not one of our preachers. Any victories that we had were mainly because others came to help – and had prayed.

On a particular day some friends from America, Brother and Sister Schaffer, came to Nigeria to see us at our Bible College. They knew in their spirit that when they had prayed on a particular day, some African had experienced a miracle. So on this trip to Nigeria they were hoping to meet that person. One of our helpers in the Bible school had taught at one time, but he did so many other things as well. He was from another tribe altogether. They were engaged in a conversation with this man when God told Sister Schaffer, "This is the man." She asked, "What happened to you on this day? We were praying and knew we had a victory, but we did not know what."

He said, "Well, I will tell you what it was. My wife and I had trekked as far as we could. The war was still on, and I told her, 'You keep going because I cannot go any further. I am totally and completely given out. I have no more strength.' Then all of a sudden both of us felt extra strength. My wife said, 'Something is happening.'" So they started on their way again to a town called Enugu, one of the major towns in Eastern Nigeria. When they got there, they discovered that peace had been made between the fighting forces, and there they were, both still alive and doing well.

At the time they had wondered who in the world had prayed for them. What a joy it was when they found out it was the Schaffers who had prayed for them on that very day. If I were to really get into some details we knew the times when people in America prayed. It was not just a crisis and a victory – it was because somebody prayed and God faithfully answered their prayers. To me this is one of the most victorious things in the world, how God answers our prayers.

I could recount many times when God answered prayer for our children. I am not talking about just spiritually. One week they went through one of the most unusual crises I have ever heard about in my life. Our daughter, Tammy, was a toddler. She did not know what she was doing when she picked up a colorful cork and lure with three fishhooks. I am sure she thought it was candy.

She popped that lure into her mouth, and one of the hooks went through her tongue and the other went into the jaw. You talk about an emergency! We did not know what to do. Then, during that same hour our son, Dan, was with a friend who picked up an old BB gun, not knowing it had BBs still inside. He pointed it at Dan and shot him straight in the eye. Dan had a BB inside of his eye. We had no earthly idea what to do, especially since it was a little kid's eye. These were two big-time crises within one hour involving our two children.

Here are the two things that happened because of the prayer of a man who lived near Chattanooga, Tennessee: He later told us he got up in the middle of the night, feeling he should pray for the Webbs' children. And he did pray. I do not know for how long, maybe two hours. But he prayed. At that same time we were able to get to a doctor who was able to look at Dan's eye and flip that BB out of his eye. And we were able to get the hooks out of Tammy's mouth without causing a major infection. I believe in both cases, the crises were overcome because God led a man to pray – and He was faithful to answer those prayers.

Yes, as missionaries we went through many times of crisis. We can think of and remember, "many dangers, toils and snares I have come through." But because somebody remembered to pray, someone got down on their knees and cried out to God on behalf of the missionaries, we came through each one.

Bringing It Home

Although all believers in Christ are called by God, there also are out-of-the-ordinary callings and specific calls of God. Moses, Joshua, David, Samuel, Paul, Peter and many others in the Scriptures each received specific calls from God. Missionaries are often called for serving specific populations or to go through difficult circumstances and situations.

But regardless of the type of call, wherever God has chosen to place us, we are all challenged by Jesus' command in Matthew 28:19-20: "Therefore go and make disciples of all nations, baptizing them in the name of the Father and of the Son and of the Holy Spirit, and teaching them to obey everything I have commanded you. And surely I am with you always, to the very end of the age."

What inspires you most about missionary Robert Webb's story?

Where and how do you believe God is calling you to serve him?

9

FREED FROM ANGER, SET FREE TO GROW

By Claude Flamand

*C*laude Flamand has been blessed with a rich career in ministry, serving as a pastor, Teen Challenge director and Living Free director for France, as well as a businessman. Today his extensive ministry is concentrated primarily in France and Belgium. He is a wonderful communicator of the gospel to hurting and hopeless people. In this brief chapter he shows us how painful experiences in childhood can later influence us with anger and other emotions, but also how such experiences can serve to guide us to a deeper encounter with God's faithfulness.

✣

As I was growing up, I was filled with anger. It lived inside me all the time, and I vented it on everyone and everything. Even after I came to know Jesus Christ, being saved as a teenager, and later becoming a pastor, that anger remained present and evident in my life. Through the years, I asked myself, "Why? Why am I so angry?" I could never find the answer – and this anger continued to control my life.

In 1992, I was participating in Living Free training and taking part in a group discussion. The leader asked the question: "What is the first memory you have of Jesus?"

As I closed my eyes and tried to remember, suddenly the memories flooded my mind. When I was nine years old, my mother was expecting a baby. My younger sister and I were so excited. We were going to have a brother! And then, when she was six months along, my mother lost the baby.

My father took me to visit my mother in the hospital. She and I wept together, and she tried to comfort me by telling me that the Bible says if we truly desire to follow Jesus, we have to carry a cross every day. I looked up to see a minister standing near her bedside, and he was affirming her words. Misunderstanding their message, my young mind concluded, "Jesus killed my brother."

Suddenly, reviewing this distant memory at the Living Free training session, I understood: I had been angry at Jesus all these years! This realization, understanding how I had wrongly interpreted the miscarriage of the baby I had hoped to enjoy as my little brother, opened the door to freedom.

As I shared this revelation with the group, everyone prayed for me. At that time God touched my life and healed me. I was able to let go of the past, and to accept God's forgiveness. I was at last free to grow into the person He had designed me to be.

Bringing It Home

One of the wonderful ways in which God is faithful is setting us free from past or present disappointments and setbacks. "Childhood trauma and rejection often hinder our spiritual and emotional growth" (*Free to Grow*, Lee, page 15).

With God's help, we can face and overcome our disappointments, rejection and setbacks. Jesus says, "Then you will know the truth, and the truth will set you free" (John 8:32). The Scripture also says, "but I will not take my love from him, nor will I ever betray my faithfulness" (Psalm 89:33).

Can you identify a painful area of your life (from the past) that continues to bother you today? If so, what is it? And how, like Claude

Flamand, can you acknowledge it, turn it over to the Lord, and allow Him to set you free from your feelings of continued hurt and sadness?

In prayer, identify your disappointment and ask Jesus to walk with you to total victory. Being faithful, God will do this if you ask Him.

10

'GOD, I DON'T THINK YOU ARE CHALLENGING ME ENOUGH'

By Hugh O. Maclellan, Jr.

*H*ugh O. Maclellan, Jr. served as Chairman of the Board of The Maclellan Foundation, Inc. for 20 years. The Maclellan Foundation, Inc., based in Chattanooga, Tennessee, is focused on supporting Christian causes at home and around the globe. With a heart to invest in evangelical, faith-based solutions throughout the world and encourage wise giving among Kingdom Investors, The Maclellan Foundation, Inc. partners with many ministries worldwide.

Without question, no one has ever come close to influencing my life – and changing it – the way Jesus Christ has. In 1970, when my wife, Nancy, and I were 30 years old, a young minister and his wife came into our church. We were in a "modern church," and went to Sunday school, but did not understand what a life of faith was all about. The young minister invited our age group to meet on Friday nights for discussions in small groups. Nancy and I were tired of the cocktail parties and going to the movies, so we agreed to attend. The minister and his wife broke the couples up into small groups and moved us into the Bible. Within five or six months we were more excited about the Bible than we could have imagined. We had never before understood the depth of the Bible and its application to our daily lives. Our eyes had been opened.

A few months later, the Bill Gothard "Basic Youth Conflict" ministry held a three-day meeting in Atlanta, and Nancy and I were among the 10,000 people attending. I remember on the second night she and I knelt by our bed in our motel room and prayed, "Lord, we would like to have you as Lord of our lives. We give you our children, our time, our weekends, and we even want to give you our money which is mostly tied up in Provident stock – but please don't sell it now because the price is too low." It was very scary as a young couple to make that kind of commitment. But here's the thing. It not only changed our lives; it changed our church, too. By the end of three years there were over 100 of us, ages 30-50, who had committed our lives to Jesus Christ.

Looking back, I knew I had accepted Christ in 1952 as a 12-year-old at a Billy Graham crusade in Chattanooga, but nobody discipled me. I went through college at Vanderbilt University, and Nancy and I attended Presbyterian House on campus every Sunday, but the leader never mentioned Jesus Christ once! So everything Nancy and I were learning in the small group Bible studies, along with other events we attended, was new to us – and very inspiring and motivating.

Some time later, Billy Graham's brother-in-law, Leighton Ford, invited Nancy and me to a Lausanne Covenant Executive Committee meeting in Bermuda. There we met some of the world's top Christian leaders, a real revelation for me. I said, "Nancy, look at all these leaders from around the world who are strong Christians. I thought only American leaders were strong Christians."

I was excited and invited some of these leaders to Chattanooga to meet our family foundation trustees. Les Thompson, a missionary from Latin America, was the first. He explained what God was doing in *every* country in Latin America. What we heard blew their minds. A primary reason this was happening in Latin America, Les explained, was there had been an earthquake in Guatemala where 60,000 people died.

Many "do-gooders" had gone down to help in the aftermath of the earthquake. During that time the Holy Spirit moved in their lives and started spreading the gospel through all of South America. One Catholic priest took his message of evangelism and discipleship back to 300 parishes. He taught the "Four Spiritual Laws" and emphasized that Jesus Christ is not only Savior, but also Lord! Because of Les Thompson telling the trustees of what was happening in Latin America, the Maclellan Foundation started investing in Latin America. Then we started to support works in Africa, as well as Russia just before the Berlin Wall came down. So when that momentous event came about, we were already prepared to help in reaching young people who had never been allowed to attend Sunday school or youth group.

One day our Foundation consultant, Pat MacMillan, suggested I go overseas and "kick the tires" to see what was happening. On that trip I saw the "Jesus Film" in action. The audience cheered and clapped when Jesus healed people and cried when Jesus was crucified. Everywhere the film was shown, the town would immediately start a church with many attending. The reason was simple: Up until that time they had heard about Jesus, but knew nothing about Him or His life! The "Jesus Film" showed His life, death on the cross and resurrection from the dead. For the first time Jesus became very personal to them. God allowed me to be part of the promotion of the "Jesus Film" worldwide for the next 15 years. In addition, thousands of ministries used the "Jesus Film" to start churches. What an investment in eternity!

After coming back from an exciting Asian trip, I attended a Campus Crusade for Christ dinner in California where its founder, Bill Bright, spoke about Gideon's 32,000 troops. Bill explained, "God said 32,000 was too many, so Gideon cut it down to 10,000. God said that was still too many, so Gideon cut it down to 300 people." Then Bill Bright made a tremendously impactful comment. He said, "That is all God needs – 300 faithful, faithful people." I was so moved by his comment that I went up to my room and wept. I felt the Holy Spirit saying to me, "That is all God needs, Hugh – 300 who are faithful, faithful. Don't worry about other people. You can be one of those faithful 300 people!"

I immediately went back home and wrote a 10-year life plan. In that 10-year plan I wanted to go all out for God with my life, my time, my talent, my treasure. Here is how I decided to go about it:

My time – I dropped out of the Rotary Club for two years so I could begin discipling people one on one. **My talent** – I knew I had the gift of seeing the bigger picture and being somewhat of a visionary. But I needed to hire other people with administrative skills and connections to complement my strengths and help me in pursuing the vision. God blessed that effort. **My money** – I had dinner with Billy Graham one night and afterwards said, "God, I don't think You are challenging me enough in my giving." (Don't ever pray that unless you are ready to be challenged!!) That's when Chattanooga Christian School started, and at the same time I was asked to help take over a college who had lost its Christian mooring. To support both as we sensed God leading required that Nancy and I start giving bigger. We resolved to give 70 percent of our income that year and in the years thereafter; that proved to be the best thing that happened to us financially. It required us to stop buying expensive gadgets (like boats or a second home) that always require more of your time and money.

In seeking to define what faithfulness to God means, I would say: Have that very important quiet time in the morning and **use a journal**. It is only when you are writing down what Scripture says, and what the Holy Spirit is telling you, that you begin to see where you have been ignorant – and when you are arrogant! Then, by reviewing what you have written in previous days, you will be able to see how God is working consistently in your life on a daily basis! And in the process, as you see your faithfulness growing and deepening, you will also see how faithful the Lord has been over the entire time.

Bringing It Home

As Hugh O. Maclellan has shown us in his very personal story, when we submit to the lordship of Jesus in our lives, He provides us with new meaning and purpose. We discover that serving Jesus is the overflow of an enduring, eternal personal relationship with Him.

And as we are faithful in seeking to obey His guidance, we will see how His faithfulness surpasses anything we could ever imagine. "Now to him who is able to do immeasurably more than all we ask or imagine, according to His power that is at work within us" (Ephesians 3:20).

In what ways has God changed and challenged you to walk more fully and faithfully with Him?

How often do you have a "quiet time" with God? What is it like, and do you find it a time when the Lord truly speaks to you? Or is it merely a habit, something to mark off your daily to-do list? If so, how could you change that so it could become a dynamic, rich time of intimate fellowship with Him?

As you read and meditate on the promise God gives in Ephesians 3:20, how can it give you increasing confidence and enthusiasm in your prayer life?

11

FINDING FAITHFULNESS EVEN IN THE SILENCE

By Tammy Webb-Witholt

Tammy Webb-Witholt was raised in Nigeria, West Africa, by her missionary parents, Robert and Dorothy Webb. Although she felt called into ministry at the age of 18, she spent the next 11 years as a prodigal, fleeing from God. In 1990, she discovered the redeeming power of God's love. Tammy graduated from Belmont University in Nashville, Tennessee, and in 2004 married her longtime friend, Wolter Witholt.

Many people find themselves spiritually warmed by Jesus' parable of the "prodigal son," but I know from personal experience that having a prodigal child is anything but a pleasant experience, especially at times when God seems silent and unresponsive. How do I know? Because at one time I was one of those "prodigals."

I can attest with complete certainty that God is faithful to the prodigal. There are difficult seasons for the parents when there seems to be nothing but silence, and it becomes tempting for them to wonder if God is truly faithful to His promises. I think what they need to know is that God is out there, preparing to ambush the prodigal - I like to call them "Holy Spirit ambushes."

At one time I was thinking of writing an article about Bill Gaither songs and the role they have played in our lives. When Mom and Dad were missionaries in Africa, Mother always used to sing, "He Touched Me." Every time she sang it there would be such an anointing and people would start weeping. That song, which I heard countless times during my childhood, stayed with me, even as a little girl living in the dormitory with other missionary children.

I remember we would sing silly songs like "Found a Peanut, Found a Peanut," or "100 Bottles of Beer on the Wall," but as we were coming back from a hike one day, I said, "I know a song. Let's sing that song, 'He Touched Me.' The other children all looked at me in surprise, as if to ask, 'What is that song'?"

One night in California, when I was a prodigal as an adult, it just got to be too much for me. Everything was stress, and I had lots of questions but no answers. So I took off running. It had been raining a little, but after I ran about three-quarters of a mile, it started raining really hard. I had been running full out, as fast as I could, because I wanted to run away from everything – life, just everything. I ducked into a little doorway and stood there trying to get dry, sorting through all of my emotions and thoughts.

About that time I heard some faint music and tuned my ear to figure out what I was hearing. As it turned out, I had dodged the rain by seeking shelter in the doorway of a little storefront church. There was an Hispanic choir rehearsing and at that very second they were singing, "He Touched Me," in Spanish. I have to admit, that got my attention.

There I was, running from all of the questions and emotions churning in my mind and heart, even though nothing had happened. I had not been in a fight with anybody or anything; I just felt things were too much. "Is this God thing real?" I wondered. "Can I trust it?" Then there were all the emotions I was struggling with as a young adult. We all face life with our different personalities, and try to find our answers in different ways. But as I heard "He Touched Me," even being sung in Spanish, I knew at that moment that God was faithful and there was nothing He could not handle. He can handle our questions, He can handle our anger, He can handle anything we are struggling with at any time.

There are consequences that come with being a prodigal. Parents of prodigal children need to understand that even if their children are in a distant land, that doesn't mean the Holy Spirit can't reach them. He is able to assault them, ambush them at any moment; even if they are under the influence of a substance, He can step in. The truths of God that have been planted into their lives and memories will come out.

It is humbling when you realize that God is the faithful Father that sometimes waits, but also the One who sometimes seizes a moment when He can speak to this child who is running.

God is faithful, even in times of silence – to the prodigal and to the parents as well. This silence can be painful. The parents may not see God at work, that He is quietly answering their prayers. They may not see it for a while. I have witnessed this as I have prayed for so many parents. I have seen and felt their pain, knowing I was there at one time.

People trust me because I was a prodigal. They trust me to tell them what's really going on with their kids. Parents do not want to tell others their kids are out living a wild life, but they will tell me. Why do they tell me? Because they know that is what I did. I have prayed with them and often have prayed these words, "Lord, I know you are out there with their child wherever they are. They can never run so far that your Holy Spirit can't ambush them."

I have had so many parents come back and bring me testimonies of what God has done. Maybe their child has not come back yet, but they have given testimonies of things that happened that had to be God doing something that shook these kids up or made them think. It could be anything – even a Bible verse etched in stone at a university, and it just "happened" that they saw it. God can show up anywhere, but the parent has to keep trusting He is big enough to go after those kids.

Faithfulness happens when no one is watching. Mom and Dad taught me that, and God has taught me you have to keep the right attitude. You don't go around and start bad-mouthing people that you think have wronged you. God says, "You keep the right attitude before Me and trust that I will make a way. Don't use man's tools and weapons to get back."

Sometimes I hear a mom and dad talking about, "What if this (or that) happens?" Well, the truth is, God is as faithful now to work out the details of their lives as He was when they were 20 years old themselves, going out on adventures of their own. So we can trust He will be faithful with their children.

Bringing It Home

As Tammy Webb-Witholt has pointed out, God is faithful to the prodigal, and He is faithful to the parents of the prodigal. He is faithful to the skeptic, the hopeless, the learned, and the unlearned. His unlimited, unconditional love and faithfulness reaches out to all of us.

As David says, "Your love, O LORD, reaches to the heavens, your faithfulness to the skies" (Psalm 36:5). Most of all, "if we confess our sins, he is faithful and just and will forgive our sins and purify us from all unrighteousness" (1 John 1:9).

What are some of the struggles that the parents, relatives or friends face in their desire and efforts to help the prodigal?

Why is it so difficult to be faithful during the silent times, when we are waiting for the Lord to answer?

12

IF WE DO THE FIRST THREE THINGS,
HE WILL DO THE FOURTH

By Thomas E. Trask

*T*he Rev. Thomas E. Trask served as the General Superintendent of the Assemblies of God for 14 years. The Assemblies of God are the largest Pentecostal denomination in the world. The Rev. Trask is also a former pastor of Brightmoor Tabernacle in Detroit, Michigan. One of his main themes through out his ministry has been the importance of prayer and fasting. During his ministry as General Superintendent, Dr. Trask said, "I've seen congregations making prayer a priority. When the church prays, God blesses."

In any discussion of the faithfulness of God, we need to consider the importance of a person knowing the will of God. I am a strong advocate and have been for these many years that we can know the perfect will of God. Is there a permissive will? Possibly. But why would one settle for the permissive will when you can have the perfect will of God? So I reflect upon an experience I had years ago when I was serving as District Superintendent of the Assemblies of God for the Michigan District.

I had been serving in this post for three years when I was approached by Brightmoor Tabernacle, a church in the metropolitan area of Detroit, Michigan. It had been served by Bond Bowman for 43 years. He was retiring, so the board of the church came to me and said, "We would like to have you consider being pastor." I said, "I am honored, brethren, but let me do this – let me help you find a pastor. I will give you names of men and you can go to their churches and visit with them." So we did that.

They came back to me about three months later and said, "We did not see anyone else that we were comfortable with, but what about you?" I said, "Look, I have not made that a matter of prayer because I thought I knew the mind of the Lord." I had only been in office for three years, and usually men aren't elected to those offices for that short period of time. I told them I was going overseas to preach in Indonesia, and that I would fast and pray until I get the mind of the Lord for this matter. So I did just that. When I arrived in Indonesia, I said to the missionary there, "I am going over to the chapel – and I am going to be there until I get an answer from the Lord."

My favorite scripture is found in Proverbs 3:5-6, "Trust in the LORD with all thine heart, lean not unto thine own understanding. In all thy ways acknowledge Him, and He shall direct thy paths" (KJV). I believe that and I have believed that for a long time. So I began to pray, "Lord, I will do what ever you want me to do, but I am sure your will is that I remain in the office of District Superintendent."

I wrestled with the Lord a lengthy period of time. I could not get peace. Finally I broke and said, "Okay, God, I will do what You want me to do, but You have to show me that this is Your perfect will for my life." I prayed this because that portion of Scripture says if we do the first three things – "trust in Him, lean not to our own understanding and in all our ways acknowledge Him" – He will do the fourth one: "direct our paths."

In the Assemblies of God, it has historically been a dangerous thing to follow a man (pastor) who has been at a place for a long time, especially 43 years. Usually there has to be a buffer in that transition.

So in my prayer time I said, "Lord, I am not cut out to be a buffer, but if that is what you want me to do I will do it. But here are some conditions I need for You to reveal to me that this is your perfect condition: Number one, I will need a strong vote from that congregation. (It was a congregation of about 700.) Second is I am not a maintenance man. I am not interested in just going in there and maintaining what they have had in the past." (Bond Bowman was a very strong Pentecostal leader, but he had suffered a massive heart attack and had been out of the pulpit for seven months, so the church had been in decline.) So I prayed, "I ask that You give us a revival and help us build Your church."

At the time Brightmoor Tabernacle was located in the inner city, which was in the beginning of decline. When I had first arrived in Detroit, the city had a population of two million people. Today it is less than 700,000 people, so you can imagine the crime and decay that has taken place in the city as a result.

Closing my prayer, I told the Lord these were some things I would need as confirmation. When I said that, He spoke to me and said, "I will do that, I will promise you."

When I went back to the missionary compound, the lead missionary asked what I was going to do. I said, "I am going to go back to Detroit (the state office of the Assemblies of God was in the suburb of Dearborn at the time) and I am going to resign from the Superintendent's office and begin the process of becoming the pastor of Brightmoor Tabernacle." He said to me, "You're crazy, that is foolishness." I said, "Well, foolishness or not, I know what God has spoken to my heart and I am going to obey and leave it to him." And that is what I did.

After returning home I met with the church board, with Brother Bowman in the meeting to make sure the church had promised to take good care of him after 43 years. I said, "Gentlemen, I am willing to submit myself as a candidate for the pastorate, and if that be the will of God I will obey that." We proceeded and in the election I got all but two votes. Two ladies came to me afterward and said,

"Brother Trask, we did not vote for you. We are sorry." I told them that was okay.

I resigned the Superintendent's office and became pastor of Brightmoor Tabernacle. It was a church of about 700 at that time, and the need to provide security for those people who were coming from the suburbs to the inner city was essential. So I had security guards patrolling the parking lot. One Sunday morning a lady came in after the service and said, "Pastor, someone stole the hood off of my car." That gives a little insight into what was happening at the time.

The congregation had purchased 12 acres of land in a western suburb before I became pastor. I thought that was evidently where the Lord wanted us to relocate. So after I had been pastor for two years, we began to lay plans for relocation. We planned for an auditorium that would seat 2,800, but ran into a snag with the city because of the parking needs and traffic that would be generated. Just a mile to the east of us was a large Presbyterian church of about 4,000 people, and the city did not want that kind of traffic in the neighborhood where we intended to build. So they would not put our request for a permit on the council agenda.

This went on for a year, even though we had the plans and were prepared to break ground. Finally, after about a year and a half, the mayor called and said he had our project on the council agenda and had the votes from the councilmen for us to get our permit. The Monday night when the council was to consider the matter, which had been announced to residents of the city of Livonia, a western suburb, so many people showed up you could not get near the council chambers. The councilmen ran scared in the face of opposition, and our permit failed to pass by one vote. The mayor called me the next day and apologized, saying it had become a political thing. He told me to take the city to court and we would get permission from the judge to go ahead with the project. "We did what we had to do, but you will get what you need," he said.

We did take them to court, but in the middle of the court hearing one of my deacons came to me and said, "Pastor, you know those 24 acres that are north in Southfield, Michigan? They are beautiful acreage. Why don't you go with me and I will show them to you." So we went.

The property was owned by the Shriners, who had one of the most beautiful temples in North America in downtown Detroit. They had been thinking they would have to move from downtown Detroit because of the race riots back in those days. So the Shriners had made a study of the geographical center for the metropolitan Detroit with accessibility by expressway and had bought those 24 acres in case they needed to move. But the Shriners had owned the property for 10 years without using it; after the race riots had ended, they determined they were going to remain downtown.

I made an appointment to go see Mr. Kelstrom, the Shriners' potentate. These officials are businessmen who offer one year of service without any remuneration from the organization. He was a kind and wonderful man. I said, "Mr. Kelstrom, you own 24 acres in Southfield, Michigan with accessibility by expressway, and we would like to make you an offer for relocating our church." He went to pull the file on the property and said, "We paid $450,000 for that property 10 years ago," and noted the plans at the time were to relocate their temple from downtown Detroit to that suburb.

Then he said, "Okay, what is your offer?" I answered, "I would like to offer you $450,000 cash." Mr. Kelstrom responded, "Reverend Trask, I can show you offers that we have had over these years for that choice piece of land, many times that amount, and I am sure it cannot be bought for that." He asked if that was my best offer and I replied, "Yes, that is my best offer."

That was on a Friday afternoon, and he explained the Shriners' board was scheduled to meet on Monday night. They had a lot of properties in the area, and according to their constitution and bylaws they were obligated to bring all offers for property to the board. He said, "I will do that for you Monday night and will call you Tuesday, but I can assure you they are not going to accept your offer." I told him I appreciated that. After some small conversation, I thanked him and left.

The next Tuesday morning Mr. Kelstrom called as he had promised. He said, "Good morning, Reverend Trask. I don't know what got into my board, but they voted to sell you that piece of property for $450,000 cash." Amazing, you might say. In a way, yes. We were able to acquire the property at the same price it had been purchased 10 years earlier, and our bid was much lower than others that had been offered previously. But in my view it is simply a very tangible example of the faithfulness of God as we obey his voice and do his will. As we acquired this property, Brightmoor Tabernacle turned around and sold the other piece (the 12 acres we already had), ending up with 24 acres and accessibility by expressway. That was phenomenal, something only God could have done.

I promised Mr. Kelstrom we would bring him a deposit on the land. I also told him we were going to need his help because we had been turned down in Livonia, so we would need to go before the Southfield city council to get permission to build. Little did I know that the mayor of Southfield was a Catholic who had married an Assembly of God woman. When I met with him, he said, "Reverend Trask, I want you people in my city." I responded, "Okay, we have the plans drawn and are ready to go."

In that city council meeting the mayor sat with me in the audience. When our hearing came before the council, he stood and said, "Gentlemen, I want this church in Southfield, Michigan. I want you men to pass it tonight." And they did, so we were able to start building on the property just a short time later.

Over the years this church we had the joy of pastoring grew to more than 2,000. What it taught me, and I could give other testimonies about this, was that if we will be faithful in doing what God's Word tells us to do, He is a God of covenant and will keep His promise. Before accepting the role of pastor, I had asked Him to do two things: 1) give me a strong vote of support from the church members, and 2) enable me to see the growth of the church since I did not want to be a maintenance person. God was faithful in doing both as a result of our being obedient to the voice of His Spirit.

A similar thing happened years later while I was still pastoring Brightmoor Tabernacle. The man who had followed me in the Superintendent's office came to me and said, "I am going to have to resign and want you to call a special council to elect a new Superintendent. My wife is not well, and she needs my care." We were dear friends and he had made Brightmoor his church home, so I agreed to do that since I had been elected as District Assistant Superintendent while pastoring Brightmoor.

I knew we were loved by the people in the Michigan District, so I took time to go to our campgrounds where we had a mobile home so I could fast and pray to get the mind of the Lord in this whole matter. The assistant superintendent had asked me, "You will come back into the district office won't you?" I had said I was not interested in coming back to the district office. I was so fulfilled in pastoring the church and seeing how God was blessing. People were being saved and filled and delivered, week after week. We had built the congregation on prayer and the work of the Spirit. So I said, "I am not interested. I am having the time of my life pastoring."

But I knew I would have to make a decision, so I took the time to go out to the campgrounds and pray. I asked the Lord to show me what to do. I was willing do whatever He wanted me to do, but needed Him to show me clearly so I could be assured that He was in it.

The Lord did show me what to do. We went to Lansing, Michigan for the specially called District Council and were sitting in the green room off to the side when the outgoing Superintendent asked me, "Tom, what are you going to do?" I said, "If I am elected on the nominating ballot I will accept it as the Lord's will. If not, I am going to withdraw my name." He got upset with me and responded, "You can't do that! You know everybody puts their name on the nominating ballot so they can go home and say they were nominated for district superintendent." I told him I understood that, but insisted this was what I was going to do.

We went out and started the council meeting. On the nominating ballot the vote count was not shown, but the head of the Teller's

Committee came and handed the Superintendent and the gentleman sitting beside me on the platform the nominating ballot report. I needed 383 votes to be elected and had 377. I was just short of the number required for being elected on the nominating ballot, so he handed the report to me and said, "Look at this." When I saw the result of the voting, I proceeded to withdraw my name.

Then members of the council asked, "What is Brother Trask's problem?" The chairman turned to me and asked if I wanted to make a statement. I replied that I had no statement to make, but they would not go on with the council until I did. So I said, "Look, I have made this a matter of prayer and if I had been elected on the nominating ballot I would have accepted. But in as much as I did not, then I accept that as the Lord's will." When they heard that, they asked, "Why didn't you tell us?" I said, "I was trying to ascertain the Lord's will in this matter and I am comfortable with this, so you must go ahead and proceed to elect a new superintendent."

Our son, Brad, who was on staff at Brightmoor, was in the congregation and several of the fellows got around him urging that he get a hold of his dad and tell him he had made a mistake. "We want him to serve," they said. So Brad came around behind the platform, knelt down behind my chair and said, "Dad, you have made a mistake. They want you to serve as superintendent." I replied, "Brad, it is okay. I cannot change the rules on God in the middle of the game. It is going to be okay. Just trust me."

Seven ballots later the council elected a new superintendent, and we went back home to Detroit that night. When I walked in the church office the next morning, I was greeted by balloons and a "Welcome Pastor" sign (everybody had known what was going on). I was thrilled at how the Lord had shown us His will, and we continued to pastor at Brightmoor.

However, two weeks later to the day (it was a Wednesday), I came home from the church office and as I walked into the kitchen about 5 o'clock, the phone rang. It was Brother G. Raymond Carlson, the General Superintendent of the Assemblies of God, who had been my district superintendent when I was pioneering a church in the Minnesota District. He said the Executive Presbytery was in session. "Raymond Hudson, our General Treasurer, has resigned and these brethren have elected you as General Treasurer." I replied, "Brother Carlson, why would I want to be General Treasurer? I am a pastor and I'm having the time of my life." I explained I would need some time to pray about this. He told me I would have until 8 a.m. the next day because the men are in session and needed my answer.

My wife, Shirley, and I were in turmoil with this unexpected news, but I promised to call Brother Carlson the following morning. So Shirley and I prayed that night. We sought God, and He spoke to our hearts and assured us, "This is my will for your life." So I called them at 8 the next morning and said, "Brother Carlson, we will accept the decision of the Executive Presbytery."

I have presented these examples of how the Lord has shown His will in my life because it is important for each of us to know we can count on the faithfulness of God if we will abandon ourselves to His will, His purpose, and His plan. It is perfect. You will always have the fullness of joy and will know of His faithful hand upon you. It's when we try to direct and make our own determinations that we fail. But if we trust those scripture promises to commit our ways, trust in the Lord with all our heart, and lean not to our own understanding, acknowledging Him in all our ways, He has promised that He will direct our paths.

As I reflect back on how He has guided, I can see God's hand in preparing me to be the General Superintendent of the Assemblies of God. For those who are in the throes of making decisions, whether it involves the ministry, business or whatever, we can count on God's faithfulness if we will bring ourselves to the abandonment of our will and say, "Lord, it doesn't matter what my will is. I want to do Your will. I want to fulfill Your pleasures and Your desires." He will remain faithful. He will do what He has promised to do. And He will direct our path.

Too often we make our own decisions on money, prestige, position, or whatever the case may be. That is not what it is about – it is doing what He wants you to do, so that when you come to the end you can say, "Lord, I have had the joy of being obedient to Your will." There is absolutely nothing greater.

Bringing It Home

The Rev. Trask emphasizes Proverbs 3:5-6, "Trust in the LORD with all thine heart, lean not unto thine own understanding. In all thy ways acknowledge Him, and He shall direct thy paths." As he says, if we do the first three things, then God will do the fourth.

Where do you see your life as it relates to the following areas:

- Trusting in Him?

- Leaning not on your own understanding?

- Acknowledging Him in all your ways?

In what ways have you seen the LORD direct your paths? How do you feel when you reflect on the direction He has provided, especially at times when you would have chosen a different path?

13

JESUS: CLOSER THAN A BROTHER

By Maury Davis

*T*he Rev. Maury Davis is the senior pastor of Cornerstone Church in Madison, Tennessee. Pastor Davis's testimony is one of a remarkable journey that has taken him from inside the walls of a penitentiary after committing a horrific crime to the unlikely opportunity to become pastor of one of the great churches in America. A man with a great passion for his Savior, Jesus Christ, Pastor Davis knows firsthand the faithfulness of God in granting the desires of one's heart, even when those desires seem impossible.

The first 18 years of my life I had never been to church. Then, after committing a horrible murder in Dallas, Texas and being arrested, I became an inmate in the Dallas County Jail. It was there that I had my first encounter with God, being led to the Lord by the kind and compassionate ministry of a local pastor, Don George. From that moment I began learning about God's faithfulness, realizing that for me it had been at work long before I entertained the first thought about Him. God, in spite of the heinous crime I had committed, was faithful to me before I knew He even existed the way most people in church do.

So it was there, in prison, that Jesus Christ became my best friend and I began what would become a lifelong walk with Him. In the process, members of my family also got saved and He was faithful to bring the whole family in. In May 1975, about five months after I was arrested, I went to trial and was sentenced to prison for 20 years. Although I knew God had forgiven me for taking another person's life, that did not free me from the consequences of my sin.

Today I still possess a letter I wrote as a 19-year-old inmate, not long after my conviction. Reviewing this letter, it always reminds me of God's promise in Psalm 37:4, that if we delight in the Lord, He will give us the desires of our heart. In His faithfulness, the Lord says he will do this even when the desires He places on our hearts seem like "mission impossible."

In the letter I talked to my family about the possibility of parole, which is what everyone is looking for once you know you are going to prison. But I also set out some goals in life. Looking back on them now, I guess they represented the birthing of a dream God was giving me. This is exactly what I wrote: "I will be here about 3 more weeks before they send me down, and then it will be 3 weeks before I will be in touch, but you all don't worry because I will be fine – because for the first time in my whole life I know what I am fixing to do. I am going to go back to school in prison and study psychology, then I am going to take a correspondence course and get a degree in ministry, so that when I get out I will be able to find a use for myself and hopefully, be able to help others."

It seems so amazing now, at 58 years old, to read that letter written 40 years ago and realize everything I had in my heart at that time, God has allowed me to do. I got out of prison after serving for 8½ years of tough, hard time – as difficult as anything you can imagine. Despite that, God was faithful to not let me become calloused. He also was faithful to cause me to become more spiritual and more tenderhearted toward others in an environment that obviously is not intended to do that. God was faithful to keep my family in His protective care, and upon my release was faithful to give me a job as a janitor at a church in Irving, Texas. Then, one after another, miracles and more miracles began to happen.

A former prison inmate, I became the youth pastor at the church, and then had the privilege of traveling all across America working in schools. One time I was in Tuscaloosa, Alabama for six weeks, working and counseling with some students after a rash of public school suicides. I remember thinking at the time how amazing it was that God had allowed me to help kids who were having problems similar to what I had experienced.

Today, sitting in my office on the campus of Cornerstone Church, I am the father of four children, all married. Both of my sons are in vocational ministry, and both of my daughters are faithful, actively involved participants in church. All of their spouses are also saved and serving the Lord. And my wife, Gail, has stayed by my side for 29 years. No question, God has been faithful to me.

When you look back over the years of life and reflect, "How do you have a dream and at the end of life say it all came true?" it's truly amazing. Because most people can't say that. Most people look back at their lives and wish they had not lost their dream. They would be happy if just part of the dream had come true.

But I think when you discover the goodness of God in your life, and make a full commitment to that goodness for serving Him and your fellowman in His name, the faithfulness of God manifests itself and produces results that no man by human intellect can produce. So as I sit here today, in this incredible environment, I have no doubt it is entirely a product of God's faithfulness.

Central to God's faithfulness is the assurance that He never fails. Having never read the Word of God prior to the time the pastor was guiding me to faith in Jesus Christ, there were a few scriptures he took me to that were very critical for me in my broken, dysfunctional, scared state. At that moment I had no idea what my future held. I thought I might be going to get killed or face the death penalty. I was certainly feeling alone. But the caring pastor took me to the scripture that said Jesus would be a friend to me that sticks closer than a brother, and showed me the passage where Jesus said, "I will never leave you or forsake you, I will be with you always."

Now, looking back over 40 years of serving the Lord, I realize I've never ever felt forsaken by Him. I have had people forsake me, I have had people reject me, and I've had church members come and church members go. Yet of all who have come and gone, Jesus has been the only consistent one.

I've learned He is there in the morning, He is there in the night. He shares the joys, He shares the tears, He shares the ups and the downs, He shares the sun and the rain, He shares both the blessings and the emptiness when you have it. He is there to fix it. He is a faithful friend. He is always there, an ever-present God.

Faithfulness, one of God's greatest characteristics, is something He wants us to exhibit as well. We tend to identify ourselves with what the men and women around us would appreciate, regarding that as the fruit of a man's life. We always want to get to the fruit. But more important is what produces the fruit. Faithfulness is the root of the fruit, and faithfulness is something we practice privately, not publicly.

We typically think, "I want people to see the fruit – the apples, the peaches, etc." But that is God's job. Our job is to be connected to the vine. Our job is to dig down deeply, maybe through some tough soil. We all want to be fruitful, but we don't have to focus on being fruitful. We just have to focus on being faithful. God will do the rest.

The Bible deals historically and spiritually with our character formation, with the development and realization of our dreams, the dreams God gives to us. It deals with the correction of our flaws; it deals with grace for humanity, as well as expectations for our "spirit man." It deals with our future, and our past; it deals with every significant life question.

Knowing this, when I get up in the morning and am reading the Bible, I realize I am reading the past, present and future tense mind of God, and He wrote it so that I would never have to feel like I did not know what He was thinking. Above all, He is faithful.

Bringing It Home

Submitting to a saving relationship with Jesus is having a friend who sticks closer than a brother (Proverbs 18:24). Receiving Jesus as Savior (see Romans 10:9) means He walks with us on a daily basis whether on top of the world or in a prison cell. God has said, "Never will I leave you; never will I forsake you" (Hebrews 13:5).

Why is it important to have someone stick close to you – like a brother, sister or friend?

What comfort do you get by knowing that God will never forsake you?

14

FAITHFULLY RESTORING FAMILY RELATIONSHIPS

By Wayne Barrington

Wayne Barrington, now retired, was the owner of First Financial of Tennessee, and One Stop Financial Center in Chattanooga, Tennessee. He and his wife, Rose, are an integral part of their home church, where they can be found on the front row on most Sunday mornings. Wayne, who has remained steady despite difficult times with his family, has inspired others by showing through his faithful persistence and unwavering trust how the love of God has stood by him every step of his journey.

When God wants to do a work, He will use any means necessary, even if it's unconventional or runs against what we would consider common sense. Thankfully, as He has shown me many times, God's sense trumps common sense every time.

I had built a successful financial service company in East Tennessee, and had just opened another office in north Georgia. We were quickly growing and doing well. I woke up one morning in September at 4 a.m. and felt like the Lord was speaking to me (impressing on my heart), but I didn't like what He was saying. "I want you to close your offices. Shut them down completely," God told me. I was stunned. I said, "Lord, I just recently opened the new office, and we have contracts in the works!" But I heard Him clearly restate, "I want you to close them down immediately." I argued, "But I have leases on the buildings!" My thinking was, "This is going to cost us thousands of dollars in leasing fees," because once you've entered a commercial lease, you can't just "change your mind." Needless to say, I did not get any more sleep that morning!

Later that day I went to talk to the owner of the buildings and told him we would be vacating, but that I understood I still had at least two years on the leases, so I needed to make arrangements for continued monthly lease payments. The owner informed me someone had just asked about my office space earlier in the week, so if I could be moved out completely and have the office painted and move-in-ready by the end of the month, he would cancel the lease with me with no penalty – and even return my security deposits. Unbelievable!

It was around the 15th of the month, so we only had two weeks to do everything. We got busy and were able to get everything moved, painted and cleaned. When I came into his office on August 30 to return the keys, the building owner had a check waiting for me – the return of my security deposits.

It was an unusual feeling not having to "be somewhere" every day – I felt lost. I asked God, "Now what?" After a couple of weeks of working around the house, I felt He was urging me to visit my parents and brother in Warner Robins, Georgia. I gave them a call, asking if I could come and see them for a few days. That "few days" eventually turned into almost two weeks.

When I was a child, my parents and I had a terrible relationship, and as I got older we just seemed to tolerate each other. I had a particularly bad relationship with my mother because of her abuse, deception, and the horrible things that she had done to me when I was young. Not only did her abuse shape my attitudes toward life from childhood, but also my opinion of "Christians." I would describe her as a "holy" person on the weekend, and a holy terror the rest of the week.

As an adult, I had chosen to stay away from the abuse for my own self-preservation and sanity. Even after I became a Christian later in life, I had forgiven her but could not seem to let go and forget. My wife, Rose, once commented, "As your parents get older, they may eventually have to move in with us." My reply was, "They can come to our home for Thanksgiving, Christmas, or some other holiday, but THEY WILL NEVER live with us! I WILL NOT have that strife in our home!" I did not realize that God wanted to remove that "broken" part of my life, and give me something wonderful in return.

As I was visiting with my parents and my brother, Roy, I began sharing what God had done for me since I had given my heart to Him. Several opportunities came up for me to talk about the Lord, and how He had changed me, saved me, given me another chance at life, etc. My family looked at me with amazement, almost as if to say, "Who is this person, and what have you done with Wayne?" God is SO GOOD!

Previously, my brother was so "religiously" whipped that he would not even allow you to pray for him. When I became a Christian, I would try to discuss how God had given me hope, and how Roy could experience the same peace. He would scoff, saying, "That's good for you, but do not bother me with it." I would try to pray for him, and he would tell me, "Don't bother praying for me...I don't believe in all that! I don't want you praying for me, either! Don't pray, don't do anything!" He was adamant!

Little did I know Roy had been watching Rose and me. Now, ten years later, I found several things on the house that needed to be repaired and I began working on them. My brother came up to me after one of his dialysis appointments and said, "When you get finished, why don't we go out to Oakey Woods and do some camping?" (This area is a place where we used to spend a lot of time together as children, and it was very special to both of us.)

A few days later, while we were sitting by the fire, he said, "I wanted to ask you some questions, and I did not want Mom and Dad around to hear or comment. If they hear me ask you, they will give me the same old, same old." I said, "Okay, shoot." His questions began with, "Tell me about that God stuff." I replied, "What?" He repeated, "Tell me about that God stuff." I asked, "What do you mean, 'That God stuff'?" Roy's response was, "You know, your religion." I said, "I don't have religion. I have a relationship." "Well, tell me about it," Roy said.

For the next three or four days we talked and talked. He was very open and told me that he had been watching me deal with Mom and Dad for the last several years, and stated, "It's like you even LIKE them now." (I was the oldest, so when the abuse, the deception, the beatings came from my parents, I was the first to get them, and he learned to get out of the way before it got to him.) I told him, "Through Christ, I am able to love and accept them, but I am constantly working to learn to like them."

When I got back to Chattanooga, I told Rose this had been the best visit that I had ever had with my family. I had gone to visit without any expectations – I did not expect love and friendship, only that everyone would be civil to each other. I did not need any of my family to "fulfill me," since God is my provider and my strength. It turned out to be a wonderful visit, beyond anything I could have hoped.

After returning home, I began working around the house, trying to get used to being "retired." My "honey-do" list was beginning to be significant. I also saw a doctor about hip replacement surgery I had been putting it off for months; I had been too busy. The hip joint had begun bothering me to the point that I had trouble walking, even with a cane. Now that my business was closed, I had the time to get it replaced.

Two weeks after my return from the visit with my family, on Sunday morning, November 15, while I was at church my phone began buzzing. It was my parents' number. I thought to myself, "They know I am in church, so I will call them when the service is over." But I received several more calls from their number, and then received a call from one of their neighbors. I thought, "What is going on? What is so important?"

When I excused myself and answered the phone, I found out my brother, Roy, had died suddenly that morning. I was speechless – I had just been with him two weeks earlier! This couldn't be happening! Rose and I immediately went home, threw some clothes into a suitcase, and drove to Warner Robins.

Because Roy had lived in my parents' home for most of his life, the three of them had become dependent on each other for their daily activities. Each had weaknesses and strengths, and Rose and I used to call their family unit a "three-legged stool." Now, one of the legs was missing. My parents seemed to be consumed by grief and fear – the loss of Roy, as well as, "What are we going to do? How will we be able to function?"

The funeral was four days later, on Thursday, November 19. Immediately after the service, dozens of people came to the house to "visit." In the middle of the chaos, the dishwasher overflowed onto the kitchen floor. I found not only did we have a leak, but also one that had been leaking slowly for months. There was significant damage to the floor, walls and half of the cabinets. The entire kitchen would have to be dismantled and repaired.

Rose had to go back to Chattanooga the following Saturday, November 21, to take care of her own mother. The next day, Sunday, November 22, my dad had a massive heart attack. It was only three days after Roy's funeral. And two days after that, on Tuesday, November 24, my mom also had a heart attack. Initially they were being treated at the same hospital, but Dad was soon transferred to a larger hospital approximately 45 minutes away. I was now traveling between hospitals to visit with my parents, talk to their doctors, and make plans for remodeling the house, as well as working as the administrator of Roy's estate. My Dad was released from his hospital just in time for the two of us to visit Mom in her hospital room on Thanksgiving Day.

My hip, still in need of a replacement, had never had a workout quite like this one. The pain was intense and aspirin would only go so far. I was my own worst enemy – a victim of my own "stinkin' thinkin.'" I would think, "All of this pressure and responsibility, when

I can barely make it myself. I think that I am going to die." Then the Lord gave me some scripture passages to ponder: Deuteronomy 28, Deuteronomy 31:6, and Jeremiah 29:11. He said, "Wayne, here are My promises. Be strong and courageous, Wayne! I will not leave you, nor forsake you! I know the plans that I have for you." I was thinking to myself, "I can't do this anymore, Lord. It's too overwhelming! It seems impossible for one person to be able to handle all of this with the integrity that You want." God simply replied, "Nothing is impossible with Me. I have you in the palm of My Hands. Trust Me! Trust in Me! Trust in My plans for you!"

Over the next few months, I would sleep for a couple hours a night, get up and go to work. During the night, I would work on Roy's estate. During the day, I would work a little on the kitchen in between other appointments with doctors, attorneys, or the county clerk. Sometimes, I would try to catch 10-15 minutes of sleep while waiting in the doctor's office for one of my parents' appointments. You do what you can, with what you have, for as long as you can. And, in all things, God remained faithful!

One night, again at 4 a.m. (God seems to really like waking me up at 4 in the morning to get my attention), I woke up and felt God was telling me to go to the "country home" in Kathleen, Georgia. This was the original residence my parents lived in before they bought their house in the city 35 years ago, and Roy had been using it to "get away for the weekend." Since this home was only 17 miles from their current home, he also had used it for storing mountains of paper he wanted to save. This included old magazines, interesting newspaper articles, ads about things he wanted to do or see, junk mail, and a host of other scraps of loose paper – stored in 50 banana boxes in the spare bedroom, as well as behind a sofa in the living room.

Still sleepy, I argued with the Lord again, saying, "Lord, I have so much to do here. I don't have time to go there. I just need some more sleep." But God would not let me rest. He said, "Get up and go to Kathleen!" After arriving in Kathleen before sun-up, I looked around and said, "Okay, Lord, You've got me here. What now?" I heard Him say, "Sort the boxes." "Sort the boxes!" I retorted. "You got me here so that I can start ANOTHER project? I don't have time to do what I have to do in Warner Robins, and now You tell me to start wasting my time looking through boxes of junk?" I was tired and irritated. But God was unrelenting. He reminded me again, "I know the plans I have for you, Wayne. Trust Me."

So for the next three weeks I added another 34 miles and 2-3 hours of "sorting" to my daily routine. Dad was in and out of the hospital with his heart, had surgery to implant a pacemaker, but soon had problems with the device. After another surgery to put in a different pacemaker, and more recovery time, his hospital stays were getting longer and more difficult to spring back from. My mother's kidneys were failing, and she was going to dialysis three times a week. There was one positive: With my dad in the hospital, we were spending much more time together. I even became comfortable talking about some of the things that happened to me as a child.

It seemed I was either on the road all the time, in the middle of the kitchen repair, or sorting boxes in Kathleen. Everything seemed like a blur. One day, while sorting another box literally consisting of junk mail, I was tempted to just burn the three boxes that were left. I thought, "If you've seen one piece of junk mail, you've seen them all. I have gone through 47 boxes of junk so far. Why am I doing this, Lord?"

Then as I picked up one piece of mail from an insurance company, it had Roy's name on the front, was marked that it was for $25,000, and it looked "official." But many of the pieces of junk mail I had been sorting for the last three weeks had been insurance company promotions and sales pitches, so I just tossed that letter into the "gone through, and ready to burn" pile. That's when I felt the presence of the Lord touch me. This piece of mail had looked different, so I set it aside and returned to sorting.

Later that morning, as I was examining the letter and the enclosed paperwork, I realized this was an actual policy for $25,000, but it was expired. As I examined the policy, I realized it had not expired until 3 days after my brother had died. Since I had to go into Macon again that afternoon, and the insurance company that issued the policy was also in Macon, I took the policy with me. When I called them, they asked me to bring the policy by the office and they would have a look. After examining the policy, the lead agent asked for a certified copy of Roy's death certificate and informed me they would begin processing the policy.

On May 19 the following year, Dad had another massive heart attack and died. In addition to her grief, my mother was worried about money and how she would make it without his retirement income. Two days later, the insurance company called and asked her to come and sign for the $25,000 check, payment from Roy's insurance policy. Did I mention that God is faithful?

Approximately one month later, on June 22, my mother succumbed to her own health issues. During the previous couple of months, God had allowed me to forgive my mother for all of the terrible things that she did to my brother and me, and we were able to talk on a level I would have never believed possible. Through Christ, I learned to love her as I never had, and even to *like* her for her strengths, while dismissing her weaknesses.

Sometimes, it seems crazy to listen to what God tells you to do. When I had shut down my company's offices about eight months earlier, that also meant eliminating our health plans and employee insurances. Needing to have hip surgery and being without health insurance is a scary and expensive proposition. The surgery would cost approximately $50,000 in total, including rehabilitation therapy. The hospital would give a 51 percent discount for clients paying cash, but that would still mean my having to pay about $25,000 out of pocket! But God's faithfulness manifested itself again. In His infinite provision the Lord had brought peace to my mom with a check for $25,000; then a month later, because of her death, the funds were passed to me, just in time to provide a much-needed hip surgery.

This testimony is not about surviving a grievous family ordeal, or about getting $25,000 for hip surgery. The thing that was most valuable to me, and for the sake of the Kingdom of God, was that my mother was the last one to die. This gave me the opportunity to be there with her every day, to build a relationship that I would never have had except through all of the trials that we went through. I was able to forgive her for all the bad that was behind, and look ahead to the future. My mother was not one to ask for forgiveness or admit she was ever wrong, even in her dying days, so it was more about me being able to forgive, and expecting nothing in return. And I was able to tell her with genuine honesty that I really did love her.

After my entire family had died, incredibly within only an eight-month span of time, Rose and I needed to sell the two homes that were in the estate. We had decided to sell the Warner Robins home first, since there was less work to do on it to get it ready to put on the market. We listed with a real estate company for a six-month period, but the house just sat. And sat. And sat.

During those six months, only three people looked at the property, and two of those people were other realtors. In addition, property values were plummeting and the house had lost 25 percent of its value due to the "housing bubble" that had burst the year before. I had lowered the price twice in the six-month period, and the realtor suggested I lower it again and list it for another six months. I felt sick, because I had gotten ahead of God. I had never asked Him which property to sell first, or even if we should sell at all. Rose and I began to fast and pray about what we should do.

After the contract had expired, I was in the realtor's office contemplating relisting the property when I heard, "Do not relist Warner Robins, but immediately list Kathleen. List it today!" Again, as I'm inclined to do, I argued, "Yes, Lord, We want to sell the property in Kathleen, but I don't even have it clean enough to show, and it is going to take a lot of work." All I heard was, "TODAY! NOW!" So I did as God directed – I listed the house in Kathleen.

We immediately entered the data into the computer while we were at the real estate agent's office, then drove down to the property to take pictures and measurements for her "online tour." As we walked around the house, I gave her the history of the property and shared a few cherished memories I had experienced while living there as a boy. A peace came over me, and I knew God would handle all of my anxiety about the work that needed to be done to make a sale on this property. After we got back to the office, I decided to rent the Warner Robins property rather than drop the price any further. So I went back to the Warner Robins home and put out a "For Rent" sign in the front yard.

Twelve hours later, I got a phone call from the realtor. She had a contract on the property in Kathleen, and they were in a hurry to move in. Nothing had to be done to it. The buyers wanted the home and property exactly like it was. They were going to remodel it anyway. About the same time, I got a phone call from the rental agency listing the Warner Robins home. They had found "the perfect couple." The house was rented, and the couple has been there to this day.

God carried us through a time of great loss. He gave me the opportunity to find healing from many years of emotional pain. And He orchestrated real estate transactions in ways I could not have imagined. Yes, indeed – God is faithful in ALL things!

Bringing It Home

Living a godly lifestyle can resonate with our immediate and extended family, providing them with an example that no words can express. But this requires commitment to our Lord Jesus Christ, trusting Him even when circumstances would tell us to respond differently.

Joshua says, "Now fear the LORD and serve him with all faithfulness" (Joshua 24:14). He further states, "But as for me and my household, we will serve the LORD" (Joshua 24:15). In Acts 16 when the jailer asked Paul and Silas, "'What must I do to be saved?' They replied, 'Believe in the Lord Jesus Christ, and you will be saved – you and your household....' He (the jailer) was filled with joy because he had come to believe in God – he and his whole family" (Acts 16:30-34).

Are you facing difficult challenges with your immediate and/or extended family? If so, what are they, and how do you think God might be desiring to work and exhibit His faithfulness to you and to them?

Was there anything you noticed about Wayne's story that especially resonates with you? What can you draw from his experiences that you could apply to your own life and circumstances?

15

GOD CAN USE ANYTHING, EVEN A JAMES BOND MOVIE

By Kim Ketola

Kim Ketola hosts a weekly radio program, "Cradle My Heart Radio." *Her mission is to prevent abortion and to help those it has hurt. She is the author of the book,* Cradle My Heart, Finding God's Love After Abortion. *In this personal story, Kim tells us how God worked through her to bring a life-changing message to her brother as he battled cancer.*

God has given me a personal mission to be engaged in the pro-life movement, seeking to dissuade women from having abortions and coming alongside to assist and minister to those who have been hurt by abortion. One reason is that these women – and their unborn children – may through faith one day have the joy of experiencing the faithfulness of God in a heavenly reunion. But for now I would like to tell you about a very different scenario in which the Lord demonstrated His faithfulness to me – also in a "pro-life" way.

My brother, Grady, was one of those people with a larger-than-life personality. We were not particularly close growing up, he being the middle of three younger brothers, and my sister and me being the older siblings. There were three years between the girls and the boys, so Grady and I didn't forge a very close relationship as siblings. But he had a daughter about the same time I did, so the cousins drew us together and we used to visit a lot as our kids were growing up.

Grady became ill with multiple myeloma a couple of years ago, and I went to help with his care while he was being treated at the VA Center in Dallas. For about five weeks Grady was confined to the ICU because they did not discover the cancer until it has ravaged his spine and his kidneys. We nearly lost him several times during those days.

As our kids were growing up, during our many visits Grady and I talked about religion a lot. He did not believe. He was more of a philosopher on life. Things got a little contentious in some of those conversations, especially because my husband, Bruce, and I were very much being motivated at church to get involved in personal evangelism for the first time in our lives. We were pretty much like bulls in the proverbial china shop. We were not subtle. We warned Grady about hellfire and brimstone a lot. Some of those conversations he clearly did not appreciate.

Years before Grady's illness, I had become our mother's caregiver at the end of her life. As Mom was leaving this life, he told me at one point that he had watched a television program that somehow connected the science of astrophysics in deep space to the belief that there must be a God. Something in this program had convinced Grady of the existence of God. Then he went on to tell me that he believed in Jesus Christ because he had seen the way I had cared for Mom. Her personality had changed, making it difficult to show love to her during those days. Grady said he could see how her personality had changed, yet I was still able to love her. So he concluded there had to be something supernatural at play.

When Grady became ill and while he was ailing, I tried many times to have conversations with him, but he assured me that he believed in Jesus. He didn't attend church and had many reasons for that.

One day a psychologist came into the room and asked Grady did he want a visit from a chaplain. He said no, and later he told me, "Kim, if I want to confess I will talk with you." I felt a little bit of a burden at having been appointed his spiritual advisor, but when I tried to bring up spiritual things he would always say, "I am good."

Grady rallied and enjoyed a year of recovery. Then I got a call from our brother, Rob, that it was nearing the end and they were planning to start Grady on a morphine drip. This was less than two years after we had learned about the serious health condition he was dealing with. So I returned to Dallas to be at his side. As soon as I walked in the room, Grady reached out his hand and said, "Kim, pray for me." This was very new behavior for him. I was caught off guard and remember thinking, "I don't know how to pray for the dying." I had not thought of any Bible verses to share with him, but knew job number 1 for him was that he had to forgive certain people. So that is where we started.

I prayed that although Grady had suffered very much injustice in life in the hands of people and in the grip of this horrible disease, that he would be able to forgive. I also prayed for God to grant him that grace. After I finished praying, he said, "I do forgive, I forgive everyone." This was so dear.

Our brother Rob was also in the room and his faith was a question mark as well. They had been watching a movie when I was asked to pray, and Rob asked Grady if he wanted him to turn the movie off. Grady had responded, "No, leave it on." As I took Grady's hand, I asked Rob if he wanted to join us. He said he was fine where he was, but at least he was in the room.

As we were praying this very deep and tender prayer, toward the end we prayed about our faith in Christ and His resurrection. Grady prayed asking God to take him, that he would receive relief from his suffering. When we closed the prayer with an amen, a very quiet calm settled on the room. Just then, from the television I heard, "In a moment, in the twinkling of an eye at the last trump, for the trumpet shall sound and the dead shall be raised incorruptible and we shall all be changed. We therefore commit his body to the deep to be turned into corruption looking for the resurrection of the body when the sea shall give up her dead."

A military funeral was taking place in the movie on the TV, and someone was quoting 1 Corinthians 15:52. All three of us heard it and collectively raised our eyebrows and shook our heads, knowing God had heard our prayers.

The most amazing thing about this, besides its perfect timing, was that the movie was James Bond's "You Only Live Twice," and in the scene they had faked his death and after they had thrown his body into the sea at the end of the funeral, divers dove into the water, pulled 007 out and took him to Japan, where he learned karate. It was not really a spiritual scene at all. But the faithfulness of God had used this to bring His Word to us, confirming His undeniable promise in that room at that moment when my prayers had been so inadequate.

What a comfort that was for all of us. What a comfort to me knowing that Grady got to hear that word. The Lord had arranged that. And also was a comfort to me being assured I did not have to worry about my deficiency in being able to say the right things to my brother.

Later, as I was able to collect myself, we had everyone there gather and we prayed the 23rd Psalm and the Lord's Prayer together. But none of that was as powerful as what God did during that very special moment through the television, using a James Bond movie of all things.

I believe God was so very faithful to come and minister to Grady in that moment when his heart was absolutely open to receive His message. The setting in the film was perfect, and the rest of the day we talked about Grady's love of all things military. That took the focus off his illness and allowed him to feel the dignity of those good memories. He had received his care at a VA center in Dallas, and he and Rob had served together in the Army in Germany when they were younger. I was filled with confidence that God had indeed prepared his heart to receive Jesus as His Savior.

Bringing It Home

Grady could see Jesus because of what he had observed through his sister's faithful care of their mother. Kim's actions spoke more clearly and loudly than her words ever could. She walked her faith in a loving response to her mother, despite how difficult to deal with the dying woman had become, and it was a witness to Grady. What a wonderful example of what Jesus says: "Let your light shine before men, that they may see your good deeds and praise your Father in heaven" (Matthew 5:16).

Who can you think of in your life that has shown a Christ-like walk that has influenced you in a positive way? How has this affected you?

What spoke to you the most about Kim's story? Her persistence in desiring to talk with her brother about Jesus? How God prepared Grady's heart to receive the gospel message at the right time? Or how the Lord saw fit to use a theatrical film that had nothing to do with spiritual matters to confirm His promise to both Grady and Kim?

16

WHAT GOD CAN DO WHEN 'IT CAN'T BE DONE'

By Wayne Keylon

*W*ayne Keylon became the first director of Chattanooga Teen Challenge, a center for the rehabilitation of young men struggling with alcohol and chemical addictions, and he served in that role for 16 years, followed by four years of service as the National Teen Challenge Director. Later he served as the founding director of The Transformation Project. His life and ministry have served as a strong model of a man of faith and passion.

We can learn about God's faithful provision in many ways, as He has shown me through the years. But one of my first lessons in how He provides came nearly 30 years ago while experiencing a vivid example of why building on shifting sand is not a good idea – as Jesus taught in Matthew 7:24-27. But in the process, I also learned not to be afraid of a little dirt. Even a lot of it.

It was in 1987, when I was the director of Chattanooga Teen Challenge and we had been able to purchase the old Florence Crittenton Home, which consisted of a house and eight acres of property. There was about an acre and a half of the property we could not use because it was like a swamp. In fact, nearly an acre of that area was a big hole. We worked and worked, digging ditches by hand from the hole back to a creek hoping to drain the swamp. A foundry in the area gave us some black foundry sand, so we tried to use that to fill in the hole once it was drained. However, one day a worker was driving a tractor across the area when metal in the sand blew two tires on the tractor. It cost $200 to replace them.

Frustrated, I told God we needed to build on this spot but I guessed sand really would not work anyway. We and our Teen Challenge staff had been trying to do it ourselves, but just couldn't make it work. This was where the dirt came in. I called Bob Lynch of Stein Construction Company, asking him to stop by and see how much they would charge us to fill in the area and get it ready for us to build on. After he evaluated the situation, Bob said the amount of dirt it required would cost $800,000. I thought to myself, "We need that dirt, but we do not have the money." So I told our staff and students that every Tuesday we would pray especially about this situation. For two years we prayed for 20,000 cubic yards of dirt.

Finally, about two years after we started praying, I got a call and it was Bob Lynch. He said, "Wayne, I need to meet with you this Tuesday at 8:30 a.m." I asked, "What is it about, Bob?" He said, "It's about dirt." I replied, "I don't know much about dirt, so I will have Jim Eldridge our contractor and Ted Franklin our architect to meet with us."

So we met on that Tuesday morning and I asked Bob what had happened. He said simply, "It was an act of God. The rains came and washed part of Lookout Mountain out into the road. Now we have over 20,000 cubic yards to move within six weeks, and I remembered that you had a hole to fill." He said his company would bring it to us free, adding, "We will grate it off at a six percent grade all the way back to the creek, and you will not have any rock three feet to the surface." Our local CBS-TV affiliate (TV12), which had its production studios in the neighborhood, came and did a story on us and titled it, "An Act of God."

Today, as you drive across Missionary Ridge, especially in the winter and you look up toward the mountain near the Incline Railway, there is a large area of exposed gray rock. It looks like a scar on Lookout Mountain, but it's where the Teen Challenge dirt came from. This happened, I am convinced, because some young men, whom nobody gave a chance because of their addictions, and our staff prayed for two years for 20,000 cubic yards of dirt. It amounted to an $800,000 gift. Now there are buildings all over the property, including a new cafeteria and classrooms standing on that piece of land that no one considered useable.

This wasn't the only example of faith being rewarded during my years at Teen Challenge – not by a long shot. What we always did there was pay the bills first, then salaries, and I was always the last to get paid, assuming there were enough funds. When I left DuPont, God had said to me that if I would lift up His Son, Jesus, and share His love, He would supply my needs. I have had that relationship with God for all of those years and ever since. I know that if I am doing what He asks me to do, He is going to supply the needs. Sometimes it gets tough, and all you can do is just stand. But that is enough.

One particular week we had to have $1,000 come in by Friday just to pay the bills. Things were really tight, but we had enough to pay the bills. So I called all the staff in and said, "We can do one of two things, because there is no money for salaries this week. We can throw up our hands and quit, or we can lift up our hands and start praising God." About that time all the staff raised their hands up into the air and started praising God.

After that worshipful experience, I was doing fine until I got home. My wife, Wanda, is the bookkeeper at our house. She pays the bills and keeps everything going. She was not too happy when I got home that Friday evening. She said, "Wayne, we do not have lunch money for the kids on Monday morning."

I could have called a friend; I could have shared the need and I am sure somebody would have come through and done something. But my supplier, the Person I depend upon on for all my needs, is God. So I prayed that weekend and truly did not know what I was going to say or do Monday morning. I did not know how it was going to happen, but God knew all about the need. I did not ask anybody. I did not present our need to anybody except God.

On Sunday night I told Wanda, "Let's not go to our home church tonight. Let's go to Soddy Community Chapel," which was close to our house. I do not remember what the preacher preached on, but when I got up to leave, a lady came up to me and put something into my hand. I just said thank you to her and asked if it was for Teen Challenge. I always asked that question when someone handed money to me because I never took any money for my personal use that was designated for Teen Challenge. The lady responded with "No, sonny, you have a personal need and this is for you personally."

So again I said, "Thank you," and put it in my pocket. When I got out of the church I gave it to my wife. Wanda looked and said, "It is $20. We have lunch money for the kids in the morning!" I did not know who the lady was at the time, but about five or six years ago I went to the funeral of one of our volunteers who had been very faithful. I briefly shared about that story while I was at that gathering, and a lady came up to me afterward and said, "I now see why God spoke to my heart to give you that $20. At the time I gave it, I did not really realize what your need was. The Lord just told me to give you $20."

In its first year, the Teen Challenge office was in the church building of Evangel Tabernacle. The ministry was needing a place of its own, and we were offered a residential property on Willow Street that was owned by Central Presbyterian Church, which was selling it at a reduced price of $16,000. This is how God spoke to me about buying that house.

My friend, Jimmy, and I went down to the Benwood Foundation in Chattanooga to submit a grant request. We did not have an appointment or anything. We had drafted a request for money to purchase the property, house and some furnishings for Teen Challenge and gave it to the foundation's director, Bill Walters. This was probably in the fall of 1978.

One day while sitting in my office at the church, I looked at a calendar hanging on my wall. It's hard to explain, but God clearly said to me, "Turn it over to January 1979 and circle January 19th." So

I just turned to January 19, 1979 and circled it. He also said to put the words, "House paid for," underneath the circle. So I just wrote, "House paid for," as instructed, not knowing how it would happen.

On Friday, January 19, 1979, Jimmy went to the mailbox and there was a letter from the Foundation telling us they have given us a grant in the amount of $16,000 to pay for the house. So the first Chattanooga Teen Challenge residential center was paid for by the Benwood Foundation grant, on the very day God had told me to circle on the calendar several months earlier.

These stories may not have happened if God had not demonstrated His faithfulness many years earlier, sparing my life from a potential drowning when I was 17 years old. I had gone swimming with two friends one day, and we went out past the buoys into the deep water after having had a big dinner. My mom had told me to wait at least an hour, but I did not obey her and we went to the lake anyway. We had moved out into the deep water and were playing when cramps came into both of my legs and both of my arms, so I could not swim. I was just like a rock going down and must have gone down about nine times. My friends tried to save me, but I almost drowned them as well in the attempt. Finally a lady from the beach came out, hit me with her arm and addled me, so she could pull me in and save my life.

Several years later, Chattanooga Teen Challenge had a softball team and basketball team. I invited a lady, Thelma Elliott, who worked at Martin Thompson, a local sporting goods store, and who happened to be my high school typing teacher for two years, to come by the Teen Challenge center because I wanted to thank her for helping equip our men on the ball teams. At the end of her visit, I said, "I want to thank you, and I also want to hug your neck, if it is okay." She said okay, and as I hugged her she whispered in my ear, "Wayne, I see why I saved your life when you were 17. That was you, wasn't it?" I said, "Yes, it was."

When you are about to die, your life video starts to play. I remember vividly that day, when I felt about to drown, my "video" was playing. I thought my life was over. I couldn't save myself. But in a way, this is what led me to Teen Challenge and its ministry to young men caught up in addictions. The people that we work with can't save themselves. They must have Jesus rescue them, similar to how I had been rescued when I was 17 years old.

When Thelma told me it was her that had saved my life from drowning when I was a teenager, I was about 44 years old. Some 27 years had passed before I got a chance to thank her – but it's never too late. And also with our ever-present, faithful God, it's never too late.

Bringing It Home

God uses faithful people for His purposes. The Bible tells us, "For the eyes of the LORD range throughout the earth to strengthen those whose hearts are fully committed to him" (2 Chronicles 16:9). The Scripture speaks, "The LORD…will not forsake his faithful ones" (Psalm 37:28). A faithful person of God can be the spark for "God Acts." Jesus says, "I tell you the truth, if you have faith as small as a mustard seed, you can say to this mountain, 'Move from here to there' and it will move. Nothing will be impossible for you" (Matthew 17:20-21).

In your life, how have you faced mountains that seemed impossible to overcome?

How have you handled them?

How have you seen God at work through these circumstances – in the midst of them, or sometimes viewing them in retrospect?

How has God used your faithfulness to Him?

17

TWO RED TAILLIGHTS TO SHOW THE WAY

By Beth A. Arp

*B**eth Arp is an ordained minister, along with her husband, Clayton (Skip), and both serve as appointed U.S. missionaries with the Assemblies of God. Beth is currently the pastor of a church in Louisville, Kentucky, where she has been for the past 10 years. Prior to that, Beth and her husband arrived in Louisville in 1997 and started a women's Teen Challenge center called "Priscilla's Place."*

In 1995, which I often refer to as our "year of the in-between," my husband, Skip, and I had just packed up and were headed to Ohio. We had finished our years at the Teen Challenge center in Arkansas, and were heading to a new place to live. But for the first time in all of our years in full-time vocational ministry, we were not in a position of any kind of ministry, nor were there any new opportunities in sight. We had thought another door of ministry would open right away, that we soon would be back where we knew God had called us.

As the U-Haul truck and our vehicles pulled us out of a long life in Arkansas, the taillights gave notice we were embarking on a journey toward the unknown. We had no idea what to expect. We ended up staying in my husband's parents' basement, along with our then 12- and 15-year-old kids. The basement to me felt like I was in a place of abandonment by God.

I immediately thought of Gideon in the book of Judges, who had been "threshing wheat in a winepress to keep from the Midianites" (Judges 6:11). Living in horrible conditions and surrounding despair, Gideon was fearful and felt God had forgotten him. He asked the question, "Why has all this happened to us?" (Judges 6:13) This is what I was feeling down in that basement. As nice as it was, it was still a basement, and it was definitely not a home.

As an interim step I had taken a job working with the elderly at an assisted living home close to where we were living. I found myself taking care of some wonderful people and helping them, but in my heart I knew it was not the place I thought we should be. I wondered where God was. I found myself cooking one day and becoming so frustrated with our basement living that I locked myself in a closet while I was cooking, leaned against the wall and said, "God, I have had it! I cannot live in this basement any longer! Would you please do something?"

While driving home that day, I saw a house with a "For Rent" sign in the front yard. I called and inquired about it, then went to look at it. The lady said she had just put the sign up that day, the day I had prayed, crying out to God in frustration. We took the house. Even though it was small, it was not a basement, and it was *our* space. God had been faithful that very day.

That helped somewhat, but just as gray as the skies over Northeast Ohio were at that time of the year, my heart was also gray, beset with doubt, fear, and discouragement. Where would we end up, and what would we be doing?

A few months later I landed another job in a nursing home in the dietary department, and my work started every morning at 6 a.m. Because of that, I had a 12-year-old daughter and 15-year-old son who had to get ready by themselves for school in the mornings. This was not a job I wanted, but one that I knew I had to have in order for us to live – or at least survive.

To get to the job at 6, I had to leave at 5:30 in the morning. For Northeast Ohio at that time of year, that can mean lots of snow and unexpected blizzards.

Just a few months earlier my dad had passed away, leaving me his car, so as I prepared to leave in that new-to-me vehicle that first morning, I felt apprehensive, fearful, and a little aggravated, wondering why God wanted me to take this job in the first place instead of being in a ministry where I thought we should be.

It was not only dark outside, but dark in my soul as I left my family that cold morning and headed to a workplace where I would start a job that was not to my liking, but necessary for our survival. As I drove, I not only felt like I would end up driving into a physical ditch on the side of the road, but also felt like my whole life had ended in a spiritual ditch consisting of shattered dreams and hopes. Thoughts raced through my mind at that early hour in the morning, wondering where God was in the midst of our chaos.

As I drove along, feeling scared, alone, depressed and confused, I couldn't see much at all. The snow had reduced the visibility to almost nothing. Then, seemingly coming out of nowhere, I saw a semi-truck ahead of me. Those red taillights showed the road in front of me, and I knew those taillights would take me all the way down the road to the place where I needed to turn to start the new job. So I followed those taillights until I finally saw the road and turned into the place where I needed to be. I let out a sigh of relief as I stepped out of my car, feeling a little more encouragement, knowing that once again God had sent a set of red taillights to guide me to my safe haven.

I learned that God's faithfulness can get through any storm and protect you in the midst of it. His faithfulness can keep you and sustain you, even in the in-between places, the dark places, the foggy places, all the places where you can't see and don't know where you're going. God will make a way for you, if you'll just trust Him. When you've had enough of the basement living, He'll make a way out for you and will provide you with manna in your desert.

It was at this time in my own life that God spoke to my heart and let me know that He had us in His hands all the time, even in the midst of the undesired job I had. I learned that even there, ministry was going on all along, and God was unfolding His plan one day at a time.

As the Bible tells us, God is the Alpha and the Omega, the beginning and the end. And He is even the God of the in-between. I had to realize that at those times when on this journey the way gets dark and the sun does not always shine, and life does not always go the way we think it ought to go, God is still guiding. He is still leading.

We eventually found an open door in Kentucky to start a women's Teen Challenge in the city of Louisville. As God worked, often in miraculous ways in starting this center, I realized He had been following a wonderful plan all along. I have seen that again and again over our last 18 years here in Kentucky, how God has guided and how He has been faithful in leading our lives.

I know He has many more things in store for us as well. I have learned to hold onto His hand, and to trust Him in all things. He knows how to guide us. He knows how to get us to our destination. He is faithful. He knows where we are on this journey and understands how dark the journey can get. I just had to keep following His lights in the midst of the dark, even when they looked like the taillights of a semi-truck. So, as I share from my own experience and tell others, just stay close, follow the light, and you'll reach the place He desires you to be.

Bringing It Home

God has promised never to abandon us, even at times when it seems He has. Hebrews 13:5-6 says, "Never will I leave you; never will I forsake you. So we say with confidence, 'The Lord is my helper, I will not be afraid.'" As the apostle Paul in Philippians 1:6 affirms, "being confident of this, that He who began a good work in you will carry it on to completion until the day of Christ Jesus." The times between starting and finishing the race God has set before us can be challenging, but He promises He will be there, even if it requires the use of two red taillights.

What "in-between times" have been the most difficult for you up to this point in your life?

What has been one of the most significant displays of God's faithfulness to date during your journey with Jesus? How does remembering what He did then help when you encounter new challenges?

18

CALL OF GOD: CLEAR AND STRATEGIC

By Dr. Jimmy Ray Lee

S ometimes trusting in God's faithfulness involves being willing to follow His leading even if "common sense" would counsel you to do otherwise.

Having been very active in church ministries for years, I just knew in my heart that God was calling me into full-time ministry as a vocation. At the time, I had been working for DuPont Corporation for more than 10 years and had an excellent salary and benefits. But I would often cry in my heart with desire to do more for the Lord's work. I was very hungry to give up everything for God, but knew I had a responsibility to care for my wife and two sons.

My "lay" ministry activities at the time included choir director, youth ministries leader, hospital visitation, etc. Even though I was very active, I knew God was calling me to broaden my work.

After seeking God diligently for three or four years, God began the process of my "definite call." In February 1975, I was scheduled to take a week's vacation to attend the Tennessee District Assemblies of God District Council (a ministers' meeting) in Nashville. The council was to start on a Tuesday. Monday evening my wife, Louise, received a call from my DuPont supervisor (my job was training supervision), asking to speak with me. She told him I was at the church, but she would call and give me the message that he wanted to meet with me. But instead, my supervisor said he would go to the church and meet with me there. Even though Louise had called to let me know about the supervisor's phone call, I was still amazed to see him make the effort to come to my church with special news that would affect my life forever.

He told me the company wanted to increase my job responsibilities, and that meant I needed to begin working a swing-shift schedule so more employees would be reporting to me. By doing so, he said, I could advance in the company more quickly. At the time I had been working the day shift, having Saturdays and Sundays off. So moving to a swing shift schedule meant I would have to start working regularly on Sundays.

I sincerely thanked my boss for his interest to advance me in the company. However, as he walked away, my heart was crushed. This meant I would have to not only give up our Saturday nursing home ministry (we faithfully met with people at two homes weekly) but also most of our Sunday ministries. Then I was amazed when a calm sense of peace suddenly filled my heart, giving me the feeling that everything was going to be okay.

The next morning, on Tuesday, Louise and I left for the District Council meeting. That evening the speaker's text was Isaiah 54:2, "Enlarge the place of your tent, stretch your tent curtains wide, do not hold back; lengthen your cords, strengthen your stakes." During the service God impressed on my heart to speak with my father, who pastored our small congregation of about 80 people, about going on staff for $150 per week (no benefits) as associate pastor. God firmly entrenched in my heart, "Don't base this on what you see now, but on the vision I have given you." I was fully convinced God had spoken to my heart and was directing me.

My wife and I returned home the next evening. I went to the mailbox and had a significant confirmation waiting for me. It was a letter from New Delhi, India, written by an Indian brother who had studied at a university in our city and attended our church for several years. He had gone back to India and I had not heard from him in over two years. In the letter he had written one sentence that stood out. It said, "When God speaks to you to leave DuPont and go into full-time ministry you must respond." What timing!

I met with my father and the church board, and they agreed to the $150 per week salary, with cautious concern for me and my family. God further confirmed this bold move. That year I received an income tax return for the exact dollar and cents amount to pay off our credit card bill.

On April 1, 1975, we started the full-time ministry journey by establishing an inner city ministry for children. Some 600-700 children met with us weekly at five government-subsidized housing projects. The children's ministry was the platform to start Chattanooga Teen Challenge; my becoming the founding director of Nashville Teen Challenge; and beginning both Project 714, Inc. (now National Center for Youth Issues) and Turning Point Ministries (now Living Free). God had a plan and He was faithful.

Bringing It Home

This walk with God – in truth, it's a journey – can be likened to a long-distance race. The writer to the Hebrews says, "But encourage one another daily, as long as it is called Today, so that none of you may be hardened by sin's deceitfulness" (Hebrews 3:13). As we look back over our life, we can often see the journey we are traveling. The Scripture says, "Praise be to the LORD, the God of my master Abraham, who has not abandoned his kindness and faithfulness to my master. As for me, the LORD has led me on the journey to the house of my master's relatives" (Genesis 24:27).

In what ways does your life's journey seem more like a marathon instead of a sprint?

How has God helped you overcome bumps (disappointments, challenges, confusion, etc.) along the way in your life's journey? In what ways has Jesus showed up to help you, even at very unexpected times?

19

SOMETIMES GOD EVEN USES COMMUNISTS TO FUND HIS PROJECTS!

By Dr. Jimmy Ray Lee

My wife, Louise, and I traveled to Budapest, Hungary in 1991 to do training with the Teen Challenge ministry. This was about one and one half years after the fall of the Communist government in Hungary. While in Budapest we were blessed to meet Pastor Attilla Fabian (now at home with the Lord) and his wife, Erzibet. The Lord led Erzibet to start a Teen Challenge home for girls in Budapest. The account of how this facility came to be funded was a blessing to hear.

As we sat in the girls' home, Pastor Fabian shared this amazing story:

"This Teen Challenge center is a real miracle. I must tell you it was the very last action of the former Communist government. Actually we made an application during the year while we were still under Communist rule, asking them to help us get this building for the girls' home, and they first gave us about 40% of the price which was two million Hungarian forints. However, we needed an additional three million forints.

"So we were praying and asking the Communists officials to help us accomplish the complete project because we really wanted to buy this building. We were using the building but we did not own it.

"There was one night that my wife and I were away, but other leaders were here with the girls and a lady came and visited the home. It was just after supper and the girls were having evening devotions. They were singing, and engaging in praise and worship. There was such a nice atmosphere in the home that the visitor began to weep and then she just went away. They did not recognize who the lady was at the time, but we later learned that she actually was the daughter of one of the top, top Communist leaders of the country.

"A day after her visit I got a phone call from the Minister of Health and he said, 'Please, Mr. Fabian, give us your bank account number because we want to give you the rest of the money needed to buy that property.' It was settled and the Teen Challenge Girls Center of Budapest, Hungary was paid in full."

Bringing It Home

From a human perspective it would seem impossible for the Communist government to have played an important role in the funding of the Christian-based Teen Challenge girls' home. In many ways the principles and values of atheistic Communism and those of Christianity were opposites. However, God truly is the God of the impossible. In Luke 1:37, Jesus says, "For nothing is impossible with God." Speaking in Matthew 17:20, He also declares that with faith "as small as a mustard seed, you can say to this mountain, 'Move from here to there' and it will move. Nothing will be impossible for you."

In your life, are you facing difficulties? Are there "mountains" that need to be moved? What are the mountains, those seemingly immovable objects that are overwhelming your life?

Your faith may be small as Jesus describes in Matthew 17:20. If that's the case, where can you start with God as your partner, trusting Him even with the tiny bit of faith that you have?

20

'EVEN IF I LOSE EVERYTHING, GOD, I AM GOING TO SERVE YOU'

By David Parker

*D*avid Parker is the Chairman and CEO of Covenant Transportation Group, headquartered in Chattanooga, Tennessee. In the following account, David tells how he has experienced God's faithfulness in many ways through challenging situations in his determination to build a God-honoring, nationally known trucking company.

Have you ever heard the phrase, "God is really moving"? I have not only said it, but also have seen it – both literally and figuratively. When you're in the trucking business, facing one challenge after another, it just happens.

We can all remember times when if God had not come onto the scene, we don't know if we would have made it or not. I have seen God demonstrate His faithfulness to me countless times over the years, but three or four times in particular come to mind when it seemed clear that He had brought me from defeat to victory.

I have been in the trucking business my entire life. My career started when I was 16 years old, working my way up through a company my parents owned. Eventually I became vice president of operations and vice president of marketing. Then in 1986, when I was 28 years old, my wife, Jacqueline, and I started our own company, Covenant Transport.

My parents sold their company in 1984, and I stayed on for about six months as a vice president until I decided to leave the company. Since I had a six-month non-compete clause in my employment contract, I could not start another trucking business during that period. So I felt very uncertain, just a young man trying to figure out what he was supposed to do and how to get it done.

I'll never forget being up in the mountains of Tennessee, coming to a point when I was crying out to God and saying, "God, I am scared. I think I know what You want me to do. I will promise You I will work my bottom off. I am a good operations guy, and I am a good sales guy. I will have plenty of freight and I will be able to give good service to my customers, but God, I am scared." Then I said, "God, let's have a covenant together. That is, I will work hard – but I need your help."

So a few months later, remembering that commitment, Covenant Transport was born. We started with 25 trucks and the first three years were great. Throughout 1986, 1987 and 1988, we were outstanding. We were still a small company, but by the end of the third year we were operating 150 trucks and doing about $19 million in revenue. My relationship with God was strong and I felt wonderful, like we were a strong testimony to God. We tried to live out what we talked, putting into action that God was No. 1 in our lives.

I'll never forget during 1988 when my sister gave me a word that she felt was from the Lord. It came from Isaiah 43, the first five or six verses. But as I read them, after having a great year in the business and making some good money, the message did not seem right. This scripture was talking about "when you go through the waters, I will be with you. When you go through the fires, they shall not burn you; neither shall the flame kindle upon you, because I am the LORD the God of Israel."

Those words – fire and water – sounded like problems. I thought, "I am doing pretty well. I am a testimony to God. Things are going great and we are not bashful about talking about Jesus. So I don't know about this 'fire' and 'water.'" But over the next couple of years I would find myself reading that scripture passage probably 100 times. God was preparing me, telling me that as I would be going through the water I would not drown, and as I was going through the fire I would not be consumed. Looking back, it was interesting how that scripture passage truly blessed me and ministered to me, because in January 1989, after being in business for three years, I made a bad business decision.

We desperately needed to move to a new terminal location and of the 150 trucks we had, I decided to keep about 75 of them longer than I ever did. I usually traded them every three years so they stayed under warranty, but wanted to buy this terminal and reasoned that if I kept the trucks another year there would be enough equity in them to pay for the terminal. So in January I made the decision to keep them, and by September those 75 trucks had cost me $600,000 in maintenance cost. The warranty on them had run out and they were breaking down all over the United States, resulting with major costs. As a result, in 1989 our company – the one that was built upon God, trusted in God, was created because of God, and the year before had record profits – experienced its first-ever loss of $900,000.

Some difficult things happen when all of a sudden you lose $900,000. First of all, you lose the ability to attract credit because banks are scared of you. They start running from you, and you start struggling from the capitol standpoint of needing to update your tractors and trailers fleet.

Then 1990 came around and we lost another $900,000. So in just two years we had lost nearly $2 million. It had erased 100 percent of the company's equity. Two years had wiped away the three great first years of the company. But my relationship with God remained very good. God was so faithful to me, and I knew without question that God would not leave me. I knew that He would not forsake me.

He was my refuge in the time of trouble and I hung upon Psalms 91, which promised, "he who dwells in the secret place of the Most High shall abide under the shadow of the Almighty." I sought God as never before. I prayed, I slept, and I worked. That is all I did. I would work for 15 hours a day, sleep for four or five hours a day, and read my Bible a couple of hours a day trying to figure out what was going to happen.

Losing almost $2 million in two years carried great repercussions for us. The banking relationships we had were strained, but I thanked God for our local bank. Over that period of two years I could probably count on my left hand how many times we were not overdrawn at the bank. So the pressures involved with that were immense, waking up trying to determine how much money we needed to come up with to satisfy the bank so the checks being presented could be paid that day.

I would run down to the post office and see how many of my customers had sent me checks. I would then add all that up and come up with the money. During the course of those two difficult years, maybe there were five days I was in the black. Every day Jacqueline and I lived with this. It got to where it would be $50,000 one day, then a few days later it would be $100,000, and it kept working its way up. I will never forget coming in to work one day and calculating that I needed $600,000 by 2 o'clock in the afternoon. The pressure was absolutely unbelievable.

I had second mortgages on all of my homes, every credit card had been maxed to the hilt, and at about 31 years of age I was desperately trying to come up with enough money to keep my company afloat. In my personal life and my business life, I had reached rock bottom. Jacqueline was responsible for accounts payable, and we were literally using the "robbing from Peter to pay Paul" strategy to try to pay fuel bills, make truck and trailer payments, cover maintenance costs, meet payroll and pay drivers. It was a juggling act trying to make sure things got paid. It was two years of pure hell on earth. Every day of waking up to this reality became the natural way of things for us.

But despite everything, God was faithful. He knew I had to get to this point in my life. I will never forget getting there, going through this as a born-again Christian, praying and seeking God. I finally got to the point when I could pray, "Father, I don't love You because of what I got." I remember at that same moment taking the money out of my pockets and saying, "I don't love you because of this. God, if I lose everything I have, I am here to tell You that I am going to serve You. My love for You is not conditional. My love for You is because You are my Daddy. You are my Father. You have been faithful and true to me, and I am going to serve You no matter what happens to my company."

In actuality it did look like I was going to lose the company and possibly everything we had. But God gave me a plan, a simple plan to go back to the basics: Go back to running the company, trading in the equipment when it was supposed to be traded. It was important to go back to the basics because I had incurred too much fixed cost. I had moved into the new terminal, expenses had gone up, and we were needing to grow the company to cover the fixed cost. That was part of the plan that God gave me. He said, "You have got to grow, add equipment into this, and get back on the trading cycle that the company should be in."

I'll never forget starting to go back to banks, having just lost nearly $2 million, and telling them I had a plan and with that plan the business was going to grow. The banks only laughed at me. They would say, "David, you have lost $2 million over the last two years, and your plan is to add more trucks and trailers – and the ones you have now have lost $2 million." So it was very difficult to get credit. There is no doubt in my mind that I was in the midst of spiritual warfare. Most of my life I have lived out Ephesians 6, which teaches about putting on the full armor of God. Whether in my business life or in my personal life, spiritual warfare has been something I have been very acquainted with.

God's works in my life have not been about instant healing or things being turned around in a day's time. I did not receive those kinds of miracles. I had to get down into the dirt and pray, seeking God and trusting in Him because He has always been faithful to me. I had to make sure there was no garbage in my heart; I could not let jealousy for my competitors, friends or relatives enter into my heart. I had to remain pure before God because I knew if I did not, it would impede God's deliverance.

Word on the street was our company was facing bankruptcy. We would have people not come to work for us because they thought we were going bankrupt. From the outside it probably looked that way, but I can only say that God was faithful in so many areas during the two or three years we were going through this. There were amazing things I experienced and saw as God was moving in the midst of the fire and the water, in the midst of times when I was sometimes wondering, "God, where are You?"

We had a driver who was delivering a load at a shopping mall. The tractor-trailer had pulled up and the lady truck driver was sitting in the passenger seat. Someone knocked on her door, and when she opened it, a man was standing there. He looked at the trailer, read the words, "Covenant Transport," and said, "The owner of this company is a man of God and he has made a covenant with God. Would you give him this cloth? Tell him God is going to deliver him and bless him beyond his imagination." The cloth had the words, "Elam Blessing."

The truck driver later said that she turned around to put the cloth in her purse so she could bring to me, and when she turned back the man was gone. He had just disappeared. She thought he might have been an angel, even though to this day I'm not sure if she was even a believer in God.

Actually, I did not learn about this right away because the truck driver did not call to tell me what had happened and I did not see her until two weeks later. As it happened, when she came in to tell me, I was in the midst of one of the worst days I had ever experienced. I had no idea if I would be able to make my payments and meet my payroll. So after the truck driver told me this story, I just broke down and prayed silently, "God, you are still there!"

Out of curiosity, I looked up the word "Elam" and found out it means "safe." I knew this meant God was promising me a "Safe Blessing." That's what He does – He pokes through. Besides the faith we have in our hearts, something tangible from God always pokes through. That's His faithfulness at work.

Another episode that touched my heart during our time of struggle involved a gentleman who leased trucks to me, about 40 or 50 of them. He owned the trucks and I was running his trucks. He called one day and asked me to go to lunch. He was not a Christian man, but at lunch he just shared his heart. He told me he was very depressed. "Things are going so badly for me," he said. "I owe the IRS $50,000 in payroll taxes and I cannot pay them, and they say they are going to come after me."

I was able to testify to this gentleman about what I had seen God do in my life and my business, even though I was still in the midst of my problems. I was able to tell him, "You owe the IRS $50,000, but a few years ago I owed $300,000 and they came to my office and I could not pay them. I did not have the ability to pay them, but God delivered me from that and helped me."

After lunch the man drove me back to my office. As he was letting me off, he paused, looked at me and said, "David, I have to tell you something. I believe you saved my life today because I was contemplating suicide."

I walked back to my office still in the midst of turmoil, still in the midst of the heat of my business challenges. The battle was raging. It wasn't like I was on the mountaintop; I felt like I was stuck in the valley with nowhere to look but up. But the Lord spoke to me and said, "Today, you ministered to your first person. Today you found out why I have allowed you to go through what you have gone through. How would you know that people hurt without your own hurting, and how would you know that I deliver without being delivered? God gave me that insight in my office that day, and despite the circumstances that continued to swirl around us, it was a special time for me.

Those "divine interruptions" were special, but I always had to get back to the equipment, my plan, and what I am going to do and how am I going to do it. Two lending institutions, a local bank and one out of Chicago, stood right beside me through all of this. There was nobody else – no other lending institutions, no people. No one had any confidence in me except for my wife and parents.

My father understood I knew how to run a trucking company and that I knew what I was doing, and felt confident my plan would work. In late 1990 he loaned me $1 million to buy the tractors and trailers and equipment I needed to start executing the plan that God had given me. I offered to give him 50 percent of the company, and my heart was right in offering that to him, but the reality was that I had wiped out 100 percent of the company's equity. We had a negative equity on our books. In other words, if I had sold every tractor, trailer, picture and desk we had at the company, I would still owe money. So my father said, "Thank you, but no thank you. I think your plan will work. Here is the $1 million, but I don't want any of that stock. I don't want my name on that stock because I don't want the liabilities." So I took his $1 million and it allowed me to start growing – and we did it aggressively.

I was always a giver personally because I have always believed you cannot out-give God. All of my life I was taught that if you give in the right spirit, you cannot out-give God. It's not a game, like saying, "I will give you $5, God, because I know you will give me $10 back." That is not the right spirit. The proper spirit in giving is this: "I don't care if you give me anything; here is $10 dollars because I want to bless you, God."

But I have learned from experience that when God sees that kind of heart, He gets excited and says, "I have a guy here that gives in the right way, so instead of $5 I will give him $10, because I know he will give it back to Me."

So I started giving from the company, as well as the giving I was already doing personally. In March of 1991, I decided the company needed to give to the Lord's work, so I gave $5,000. This is from a company that had lost $2 million in two years. We wound up having our most profitable March in the history of the company.

In April of that same year, the very next month, I gave another $5,000, and it became the most profitable April in the company's history. I will never forget how that month the Lord impressed upon my spirit that the chains had been broken. Because of my faithfulness to Him, He would be faithful to me and would deliver me. So I pondered that assurance in my heart.

Just a few months later, in the fall of 1991, God impressed upon me that the year of 1992 would be a jubilee year for the company. I believed that, but we were still experiencing the after-effects of our financial struggles. Things were starting to get better. At least I was beginning to make money and we were starting to make profits, but I still had to get cash flow. That was still somewhere down the road. Believe me, you have to make a lot of money before you start catching up on $2 million in losses.

True to God's promise, 1992 was our "year of jubilee," the most profitable year of the company. We did $55 million in revenue, were running 350 trucks, and by April 1993 we had paid back every penny that any bank had loaned me. Soon I was also able to repay the $1 million my father had loaned me, as well as any interest we owed. And we now had $1 million in the bank – cash flow.

By the end of 1993 we were doing about $82 million in revenue and decided to take the company public. We were on an upswing, profits and revenue were growing, and we were adding trucks, 300 to 400 per year. After much prayer, I believed it was God's will for us to take the company public, which is what we did in October 1994. At that time I paid my father back the $1 million loan, we were one of the most profitable trucking companies in the United States. So I decided that I was going to give my father 25 percent of the company.

We went on the "road show," taking our company to Wall Street and all that transpires in doing that. Then came the day of reckoning, when all the banks get together to look at how many people are interested in buying some of the stock. That marked yet another amazing chapter in God's faithfulness to me and my company: In October 1994 our company, that had been broke and had negative book equity in 1991, was informed by Wall Street traders that it had become a company with a total worth of over $200 million! My father's $1 million investment, which he had loaned me because of his faith in me, was worth $40 million at the time we went public.

God showed Himself so strong in those tough, tough times. In His faithfulness, God is not and has never been a respecter of persons. What He has done for other people, He will do for you. What He has done for me, He will do for you. What He had done for you, He will do for me. We only have to be willing to fight the fight, to persevere and keep our faith in God, because He is there.

Bringing It Home

It is comforting to know that God in His faithfulness is with us even though we may be frightened or in despair. His faithfulness to us is beyond question. The key for us in walking through the difficulties is to remain faithful to God. As the old saying goes, "Just keep on keeping on." As Hebrews 11:6 tells us, "And without faith it is impossible to please God, because anyone who comes to him must believe that he exists and that he rewards those who earnestly seek him."

Have you faced times or situations in your life or ministry that have scared you? What were those experiences like? During those times, did God seem near – or distant?

What assurance do you receive from reading and meditating on Hebrews 11:6?

21

FAITHFULNESS IN FOLLOWING GOD'S CALL, WHEREVER IT LEADS

By Glenn Burks

*P*astor Glenn Burks is known as a man of prayer, compassion and integrity. He has served in pastoral ministry and leadership with the Tennessee District Assemblies of God for more than 50 years. Ever since Glenn answered the "call of God" on his life at the age of 12, he has been a living testimony of what it means to be faithful to God over an entire lifetime, through victories and struggles, success and adversity.

"Act as though you've got a hundred years, but live like you may die tomorrow." I received this tremendous advice while was still a boy, not long after I had committed my life to Jesus Christ. Even today, many decades later, this counsel continues to inspire me.

I became saved at about the age of 12; shortly thereafter I sensed a call to the pulpit ministry. Even at that young age, I had no doubt that God had called me to the ministry of the Gospel. That was when I received those wise words from my pastor, Brother Charles Lee. I had gone to tell him that I was sensing God's calling on my life. His answer was simple, yet profound: "Glenn, you know you're young, but act as though you've got a hundred years, but live like you may die tomorrow." Through the years this has helped me to remember that the call of God is not just a temporary thing. It's a lifelong thing, and it's been that way with me. It's a call to faithfulness.

During my teenage years, I became involved in evangelism, and my pastor at that time was a tremendous help to me. He took me under his wing, mentoring and encouraging me in difficult times – including in my own home.

When I first got saved, hardly anyone in our family knew Jesus Christ. I remember telling a relative of mine who had also gotten saved that the Lord had spoken to my heart. I told her, "I believe that if you and I will pray and seek God for our family, that we will see every one of them saved." And that's what happened. Over time all the members of our family became saved and started attending the Assembly of God church we were attending. But that was just the start. Out of our family came several ministers and ministers' wives. I always embraced the promise that the Holy Spirit placed in my heart, that if we would be faithful and pray and seek God, the Lord would bring our family in – and He certainly did. Beginning with my teenage years and into my early adult years in the ministry, God showed me in many ways how faithful He is.

During my times in reading the Bible, both as a young person and later, I have studied a lot about faithfulness. Brother Lee was a wonderful pastor and such a great example in being faithful right where God had placed him in that church. In all kinds of situations, he remained steadfast in his commitment to the Lord and the work He had called him to, an excellent model for any person – certainly for young ministers – on how to pattern their lives as a man of God. I have really tried to do that. Brother Lee was my hero, and whatever I have been able to do for the Lord, I owe a great debt to Brother Lee for the example he set for me.

The call of God has always been uppermost in my mind because I never doubted that God had called me. During my teenage years, whenever anyone asked me what I planned to do in my adulthood, my response was always, "I'm going to be a minister" or "I'm going to be in ministry." There was never a time when I felt like I could do anything else; I just knew I must be faithful to His call.

Through all the years I have remembered Brother Lee's advice, "Act as though you've got a hundred years, but live like you may die tomorrow." He realized the importance of the long haul, that this was not temporary but a lifelong calling. From my early years of ministry, seeking the will of God, this long-term perspective helped as I knew in my heart that I had tried to be in God's will and depend on the leadership of the Holy Spirit.

An example was the time we were pastoring a small church and I really felt the Lord was leading our congregation to relocate to another area where the property was very expensive. At the time we could not afford the price of that property, but through miracle after miracle God worked, and we finally were able to purchase the site and get the building built. Humanly speaking, there was no way we could meet the financial obligation. I remember one day being in the church's sanctuary, kneeling at the altar praying by myself, when the spirit of God spoke to my heart and said, "I will meet the needs of this congregation, and if the people inside this congregation fail to give, I will bring resources in from the outside."

One day shortly after that I went to the mailbox and there was a one-thousand-dollar check in the mail from a family in Alabama. That totally unexpected gift increased my faith tremendously for the future, and God began to bless the church. Things began to move spiritually, numerically and financially, and I attributed that to our people being faithful to serving and honoring the Lord.

Knowing where God has placed us, and then being faithful to serve Him in that place, I think should be the desire of any Christian. We should want to be found faithful – I don't think there is anything more important than being faithful. It is important how we start, of course, because if we don't start, we'll never finish. But remaining faithful during that time, all the way to the finish, is the key to being successful for God wherever He plants us. If we stay there and strive to remain faithful until He is through with us in that work, I believe we will be highly successful in carrying out the will of God and doing the work He has set out for us to do.

When I think of "faithfulness," I would define it simply as obeying God. I think you have to demonstrate obedience to be faithful. You've got to be obedient to be faithful, demonstrating obedience to what God calls you to, and staying there and doing it. It doesn't matter what you face – adversity, good times or lean times, wonderful times, mountains or valleys, crossroads, or whatever the Lord allows to come your way. To be faithful, to me, is staying put where God places you until God releases you, and then we have been obedient to that new call as well.

Sometimes when things begin to get tough, when trials and adversity come our way, the temptation is to run or change places. But often those are times when it is God's will that we stay there even in the down times and dry times. It's reality – a part of life, and a part of the work of God. God has never promised it's always going to be easy. But He has promised, "I'll be with you always, and I'll never leave you or forsake you." So to sum it up, I think being faithful, plain and simple, is staying put where God calls you. Persevering and striving to complete whatever He has called you to do.

Bringing It Home

Remaining faithful to God always seems easy when times are good and the way seems smooth. But remaining faithful wherever God has placed us can become extremely difficult during challenging times.

Isaac experienced such a time in Genesis 26:1-3: "Now there was a famine in the land – besides the earlier famine of Abraham's time – and Isaac went to Abimelech, king of the Philistines, in Gerar. The LORD appeared to Isaac and said, 'Do not go down to Egypt; live in the land where I tell you to live. Stay in this land for a while, and I will be with you and will bless you.'" That is exactly what God did, and His promise remains true for us as well. He will always be with us, in good times and bad.

Have you experienced a time when you believed the Lord wanted you to "stay put" (instead of pursuing another job, changing church congregations, etc.) even though the present challenges seemed difficult, maybe even beyond what you could handle? What was that circumstance like – and how did you handle it? Did it become an opportunity to experience God's faithfulness?

It has been said, "Success is being faithful to what God has called you to do and where God has placed you." Based on that statement, how would you rate your own success?

22

BUSINESS BEGAN IN THE BACK OF A 1949 CHEVROLET

By B. H. Yerbey

B.H. Yerbey founded Yerbey Concrete in 1950. He chose to start the business in December, which is the worst month in the year to start a concrete business. His son, Gary, now owns the business, providing a second generation of leadership. The late Mr. Yerbey, who went to be with the Lord on November 24, 2015, was known for his integrity as well as his generous support of Christian ministries.

These days entrepreneurs, even in their first business ventures, desire to start off with nice offices or well-appointed facilities for building their companies. But when I started my company, Yerbey Concrete, in 1950, all the tools I had to do concrete work could fit into in the back of my 1949 Chevrolet. And it was slow going at first. To build the business I went everywhere I could think of trying to get work. One reason I succeeded in getting work was because I would do anything that was needed to be done in concrete work, even very small jobs like driveways, garages, or anything else I could find. The very first job I had was putting in a sidewalk – and I got a total of $7 for the work.

I loved this business so much that I actually made a god out of it. That is bad to say, but it was all I had on my mind. Just doing another job, doing another job, doing another job. Phyllis, my wife, made sure we went to church on Sunday. I might be sitting there in the church pew, but in my mind I was building or pouring some concrete. But I was there physically because of her and our family. Looking back now, I can see God was trusting me with the company, Yerbey Concrete. It was not General Motors, Exxon or some huge corporation like that, but I think God trusted me with what He thought I could handle. At one time we had about 125 employees, so we were touching a lot of lives and families.

As the company grew I got into commercial work rather than residential work. I made friends with all of the job superintendents that worked for the general contractors, and they all liked me and started asking if they could use me. So we rocked along and the business was doing well.

Yerbey Concrete was a union company at that time. We had operating engineers, laborers, cement masons, carpenters, truck drivers, ironworkers, and people with a variety of other crafts and skills. We were doing what we could to make it better for the employees, but the unions got to be a burden for us. We decided we would try to get out of the unions. The National Labor Relations Board came in and we had a vote. We lacked one vote for being able to get out of the unions, so the board said since it was such a close vote they would have to come back and have another election. When the Labor Relations Board came back, our employees had a unanimous vote to leave the unions. The board said they had never had a unanimous vote before, but it was because we took better care of our employees than the unions did.

In 1971 I decided to sell Yerbey Concrete and it sold for one million dollars, which at the time I thought was all the money in the world. However, I had a problem – I did not have an attorney when I sold the business. I sold it to a good Christian man, but did not get a guarantee on the full amount of the money. He had guaranteed the first $500,000, but not the last half. So in 1973, when the new owners bankrupted the company, the Lord gave it back to me. We bought it after the owners had filed for Chapter 11 bankruptcy in the courts, and as a result had the ready-mix concrete company along with a construction company.

As I look back now, it seems evident that the Lord gave the business back for me to run because it had been so easy going through the court system and regaining the company. After getting the concrete business back, I told Phyllis I wanted her to go to the office and run the front desk. She had never been very interested in the business, however, so she said, "I can't do that, I can't even type very well." But I replied, "Phyllis, you are going to run my front desk. We are going to be together." It was at that time I began to get my perspective and priorities in order. I wanted to put God first, my family second, and the business third, and ever since I have believed that is the way it should be.

Things worked out well. I am not saying that to boast or brag, but just to say that God was in the picture all the time in every way. I did not realize that so much until several years ago when I sold the company again, this time to my son, Gary. Looking back now I can see that from the beginning God had a plan and vision for us that I could not see at the time.

Yerbey Concrete has been good to the Yerbey family and also to a lot of other people who worked for us, some who worked for us many, many years. We had some of the best skilled people in Chattanooga at that time. It seems like every time we needed a person with certain skills, God was there and provided the specific person we needed.

One day Gary and I were sitting in the shop because it was raining and we were not able to get out and work. Business had been slow and Gary said, "You know, Dad, I know God's got a plan for us, but wouldn't it be good if He could slip us a little note and tell us what that plan is?" He didn't "slip us a little note," but always provided when we needed it.

When we bought the ready-mix concrete company back from bankruptcy courts, there were about four similar companies in the area, including Vulcan Materials, which was the biggest. We bought most all of our materials from them. One day my friend there called and asked if we had some extra concrete trucks we could rent to them. I had just secured the entire inventory from the bankrupt company through the courts, so I did have several trucks that I was able to rent to them so we could make extra income.

There is a verse that has been with me through the years. In the verse Jesus says, "Come unto Me all you who are heavy laden, and I will give you rest." There is also a song that comes to my mind that says, "Without Him I could be nothing." And that, I can say without any doubt, is the truth.

In the process of building Yerbey Concrete, we also worked to help Bethel Bible Village, a residential school that at the time helped children whose parents were incarcerated. I was asked to serve on the board of directors. They were in need of a gymnasium, and it was going to cost them $300,000. Bethel had a policy that they would not spend any more money than they had, but they did have $150,000. So they asked me to start the building and go as far as I could with that amount of money.

That seemed good to me, so I said that I would start the work with that amount. After that meeting a lady came up to me and said, "I'll give $50,000 right now." As it turned out, that was just the start of things, because when we began constructing the building – I can't raise money, I just can't – I would call and place an order for materials and tell them to charge it to Bethel Bible Village. The suppliers would say, "Oh, we will give you a special deal." That did not happen just one time; it happened all through this project and continued through the 13 years I served on the board.

And it was not just about developing a residential campus for children in trouble. I remember building a cottage on the Bethel campus and on a particular afternoon one of the young girls living on campus came over to tell me she had gotten saved the night before, committing her life to Jesus. I told her I was so proud of her. Things like that went on all the time, and it was my privilege to be a part of it.

When we started the educational building a man and his wife – he was a service station operator and she was a schoolteacher – gave us $800,000 that they had accumulated over the years. They didn't see it as a sacrifice, but as a gift of love. We were able to complete the entire building with that.

Another time I noticed the parking lot at Bethel consisted of gravel and felt it really needed to be asphalt. I ask if the ministry had any money to put toward that project, but they told me they were out of money. So I thought to myself, "Well, I will just go ahead and put concrete curbs up."

Later I asked a friend in the asphalt business to give me an estimate on the project so I would know how much money I needed to come up with to complete it. He said it would be about $20,000. Then, after a moment he said, "No, don't worry about it. I will just give it to you." That was a special blessing, but it was not anything unusual at Bethel. It happened all the time.

I have to say Bethel Bible Village paid Yerbey Concrete for much of the work we did because we could not give it all to them. I don't know how much we gave them and do not like to talk about what was given. I like the way a guy answered when someone told him how he really appreciated what the person had given. The person's response was, "Oh, don't tell me that. I wanted to hear it from the Lord when I get to Heaven."

Yerbey Concrete was a great company for us, but it would have been hard to sell to anybody except my son. Some people may think I gave the company to Gary, but we worked out a fair deal and he bought it from me. He paid me every dime of what we agreed on. There again I feel the Lord was in it, because He knew it would have been hard for me to sell and step away from it completely, because it had been my life. It was hard. Honestly, even then I had a hard time divorcing myself from Yerbey Concrete. Until the past two years I would let things worry me, but I have seen Gary do everything he said he would do.

Bringing It Home

Living a life of faithfulness calls for us to understand that God "guards the life of His faithful ones" (Psalm 97:10). This means not always seeking to be "doing for the Lord," but sometimes simply trusting Him and what He's doing. That is because in this life we will need rest to overcome. As B.H. Yerbey pointed out, Jesus promises, "Come to me, all you who are weary and burdened, and I will give you rest" (Matthew 11:28). At the same time, when the Lord gives us a mission or a difficult task to perform, we must not give up. The Scripture says, "Let us not become weary in doing good, for at the proper time we will reap a harvest if we do not give up" (Galatians 6:9). We can see this in the faithful life of B.H. Yerbey.

In what ways have you seen God guard and protect your life?

Think of times when you have grown weary in serving the Lord, as we all have done at least on occasion. Who or what has helped you to not give up?

23

FAITHFULNESS – IT'S ALL ABOUT GRACE

By David Olson

*D*avid Olson is a veteran missionary, known for his compassion and creative thinking. He has worked in many parts of the world, primarily with the ministry of Teen Challenge. David and his family have worked through some difficult challenges, but despite their adversity have remained faithful to "His calling."

"Where is God?" This is a question most, if not all, of us have asked at one time or another. And I think you will agree it is never when things are going well. We wonder where He is when problems seem beyond solution, times when it seems things couldn't get any worse. We pray, and it seems God isn't listening – or maybe He doesn't care. If you have felt that way at times, you're not alone. But through the trials of life, the Lord has been teaching our family that He really is there, He really is listening, and He really does care.

As missionaries, my wife, Celia, and I sensed our call was to live in an international community. We started off in Brussels, Belgium. In most cases for missionaries, part of God's call is that it is for the entire family, that you bring your children with you. Even in the best of circumstances, there can be challenges in having children in tow on the mission field. And ours were not the best of circumstances. There are many stories I could tell you, but I'll limit myself to two that involved one particular member of our family.

We have two daughters, Heather and Amanda, and Amanda (she gave me permission to tell her story) is a special needs child. She grew up with a learning disability, but it wasn't until we were at a juncture in life, preparing to come home for a furlough, that the school Amanda was attending in Brussels called and told us that Amanda would not be able to return because with her disability; they did not think they could help with her education any further. So we searched and researched schools all over Europe, but could not find the place where she would fit. So we came back to the United States very discouraged.

After we had gotten back to the U.S., one day the nation was celebrating "standing in the gap," but I had hit a very low spot. It seemed like God was gone, that He had abandoned us. I felt like there was a great gap in our lives, and no one was standing in it. Here was our daughter, Amanda, causing us to re-examine our thinking about what we had sensed was God's calling. At the same time, we knew God was not finished with us in missions. "What now, Lord?" I was asking.

What happened that day was that God restored my faith in Him through relationships we had with Teen Challenge, Mike and Kay Zello. We had known them for several years, but had never imagined working with them. But God opened some doors, and we found our life being transformed as we began working with Teen Challenge.

Things seemed to be going well, but then Amanda had a crisis, one that led us to Akron, Ohio and Emerge Ministries. The doctors there worked with her and us, trying to bring about some healing, but our daughter got worse instead of better. Finally, Celia and I took her to the hospital. We were very worried about Amanda's condition, but on top of it, did not know how we were going to pay for all the medical expenses. Absolutely no idea.

We were told to go to social services, but we were not residents of the state of Ohio. So as instructed, we went to the social services offices where they said we needed to talk with a certain lady, but she would not be in that day. Then, totally unexpectedly, in she walked. We came to find out she was a strong believer. We told her our story, about looking for assistance because we have a special needs daughter who urgently needed medical help. Amanda, we explained, was almost at the point of being an independent adult, but we had no way of paying for her hospitalization.

The woman at social services invited us back to her office. After some discussion, she confirmed that we were in fact residents of Ohio – at that moment in time, on that day – and gave us residential status so we could avail ourselves of the social services resources. Later, when Amanda emerged from the hospital, we did not owe one dollar to the hospital. God, in His faithfulness, had put a person in place to meet our needs. It was not because we were deserving, but simply because He is faithful, and He delights in caring for even the small details. How could we help but rejoice in His faithfulness?

Thinking back to our time in Akron and Amanda's illness, God showed us another vivid example of His faithfulness. We had arrived at the hospital and Amanda's condition had gone from bad to worse. We were sitting in a waiting room, hoping to be able to talk with a doctor soon, and across from us was a man dressed in motorcycle getup. He looked like he was rough as all get out, and I was thinking, "Well, we will just leave him alone, and he won't bother us." It turned out his name was Dale Adams.

As Celia and Amanda got up to leave the room, Dale looked over at me and said, "You have a real pretty daughter there." When you are hurting the last thing you want is for someone to try to strike up a conversation with you. I was sitting there fuming mad at God because my life was changing, I had no control over it, and had no ability to deal with all the things that were happening because of something that was the result of the medical condition of a child in my family, something over which she had no control either. The challenge was for me to step back and not take it personally, but to accept it as God's hand, even though I felt certain we would not be able to live overseas again.

When Dale started trying to talk to me, initially I just kind of shut him out. But he persisted and said, "How are you doing?" Of course, being a good, well-schooled Christian, I felt I had to tell him what I thought he should hear, so I muttered, "fine." We tend to lie to ourselves when we are hurting. Then Dale did something very unexpected. He did not look at me, but rather it seemed as if he looked through me and asked, "How are you doing spiritually?"

My only admission to him was, "Well, we are missionaries." I was avoiding his question, as well as attempting to avoid making a connection with him. But Dale would have none of it. That day he shared with me his story. He explained how, as a manufacturer or rebuilder of million-dollar cars, he had come to the point where he was losing everything because of one issue that was happening in his life. He told me the factories were having to close, taking with them the things he was doing. Then he said, "But you know, God has been faithful."

As I listened to Dale and heard his story, it resonated with me – because no matter where I was, even when I was many miles away from home, God had always provided someone to walk beside us, whether it was an understanding social services staff person, who "happened" to be a believer in Jesus, or a rough-looking motorcycle type.

At one point during her illness, Amanda had curled up in a fetal ball and could not even control her bowel movements. She just lay there. And yet, even during these darkest hours with Amanda, God brought someone along to walk with us. We read in the Scriptures that God's faithfulness is renewed every morning (Lamentations 3:22-23), but I would like to think – and believe – it is renewed every hour, because each hour can bring another change. At each juncture for us, God has been there.

My definition of faithfulness is grace – unmerited favor where God suspends the punishment for disobedience and sin, and tells us,

"Let me show you how much I love you." Grace is used in a variety of contexts, but for me faithfulness is all about grace. I certainly did not deserve the friendship I received from Dale. I've been undeserving of His favor in so many things, yet God still says, "I want to love you."

Fast-forwarding to the present, I and my family are still missionaries today. We started working with Global Teen Challenge and ministering around the world. I had been in the Teen Challenge program when I was a teenager, but never realized one day I would come back to work for them, both in the United States and overseas. One of the first things I did in ministry was Teen Challenge in Okinawa, Japan.

For the most part we have been able to stay stateside and work because my gifts are technology. I work and build resources for other people, helping Teen Challenge with their media and in launching the Global Training Network. But we also have worked in Ecuador, traveling back and forth every month in helping to build a family values television network where we have seen 1,000 people every month come to Christ. This is not because it is Christian TV, because actually it is secular programming, but with a biblical worldview. Every 30 minutes there is a commercial that advertises there is help for the helpless and hope for the hopeless. Now we are working to establish similar programming in Peru.

God has been faithful in so many ways to let us walk in the passion of His heart and our heart, seeking to serve around the world and make a difference.

Bringing It Home

The great hymn says "Grace! Grace! God's grace. Grace that is greater than all our sin." God's grace (which some have defined as GRACE - God's Riches At Christ's Expense) reaches to the depth of our pain, failure, disappointment, and our sin. The apostle Paul writes of God, "My grace is sufficient for you, for My power is made perfect in weakness" (2 Corinthians 12:9). The Scripture also offers the assurance, "But where sin increased, grace increased all the more" (Romans 5:20).

How do you perceive God's grace in your life? What does it look like – what are some examples of how the Lord has manifested God's Riches At Christ's Expense for you?

Reflect on a specific time that God's grace proved to be sufficient during an especially challenging time.

24

CHALLENGE OF FAITHFULNESS – DISCERNING GOD'S PART AND OUR PART

By Dr. Don Finto

◈

*D*on Finto, who served as pastor of Belmont Church in Nashville *for more than 25 years, continues to serve as a pastor to pastors, and has become actively involved with the expanding community of Jewish believers in Jesus, both in the United States and Israel. Don is a model of faithfulness, trustworthiness and proven leadership.*

Opposition to followers of Jesus and overt expressions of faith seem on the increase in the United States, but the religious freedom we enjoy in the nation is still something that people in many other parts of the world and other cultures can only imagine.

I immediately think of a young woman we hosted at Caleb Company (a ministry outreach), whom I met a few years ago when I was teaching at the YWAM base. She was the youngest of 10 siblings from a family in one of the former Soviet Union satellites. At age 14 she had some Christian friends who started inviting her to go to worship with them. Feeling strongly drawn to Jesus, she received Jesus soon after she started attending the services.

She then started taking her next-oldest sister just above her, and often, after the men of the house were sleeping, they would go to church to all-night prayer meetings. They would return before their father and brothers were awake because they knew that if they found out about them going to church, they would be persecuted. They were also participating in some kind of exercise program at the church, so they could honestly say they were going to work out.

Sometime later they took a trip with the workout group which the father and brothers thought was okay, but what the sisters were really doing was going to a mountain resort to be baptized. After they came home, the father found out about it. He had always been a very kind man, but he slapped them around, the brothers beat them, and they locked them in their room for days.

The girls eventually were released from their punishment and despite their family's opposition, went back to the church. One night, while they were there, the church was bombed.

This young woman's horribly disfigured body was right in the middle of the bombed area, surrounded by dead bodies. Her body was almost completely destroyed by the fire, so when emergency personnel got her to a hospital, the nurses were not even going to tend to her. They thought for certain she was dead or at the point of death. However, her sister went to the nurses and insisted that they treat her.

When the nurses learned she was Christian and no longer a Muslim, they began to mistreat her. But this woman so believed what she had learned from the Bible that she kept quoting the Scripture passage that she would be healed. God heard her prayers and miraculously healed her, and today she is a beautiful woman with absolutely no scars remaining from her experience of being burned alive, except one small gash in her hair line. When she asked the Lord about that one, He said, "Remember, I had scars when I came back!"

And now, almost as miraculous, nearly every member of her family has become a believer in Jesus. I know of this because this lovely woman visited with us not long ago.

Another fellow that comes to mind, Samer Mohammad, was a terrorist in Lebanon. He received some kind of revelation of Jesus and became a believer; upon learning of this, his relatives locked Samer in his room. He called the police and told them he had denounced the name of Allah – something like that – so they would come and arrest him, to get him out of the hands of his own family. But the family came to the jail and told authorities to release him to them so they could take care of him.

There was a Christian police officer there, however, and he would not release Samer because he knew he would be killed. Instead, the policeman helped him to escape.

I met Samer in Cyprus at a YWAM base. Also in Cyprus is a Jewish-led ministry called Gateways Beyond, a very close ministry partner of ours. We teach in their schools and they teach in ours. I also met Samer there, a former Palestinian terrorist that had hated Jews but after becoming a believer had realized, "Wait a minute, we are not suppose to hate Jews. They are the ones who brought us redemption, and Jesus is Jewish."

He was a little bit upset with the YWAM base because he felt he had not been honoring Jews as he was supposed to, especially now that as a believer he had been grafted into the family. He came into the Gateways Beyond base, looked at the senior leader and about 80 of the rest of us, and said, "Is that an Israeli over there?" The leader replied, "Yes, it is," and Samer said, "I need to wash his feet."

What a sight to see Samer Mohammad, a former terrorist, going over and getting a pan of water to wash the feet of this man who was a captain in the Israeli army. What a transformation – this can only happen in the Lord! But it was not unique; I have had bunches of situations like this.

I was a part of an organization through which Jews and Gentiles who are believers and leaders traveled all over the world to the places where Jews had been persecuted through the years. As a group, we would take responsibility for the sins of the former generations on ourselves and confess them. At one of these meetings in Switzerland, we had a trained former Nazi and a son of the Holocaust survivors who was raised to hate Christians. He had become a hippie and married a Gentile hippie that had turned away from following Jesus.

His wife had begun to feel she needed to return to Jesus, but the husband became so angry he started to read and study ways to prove Jesus was not the Messiah. As he was reading the last book on the subject, convinced that Jesus was indeed not the Messiah, Jesus spoke through the fog to him and said, "But I am." The man then became a believer and eventually a very strong leader in the Messianic movement.

With all of this having transpired years before, I found myself in Switzerland, watching these two men giving their testimonies and embracing each other in the Lord – a former Nazi and the son of Holocaust survivors. Again, this is the kind of thing that can only happen in the Lord.

I would define faithfulness on our part in very simple terms. Actually, one time a girl asked me, "How have you kept strong in the Lord all these years?" I had never been asked that question before, but with very little hesitation I replied, "Keep your eyes riveted on Jesus and take the next step." I think that pretty much sums it up. As far as our faithfulness is concerned, at those times when we fall – and we all do – we just get up quickly and look back at Jesus. We don't wallow in guilt. That does no good. We just praise Him and keep going. That is our part of faithfulness.

As far as God's faithfulness to us is concerned, I think one of the reasons that I, at age 85, am still walking strong in the Lord is because I am continuously awed by the goodness and mercy of God, and remain hungry to know Him better.

Martha, my wife, and I recently read Romans, chapters 3,4,5, 6 and 8. Because God knew us, He had to figure out a way to make us righteous other than when we got good – because we do not ever get good. The first part of Romans 3 contends that not anybody is good. You know you're not good, and I know I am not good. I am constantly awed that He gives us righteousness, His righteousness. I love

Hebrews 10:14 (NIV), which says, "he has made perfect forever those who are being made holy." This verse is so transforming.

Romans 4:5 says, "God justifies the wicked." That's really encouraging to me because you cannot get worse than wicked and He justifies us. Romans 4:7-8 tells us, "Blessed is the man whose sins the Lord does not count against him." The first time I read that verse, I re-read it in every version of the Bible I could find because I could not believe that was what it said. But that is what it says.

And Romans 5:17 talks about "the gift of righteousness." I have become overawed, and remain in awe, because I'm still not who I want to be, but I am hungry for more. God's faithfulness continues to create an incredible sense of awe in me. I never want to read Scripture so rapidly that I don't pause to ponder the awesomeness of our God when I am reading.

Bringing It Home

As some of Don Finto's examples show us, God's faithfulness to us never ends. Even when we are not faithful to Him, He remains faithful. "If we are faithless, he will remain faithful," we are told in 2 Timothy 2:13. Psalm 117:2 declares, "For great is His love toward us, and the faithfulness of the LORD endures forever." Our part, as Don said, is simple: to always focus on Jesus. "Let us fix our eyes on Jesus, the author and perfecter of our faith" (Hebrews 12:2).

How does it make you feel to know that God is always faithful even when we are not? What should be our response to this great truth?

What do you think it means for you to focus or fix your eyes on Jesus? How successful do you think you are at doing that on a consistent basis?

25

TRAVELING BY GPS: GOD'S POSITIONING SYSTEM

By Brad Rymer

*B*rad Rymer is actively involved in leading small groups and training small group facilitators. Trained in conflict mediation at the Institute for Christian Conciliation (a division of Peacemaker® Ministries), Brad is a marriage and family mediator. Brad has a keen desire to be obedient to the Lord as his story will show.

A familiar passage from the Bible declares, "A man's steps are directed by the Lord. How then can anyone understand his own way?" (Proverbs 20:24). Most of us would agree to the truth of this statement, and might be able to think of some times when we saw God was indeed directing our steps – especially in hindsight. But rarely has it been so obvious to me as it was during an encounter I had in March of 2006. This was a time when God became my divine travel agent and appointment secretary.

It seems like it was yesterday. In the middle of a fairly normal, average week, I was running some errands and returning phone calls. A former business associate had left a message for me, saying he was just calling to see how I was doing. Since his message hadn't seemed like anything urgent, I didn't respond to his call for a couple of weeks. On this particular day I was in my car, heading to meet with a friend for lunch. To make use of the time, I decided to finally return my former associate's call. At first he said he had left the message just to see how I was doing, but then added, "My father has had a stroke, and he is in critical condition and Hospice has been called in. Would you pray for him?"

I told my friend that I would, even though it had been about 20 years since we had been business associates, and at the time neither one of us had been walking with the Lord. As a matter of fact, I knew he was Jewish, and he knew I was from a Christian background, but since neither one of us had been following Christ at that point, I was a little taken back by his request. My life had certainly changed a lot since I had known him, so I affirmed I would certainly pray for his dad.

We hung up the phone and I began praying for his father, whom I actually knew before meeting my business friend. We had done some business together, so at that point I had known the dad for about 30 years.

As I started praying for him, one of the things I prayed was, "Lord, I just pray that you send someone to Harvey's side that would lead him to a saving knowledge of you Lord Jesus." And while I was praying, I sensed the Lord saying, "Well, why don't you be that person?" Immediately I started having a conversation with the Lord, which a pastor friend of mine describes as arguing with God. At least we think it's an argument, even though He isn't really talking back.

I found myself sitting there, driving in my car, having this "discussion" with the Lord: "Well, now Lord, as best I know, Harvey's in New Jersey, and I'm here in Tennessee. And besides, I've got all these appointments that I need to get to, and You know, I just don't see how I could do that." But the impression that God was leading me was pretty strong, so I didn't really need to ponder it very long. I sensed the Lord saying to me: "The most important thing to Me is that my children spend eternity with Me." I just thought, "Wow, I'm really supposed to do this. I'm supposed to go and see Harvey."

I called his son again and said, "Billy, where is your dad these days. He's in New Jersey, isn't he?" Billy replied, "Yeah, he is in New Jersey. He's in a hospital in Englewood, New Jersey." "Well, you're going to think this is pretty strange I suppose, but you asked me to pray for your dad, and when I prayed for him, I felt a strong sense that I needed to go talk to him. So, tell me what hospital he's in and what room. Give me the information – I want to go see him."

It was really strange because Billy, my former business associate who didn't know Christ when we were working together, responded, "That really doesn't surprise me." So, I called the friend I was planning to meet for lunch and told her what had come up. She said, "I completely understand. This sounds like it takes precedence over us having lunch." I replied, "Well, that's really the strange thing about it. I feel there is a tremendous importance here, but there is not an urgency yet. So I think we are supposed to go ahead and have lunch." She said, "That's fine," and we did meet for lunch since we had some ministry matters to discuss.

We finished our lunch around 12:30 and I headed home to figure out what the next step was – whether I should pack up some clothes or call the airport or look on the Internet for airline tickets. I did go online to look for some flights to New Jersey, but it said flights could not be booked if they were not at least six hours away. So I decided I would just go to the airport.

While I was getting ready to leave, my daughter called and wanted to talk to her mother. I told her what was going on. I said, "I'm headed for New Jersey, and this is sort of odd for me, but it has come up. Would you pray for me?" So my daughter prayed and I started heading for the airport with just one small bag. After I arrived at the airport, I would soon realize the things my daughter had prayed were already starting to happen.

But first, you need to know that for me, this whole thing was very much out of character. For a lot of people, such a spontaneous decision is not all that out of the ordinary. But I'm not a naturally spontaneous person. I'm about the last person in the world I could imagine God tapping on the shoulder and saying, "I want you to go to New Jersey and lead a person to the Lord."

I remember talking about this one time in our Sunday school class – whether people were spontaneous or not. One lady had said, "Yeah, I'm spontaneous, as long as you give me a two-week notice." I remember thinking, "I can relate to that. I like plenty of warning. I like to think things through and really process them." So this whole idea of going to New Jersey was one of the most unusual things I had ever done. I'm just not that kind of person.

Again I tried to convince the Lord, kind of like Moses tried to convince the Lord that he couldn't talk, so how could he tell Pharaoh, "Let my people go." I remember I was saying, "Lord, I don't like to fly, and you know if I'm going to New Jersey today I'm probably going to have to take a plane. You know I'm really not crazy about flying." I've flown all my life, but I'm just not crazy about it and never have been.

Along with my dislike of flying, I'm also not crazy about going to towns that I have never been to, especially by myself. I'd rather go with somebody that knows the town. I had never been to New Jersey in my life, but there I was heading to New Jersey. There were just a lot of things that didn't make me a fit for the person who should be on this mission.

When I arrived at the airport, I went to the desk and started talking with a ticket agent. She said, "We've got connecting flights to New Jersey this afternoon, but booking this quickly, we don't have anything for under a thousand dollars." I replied, "Well, money really is not an issue right now. The issue is I need to get to my friend, Harvey. Is that possible? I'll just look at the possibilities first, then we'll talk about the details." She said, "Oh, yes, this is possible. We can book you," so I start talking with her about the particulars.

Another ticket agent, evidently a supervisor, had been in and out of our conversation, kind of watching over our interaction. She finally walked up to the desk, looked at me and said, "Sir, I don't know why I'm thinking this, but I just feel in my heart like I'm supposed to do this. So here's the deal: I'm going to give you an airline companion ticket. As an employee, I can give these out to people. So instead of costing over a $1,000, it will cost you $262 and it's an open return."

The agent said, "Ok, you're going to New Jersey. When are you returning?" I told her I had no idea. "I don't know whether I will be coming straight back, or whether I'm staying awhile. I just need to get to New Jersey." So, this kind lady gave me a ticket that had an open-ended return for $262 on a flight that was leaving in an hour.

I had gotten to the airport in time to book a flight and get on it. I was on the plane, it took off, and then I realized how focused I had been on what the Lord wanted me to do, what He wanted me to say, and all the arrangements. The next question was what I would do once I arrived in New Jersey. I didn't know where the hospital was, or even how far it was from the airport. I felt so overwhelmed by this mission, I just started scouring scripture for guidance. I was sitting on the airplane, flying to New Jersey for the first time, and buried in the Bible looking for verses and asking for some direction from the Lord.

Things had happened so quickly, I didn't even know what city we were going to for my connection to New Jersey. So I prayed, "Lord, I don't even know where to go to the next gate to catch the next flight," and asked Him to show me the way. By the time my intermediate flight landed, I had figured out what airport I was in. I got off the plane and walked straight toward the gate where my connecting flight was waiting.

On the way to that gate, I had begun thinking, "Well, now I am kind of getting hungry." The Lord knew that too, of course, and the bottom line was He just provided – just as He had provided the tickets and the transportation to New Jersey. Over my years of walking with Him, I have learned that when He sends you on a mission, He faithfully provides all the way. I began looking at the types of restaurants that were in the main food court. I said to myself, "I don't want to eat any of that type of food." But on the way to my gate there was one restaurant all by itself that had the type of food I like to eat. So before boarding my connecting flight to New Jersey, I had time to enjoy a lavish meal. I guess I could have fasted for this trip, but with everything else that had already happened, this wasn't on my mind.

With a full stomach I proceeded to my gate and boarded the plane for my destination. Now officially en route to New Jersey, I began praying about other provision. When we landed in New Jersey, I didn't even know what city I was in. Coupled with not knowing where the town was I was supposed to be going to, again I prayed. "Lord, now I really need some guidance because I have no idea what kind of transportation I need to get there." Then I noticed a sign that said, "TRANSPORTATION," so I headed that way.

I was walking through the baggage area since I didn't have a checked bag when a guy just stopped me and asked if I was going to the hospital. I said, "Well, yes, I am," and he replied, "I'm your guy."

This was so unexpected. I never really asked how the guy knew me or where I was going. I just said, "Lord I'm in your hands", and then we got in this vehicle that was not so much looking like a taxi or limo. I said, "Lord, this better be your deal or I don't know what's happening, because this guy doesn't seem like a limo or taxi driver. He doesn't have that type of car." There I was in the middle of New Jersey, not knowing a soul, and not knowing who this guy was, but just sensing it all was of the Lord. So away we went, a stranger driving me to the hospital in Englewood, New Jersey.

Now one other thing that was going on during all of this: A major snowstorm was coming in. It was already snowing, but a huge snowstorm was supposed to be on its way. Nevertheless, this guy drove me to this hospital and by the time we arrived it was night. When I entered the hospital, most of the lights had been turned off in the reception area. There were a couple of security guards, but no one else in the lobby.

I went to the security people and told them why I was there, to see a dying friend. They said, "Okay, we'll give you ten minutes." They gave me a badge and told me what room Harvey was in, and then repeated, "We'll give you ten minutes." I began walking up to the hospital room and on my way ran into the chaplain of the hospital. I told him why I was there. Frankly, I was hoping he would come with me and take charge the rest of the way because by then I was so nervous and shaken up. But the chaplain excused himself, saying he had just finished a long day and was on his way home.

After he left I was on my own again, so I went to Harvey's room. There was nobody around, not even any nurses. When I entered his room, it occurred to me that I hadn't seen Harvey in probably 15 years. I looked at the person in the bed and thought it looked like it could possibly be Harvey, but he was in bad shape. I knew he'd had a stroke, and he had all kinds of tubes and wires connected to him. I walked back out of the room just to make sure it was his name posted on that room number. Sure enough, it had Harvey's name, so I went back in.

As I said, there was not a soul around, no one with Harvey. He had burned a lot of bridges in his lifetime, so it did not seem that surprising that there was nobody there. My heart really sank as I re-entered the room. As I approached the bed, Harvey's eyes opened and he saw me. I said, "Harvey, it's Brad Rymer. Your son, Billy, called and told me that you were not doing so well, and I'm just going to be honest with you. He asked me to pray for you, and when I prayed, the Lord sent me to come and talk to you."

As soon as I said those words I sensed the Holy Spirit envelop both of us. Now I can't describe what that looked like, or how I knew that. As a friend of mine has said, "it's just a spiritual thing." And it was, just a sense of knowing. I can't explain it, but nobody can talk me out of it. I just knew the Holy Spirit came over us.

Throughout my trip I had been scouring the Scriptures and praying, but didn't have a clue what to say. The interesting thing was that just two weeks before I had gone to lunch with a friend that had been to Israel and knew he had a heart for Israel. So I had just started asking him questions. Until then I hadn't even known how to say Jesus in Hebrew (Yeshua). I had found myself asking the friend other things about the Jewish faith and the Jewish people, and remembered wondering why I was so interested in this all of a sudden.

Well, when I got to Harvey Rose's room, I realized what my sudden curiosity was all about because of Harvey's Jewish heritage. I told him why I was there and remember him trying to mouth my name, but he couldn't speak. Not a sound. I went on to explain how and why I had come there – that his son had asked me to pray and that I had been praying for him. Then I said, "Harvey, as I was talking to the Lord about you, the Lord was just telling me that you've made a lot of mistakes in your life."

Harvey was just wide-eyed. I could tell he was very attentive to every word I was saying and was trying to talk, but he just couldn't speak. I was not using the name "Lord," I was using, *Yeshua*. I was saying things like, "*Yeshua* tells me that you have made a lot of mistakes in your life." I don't recall a lot of the things I was saying; I just felt like I was flowing with the Holy Spirit and that He was speaking through me. I didn't even know what words were coming out.

But I do distinctly remember saying, "Harvey, the thing that you have been looking for your entire life, *Yeshua* is here to give you. That thing that you have been looking for your entire life is *Shalom* (peace)." Then I said, "Harvey, *Yeshua* wants you to have His *Shalom*. All you have to do is acknowledge Him and say the name, call on the name *Yeshua* and you are forgiven for everything you have ever done – and you will enter into *Shalom*."

Harvey Rose had not been able to utter a word until that point. But as soon as I told him that, he responded, very clearly, "*Yes, Yeshua,*" and at that moment I knew something eternal had happened. He couldn't speak after that. Harvey could not say another word. Those were the only words he could say, and he said it very clearly. So I told him how wonderful it was to see him and how happy I was for him, and said a prayer over him. Then I turned around and walked out of the room.

I felt like I had done what the Lord had wanted me to do, so that was it. Then I began thinking, "Okay, I've done what I was called here for, it's night, the hospital gave me ten minutes, and I don't know how long I have been here." I knew it had been well over ten minutes by that point, so I wondered whether they were going to kick me out on the street when there was a snowstorm? I didn't know where I would stay or anything, so I decided to find the nurses' station.

When I finally located the nurse's station, the nurses there were busy and referred me to the head nurse. I explained to her that I had come there to see a dying friend, that I was from Chattanooga, Tennessee, and had no place to stay. "Is there anything you all could do to help me?" I asked. Once again, it was almost like the supervisor at the airport. The other nurses had been trying to decide what to do, most of them giving me a deer-in-headlights kind of stare, as if to say, "We don't have a clue. This is not in our protocol. We don't know what to do with you, mister." But then the nurse supervisor looked at me and said, "Sir, I'm going to help you, just hold on. I've got some other things right now. Would you just hang on?"

The other nurses kept asking me what I was doing there, and then they suddenly started asking me to pray for them – and I found myself praying for the nurses. It just blew me away, all the things that started happening. They would ask me to pray, and then they would be in tears, telling me what was going on in their lives, and how much hope and encouragement that my just praying with them had given them. Then the nurse supervisor said, "Okay, I want you to go down to the second floor. It's pediatrics – they'll have a room for you."

I went down to pediatrics and, as the nurse had promised, they stated they were going to take care of me. Then I said, "I only have one request. I have seen signs around the hospital saying not to use cell phones, but I have got to call my wife and let her know what's going on." I asked if there was someplace I could use my cell phone. They said I could use it in the room where they were putting me. This happened to be a section of the hospital where it was okay to use cell phones. When I got to the room, it was not a regular hospital room. It didn't have just a bathroom; it also had a shower. I thought it was kind of like Jesus said, "I go to prepare a place for you." I felt like I was in the place He had prepared for me that night.

So I went to sleep and when I woke up the next morning, I prayed, "Lord, am I supposed to go see Harvey again, or is there something else?" He just gave me a vision of Harvey walking up to the Jordan River and putting his foot into the river. He was barefooted and as he put his foot in the water, the Jordan River parted. When I saw him step in, I said, "Lord, have you taken him home?" I didn't really get an answer to that, but sensed my mission was over, that I just needed to head home.

I walked out of the room and started to say, "Is anybody...," but before I could get the words out of my mouth about breakfast, a lady was there with a breakfast cart who said, "What would you like this morning?" I looked on her cart and saw everything that I usually eat in the morning for breakfast was on it. I started crying, actually weeping. This lady didn't know why I'm weeping, but said, "Would you pray for me?" So I prayed for the lady with the cart.

Remembering I had to pass the chaplain's office to leave the hospital, I dropped in to see the chaplain. Since he had been out so late the night before, he wasn't there yet. Only his secretary was in the office. I told her what was going on and she said, "Sir, there's a huge snowstorm outside, but I'll try to get you a limo." She called a limo service, but they said the soonest they could get to the hospital was 45 minutes. She sent me to the lobby, and to my surprise the limo was there within five minutes. I don't know how that happened, but the limo driver said, "We're backed up, it's snowing so heavily outside." As I went out the doors of the hospital, there was a blizzard going on outside. Everything was solid white. Despite that, the limo service picked me up and took me to the airport.

When I got to the airport ticket counter, the lady there told me that because I had an open-ended ticket I could run into problems. As I was standing at the counter, an agent looked at my ticket and said, "Oh, we have to get you on quick, there's a flight that's leaving in 20 or 30 minutes. We've got to get you on quick."

I had been thinking my open-ended ticket was going to be a problem, but they were making me a priority and were shuffling me to the gate. By the time I got on the plane, it was getting ready to taxi away. The crew said it was snowing so hard and the plane had been sitting so long, ice was forming on the wings. "We are going to have to wait to be de-iced." So the de-icing equipment came up, de-iced the wings, and we got back onto the taxiway.

Then they said we had lost our place in line because the plane had to get de-iced. So we were the 22nd jet in line to take off. The runway we originally were going to take off from was closed, so we were in a long line of planes headed for the runways that were still open. All 21 planes in front of us went across this runway, but they stopped us. The pilot said, "They are just opening this runway again, and we are now number one for takeoff." So after being in the back of a line of 22 planes, since 21 of them had already gone across, we were suddenly at the front of the line. Suddenly a thought flashed through my mind: "Well, the last shall be first." I was just amazed, blown away really, because time after time things like this had happened the whole way on my trip and now on the flight back.

While traveling back home, I called my friend Billy to report what had happened with his dad. He said, "How'd it go?" I told him what I had said to his father, that the thing he had been looking for all his life, eternal Shalom, was available to him. Then I said, "Billy, it is for you, too." Then he replied, "Brad, I'm a believer." Since then some amazing things have happened in Billy's life.

It's been about eight years since that trip. I learned that after I left the hospital on a Thursday morning, Harvey Rose died the next morning. His wife, who may have been his former wife at the time (I'm not really sure) called to tell me that she had heard through her stepson what I had done and thanked me for it. She even said that Harvey had passed in peace. Thinking about all that transpired during such a short span of time, I realize I didn't do much. All I did was be obedient. God did all the rest, faithfully guiding every step and every detail of my journey.

Bringing It Home

People turn to various places and sources to find peace. The Scripture shows us the only way to peace and the true source of peace. The way, it says, is that, "We have peace with God through our Lord Jesus Christ" (Romans 5:1). The source, Jesus says, is Himself. "Peace I leave with you; my peace I give you. I do not give you as the world gives. Do not let your hearts be troubled and do not be afraid" (John 14:27).

How have you experienced direction from God in your life? Has it ever come to you in unusual, unexpected ways?

When you feel troubled, lacking the sense of peace that seems to be a universal human need, in whom, and where and how do you place your trust? How do you find that working for you? Can you say that you are experiencing the Shalom of God? Why or why not?

26

ACTING BOLDLY BASED ON WHAT GOD HAS PROMISED

By Andres Augusto Bunch

*A*ndres *Bunch is pastor of Iglesia Christiana El Pacto in Bogota, Colombia. He has been deeply involved in ministry to drug addicts, homeless and others in despair for more than 25 years. Andres' ministry extends from the slums of Bogota to people in high places in the Colombian government. In addition to their ministry responsibilities, both Andres and his wife, Beatriz, are respected attorneys in Colombia.*

There is a myth sometimes spread through Christian circles that following Jesus Christ means living a life with few if any problems, especially if you are serving in vocational ministry. Yet God has taught me that often the best way to see and experience His faithfulness is to watch what He does in times of struggle and uncertainty.

I have been married to my wife, Beatriz Arguello, for 28 years. We have a son, Andres Mauricio, who along with his wife, Laura Gonzalez, serve as youth pastors at our church. God has remained faithful on many occasions in the midst of difficulties we have faced, and has been gracious to honor me for my striving to remain faithful to him. Let me share just a few of the situations in which God manifested His faithfulness in ways I could never have imagined.

My wife and I obtained law degrees and both worked in the legal field. During that time the Lord brought to our office a missionary from Norway who started a ministry in Bogota helping homeless drug addicts. When the missionary left, I assumed the leadership responsibilities for the ministry, while Beatriz started working at a high-paying job for the Colombian government. The extreme differences in the kind of work we were doing caused a major crisis in our marriage; as a result, I was unexpectedly facing the possibility of a separation from my wife or leaving the ministry to the drug addicts.

The question I had was, "What if I leave everything and my marriage is not restored? Then what?"

Seeking direction from the Lord, I started a serious process of fasting and praying, clinging more to God and depending on Him. I was dealing with all kinds of problems and didn't know what to do. One night I went into my small son's, Andres Mauricio, bedroom and opened the Bible to Luke 14:26, where Jesus said, "if anyone comes to Me and does not hate his father and mother, his wife and children, his brothers and sisters – yes, even his own life – he cannot be My disciple." Convicted, that night I put Christ in the center of my heart.

When I surrendered everything to the Lord, He started working and His faithfulness reached out to me. My wife had a knee injury and I had to start helping her to do things she could not do on her own, things like bathing, getting dressed, and going to the doctor's office. Through this the Lord started restoring our relationship and our love for one another. Shortly after this Beatriz left her job, along with her good salary, and came to my office at the church to serve the Lord and live by faith.

The Lord not only demonstrated His faithfulness by restoring my family, but also extended the calling on my life to my spouse. We were, as Philippians 2:2 states, "being like-minded, having the same love, being one in spirit and purpose."

Another time, when Andres Mauricio was 18 years old, he decided to study for ministry at a Bible school in another country.

Both my wife and I felt this was not the time or the place for our son, but he insisted so strongly that we gave in to his desires. So he ended up going for his studies to Argentina, a country very far from Colombia.

The Bible school he attended had a very traditional and legalistic style of teaching, where the role and work of the Holy Spirit was not recognized or a part of the curriculum. This undermined my son's faith to the extent that when he would call us, he would sometimes threaten to take his own life.

This was, of course, an extremely painful and confusing situation for us as parents. The only thing we knew to do was to get on our knees and ask God to take control of our son's mind and emotions, and that He would watch over Andres Mauricio's life and carry out His purpose in his life. We couldn't do anything else since we were too far away to hug him and or have him with us, and could not bring him back home immediately. We were simply trusting in God's promise to watch over our son and protect his life.

When Andres Mauricio finally returned to us, his faith was shattered. He said he did not want to continue believing in God. Even though his faith seemed almost dead, we continued supporting him with love and trusting in God's faithfulness to us.

After a few months, Andres Mauricio's faith was restored and he decided to train for ministry at a Bible school in Colombia, much closer to home, as he felt God's calling on his life was confirmed. Today, as I said before, our son is married to a woman who loves God. They have given us two beautiful granddaughters, and are serving by our side as youth and children's pastors in our church.

Later, in 2013, I experienced another difficult time and saw again that by remaining faithful to our faithful God, the Lord would honor my faithfulness. One Sunday during a church service a homeless man, addicted to drugs and alcohol, showed up asking us to help him rehabilitate. We had already helped him three times, but gave him another opportunity without taking into consideration the protocol for rehab centers according to the Colombian laws.

A few hours after arriving to the rehab center, this man started having typical withdrawal symptoms. The second day he lost his vision and while walking to the bathroom, he fell and died. That morning the government officials in charge of removing his corpse arrived and initiated a homicide investigation. We conducted the man's funeral, but none of his family members were present.

Shortly afterward, the district attorney's office subpoenaed the employees of our rehab center and myself as its legal representative. They started a preliminary investigation against me since I was the primary representative for the organization that got the man into the rehab center. The investigating official was strongly against me because he said that as a lawyer I knew the law. I was accused of manslaughter and had to respond.

On our way home, my son and I were thinking about all these events, as well as how we were going to face this legal process. The most serious thing was that in the office files in the last 15 years, there existed no evidence of this man having been admitted to our organization. Some of my colleagues offered to defend my case, and others considered talking to a district attorney who would talk to the attorney prosecuting my case and discuss the situation to find a way out.

My wife and I, along with my family and the office staff, started praying and fasting. Finally I decided not to do anything. I would not hire a lawyer or seek friends with influence, but instead I would pray and claim the promises of the Word of God for my life. In prayer, I declared my faithfulness to the Lord, declared His Word, and told Him that I did not mind going to jail for serving the weak. If that was His will, I was willing to go.

Psalms 41:1-2 says, "Blessed is he who has regard for the weak; the Lord delivers him in times of trouble. The Lord will protect him and preserve his life; He will bless him in the land and not surrender him to the desire of his foes." I told God I was ready to face whatever would happen. I made sure that the kingdom of darkness heard my decision, and started praying and praising the Lord day after day, and little by little I was casting my cares on the Lord.

God showed His faithfulness in a very clear way. Four months after the charges were filed, the district attorney permanently closed the case. One more time, God was with me and the ministry. We celebrated this victory by returning to the streets to conduct "love brigades" to help the homeless.

Now I can say what I consider faithfulness to be: It is the decision to continue believing the Word of God and act boldly on what God has said. It is the fulfillment of His Word in our lives, based on His love, not on our response.

Then, faithfulness on our part has to do with remaining steadfast, convinced of the love God has for us, and trusting in His work, regardless of the circumstances.

Bringing It Home

Working within biblical truth, God may call us to act boldly. "Now Lord, consider their threat and enable your servants to speak your word with great boldness" (Acts 4:29). Jesus sympathizes and understands our weaknesses. He was "tempted in every way, just as we are – yet was without sin" (Hebrews 4:15). As we face challenges and difficulties, may we remember Hebrews 4:16, "Let us then approach the throne of grace with confidence, so that we may receive mercy and find grace to help us in our time of need."

Describe a time when you felt that you acted boldly for Jesus.

As you reflect over the course of your life, can you think of occasions when and where you have received mercy and found grace "to help (you) in (your) time of need"?

Describe one or two of these times – what were the circumstances, how did God act, and what was your response, both during and after the events?

27

WHEN IN PAIN, JUST START SINGING

By Bill Lickliter

*T*he Rev. Bill Lickliter, pastor at First Assembly of God in Clinton, Kentucky, is known for his great compassion for the lost and hurting. Pastor Lickliter has served congregations in Arkansas, Kentucky and Tennessee, and has experienced and observed more examples of God's faithfulness than he could ever recount. This story, which he witnessed firsthand, is one of the most vivid.

ℒ

What do you do when you're at wit's end, pain is excruciating, and it seems nothing you have tried to do is working? Well, although I wouldn't suggest doing this in every circumstance, sometimes the very best thing you can do is to sing. Let me explain what I mean.

The story about how God used a process to intervene in a seemingly hopeless situation on a particular day and in a very unusual way begins on July 9, 1999, while a group of people was busily taking down the set we had used for a major production we had presented on the Milan (Tennessee) High School football field. This musical production was called, "Nation, It's Time to Pray." About 13,000 people had come to the football stadium, and after the presentation we had a crusade. Steve Gaines, now the pastor at Bellevue Baptist Church in Memphis, served as the evangelist for this crusade.

Twelve churches were involved and the set itself cost $90,000. We raised $100,000 for the set, enabling us to cover all expenses and have some funds left over. The set had filled up the end zone of the football stadium, and after the production we wanted to keep as much of the equipment as we could. So we contracted with a "home-mover" to move the set in sections, and transport it to a farm nearby so we could come back the following year and not have to incur as much expense in rebuilding it.

After they removed the bracing for the set, one portion of the set remained that looked like a beach house, like a large garage or a house. It was standing on poles, because the stage bracing had been taken off so we could move it. Then we determined it would have to be cut in half to be moved, which is why the braces had been removed. One of my deacons, Bobby Ross, was in charge of taking it down and getting it cleared out from the football field. My associate pastor, Steve Martin, was working with him on the field, as were several others.

It was about 3 in the afternoon, and Steve and Bobby were walking underneath this particular building, picking up paper. Bobby looked over at Steve, and the last word he said was, "Praise the Lord." They were just kind of working, experiencing the joy of the Lord. Suddenly there was a strong gust of wind. I did not see what happened personally, but from what I've heard, it was almost as if the house was lifted up and fell straight down, directly on both men.

Bobby's injuries were so severe that he didn't survive. He passed away even though there were a lot of people that tried to save his life. Steve Martin was pinned underneath. The lower middle area of his body had been crushed, but they got the debris from the house off him and flew him to the trauma unit in Memphis by helicopter.

For the next two weeks Steve was in extremely critical condition. The surgeons had actually opened him up, but could not do what they needed to do to be able to close him up, so the wound in his mid-section had to remain open for nearly two weeks. Understandably, he was really experiencing severe pain from this. For whatever reason, the hospital and medical staff seemed to keep delaying the completion of his surgery, even though it was desperately needed. So Steve had no choice but to just hang there in agony for quite some time.

After the memorial services for Bobby Ross, which were attended by many people across the city, and then taking care of other arrangements, we would go down every day to Memphis to visit and pray for Steve. It was already such an inexpressible tragedy that we had lost Bobby, and if we had lost brother Steve, it would have just doubled our grief. So we were all just praying, "God, let him live, and help these doctors to be able to do this surgery that he needs to have done." After almost two weeks had passed, I visited Steve again. I don't have all the details on why he remained opened up, but there was no question the rest of the surgery had to be done.

For Steve, it had gotten to the place where his pain could not be controlled with morphine or any other pain medication as it needed to be. He was suffering so badly, and nothing was easing his pain or dulling his situation. It was so hard for me to watch this. I was actually there that particular day by myself, just he and I. No one else was in the room.

At that moment I prayed, "God, I don't know what to do. I really cannot help him. How do you want me to pray, and what do you want me to do?" It was as if the Lord gave me kind of a strange instruction. I was asking God to guide me in a prayer, but the Lord told me to start singing.

Even though I often visited people in hospitals, I didn't do much of that there. But apparently God wanted me to sing, so I did. I started to worship the Lord, without fear of who would be coming in. I started singing choruses and hymns. I sang just about every chorus and hymn that I could. After a little while, Steve actually joined in and started singing with me. I ended up singing over him for two hours.

Sometimes as he was singing, Steve would grab one of those triangles that hung above his head, hold onto it and try maneuvering around with it to get any kind of comfort. We just kept singing and singing. After we had been singing for a couple of hours, his pain subsided. It seemed as if God had moved in.

The doctors had thought Steve was going to have to stay open possibly for a couple more days until he was physically able to endure the surgery, but about that time they actually came back into his room and when they saw how he was doing, they were able to finish the surgery and close him back up that night.

That evening and the following day, when I saw Steve, he looked and felt a hundred times better than he had been just the day before the surgery. From that point on, we knew that he was going to make it.

After recovering, Steve remained my associate pastor until 2005, so I saw daily evidence of how God had moved in a very special, very unusual way. The thing I learned through this experience is we need to go His way even if it sounds unusual. Just as in the Old Testament, when Naaman was told to dip seven times to be healed of his leprosy, and I'm sure Naaman thought another way would have been more suitable to his tastes. But after he submitted and obeyed exactly the way God said to do it, the results were there.

I believe the Lord not only touched Steve's pain but also advanced his condition to the place where the doctors felt they would be able to undertake the surgery they needed to perform. From that point on, it wasn't long until he made a full recovery. It seemed evident God was not finished with Steve Martin, as he continued to faithfully serve the Lord as an associate pastor.

For some time I had thoughts of, "Why?" First of all, there was a thought of who caused this, God or the devil? Then there was the thought about why did one man live and one not live. Eventually I just had to come back to that scripture, "All things work together for good to those who love God and are called together for his purpose" (Romans 8:28). I feel like God's purpose was evidently finished for

Bobby at that time, so he took him home while keeping Steve alive. And since the Lord knows the beginning and the end, we can have peace and comfort with that.

Bringing It Home

Walking in faithfulness with God sometimes leads us into challenging situations. It could involve taking a stand for righteousness, or going the "extra mile" to help someone. Naaman was called to do the unusual: "So he went down and dipped himself in the Jordan seven times, as the man of God had told him, and his flesh was restored and became clean like that of a young boy" (2 Kings 5:14).

Can you remember a time when you felt God speaking to you to do or say something that seemed unusual or unorthodox that glorified Him? If so, what was that experience like for you?

How has God used you to go the extra mile in someone's life? Or how has God used someone else to go the extra mile in your life?

28

GOD RESTORES MINISTRY THROUGH RELATIONSHIPS

By David Deerman

*D*avid Deerman serves as pastor for CenterPointe Church in Bowling Green, Kentucky after serving as executive pastor of Cornerstone Church in Nashville, Tennessee. He's the product of a family of pastors – his father and grandfather were both pastors, stalwart examples of faithfulness. In David's life, however, there was a time when he ran from God's faithfulness even though it was always available – and accessible. All David had to do was just turn back to the Lord and return to Him, but it took time. David's story is that of a gifted pastor who today understands deeply about God's grace, power, love and peace, not only from the Scriptures but also through his life experiences.

One of the strong, unquestioned attributes of God is His faithfulness, and we all have experienced that in many ways. But what about when we're weak, when we are not faithful, when our thoughts, words and actions are a virtual fist-shake at God, defying Him and insisting on doing things our way, not His? Does He remain faithful even then?

My long and winding journey with the Lord began when I was six years old. Raised in a pastor's home, I gave my heart to the Lord at an early age and through the years watched as my dad led his congregations and saw the testimony of God's faithfulness lived out through the generations in front of me – my dad and my grandfather. I watched my grandfather pastor small churches in New Mexico, and watched my grandmother on my mom's side serve as a pastor in Arkansas. I was fortunate to observe my dad serving as a pastor and being faithful, solid and consistent – also seeing how God blessed him as we moved from one church and built another one.

So one of the ways I learned about the faithfulness of God was by watching the faithfulness of my parents, having the privilege of being raised in a faithful home, where my grandparents and parents lived out in front of us the reality of "great is Thy faithfulness." That's a wonderful hymn, and they lived it all out, every verse, in front of me.

As I watched my dad model faithfulness to the Lord, I saw how God was faithful to him and and met every need we had. Being raised in this atmosphere, at age 18 I sensed the Lord calling me to preach, to prepare to become a third-generation pastor. I went to Bible college, and at 21 went to work with my dad as an associate minister at his church.

I married and continued to work with my dad, following what I knew the Lord wanted me to do. During this time God demonstrated His faithfulness to me in an unexpected way, enabling me to pay off my college loan through my grandfather, even though he had no idea I had that need. I worked for my dad for five years as a member of his church staff, and it was good.

Then I went to West Texas for a time, before moving to Dickson, Tennessee, in the Nashville area, in 1994. I assumed the role as pastor of a small church and it began to grow. It really was amazing how that church grew and, trusting God, we built our first building. I would lie in my bed with heart palpitations, nervous about meeting the payments for the new building, but God provided, and as the church grew, people were being saved. I was at Dickson for 12½ years, and there was not one weekend where someone did not give their heart to the Lord. Continuing to grow, we built another building and we prospered so much that at times we were able to make two and three payments per month. It was wonderful.

During that exciting season of ministry, however, especially in the last few years, my marriage got into serious trouble. Despite that dysfunction, pain, whatever you want to call it, God remained faithful. But I, who had seen firsthand what faithfulness looked like through my parents and grandparents, began to waver in my own faithfulness – to the point where I honestly wondered, if I were not pastoring this church, would I still be a Christian?

Things deteriorated in my personal life to such a degree, I resigned the church, and then I failed in marriage. I became unfaithful, to the Lord and to my wife, during the separation time and in going through divorce. Yet from an early age my favorite verse had been and remained Proverbs 3:5-6, "Trust in the Lord with all your heart and lean not in your own understanding. In all you ways acknowledge Him and He will direct your path." Sadly, for a time I forgot – or ignored – that wonderful promise and the faithfulness of God it assures us.

There, during one of the most unfaithful seasons of my life, I pushed back from God, I pushed back from ministry, I pushed back from everything I had seen modeled in the way of faithfulness. And yet, in my own selfish heart the thing that held me, kept me from losing my own mind and completely going off on some God-forsaken track, was remembering the faithfulness of God. At the same time I was living as unfaithfully as I could have from what I had been raised in, what I knew in the church world, and what had been modeled for me in going to church. I had seen so many examples of marriage staying together, yet mine had failed, and in everything else I had become selfish and sinful.

During that entire time the Lord would keep drawing me, despite my willful disobedience and rebellion. It is amazing how God, through the sacrifice of His Son, keeps drawing us even when we are pushing Him back, wanting nothing to do with Him.

Even though I had justifiably lost my ministerial credentials, God continued to draw. I would walk the beaches of Myrtle Beach, where I had gone to escape from everything I considered faithful. There at Myrtle Beach, where many people go for joyous vacations, I found myself digging ditches instead of leading people to Jesus. Digging ditches with three illegal Guatemalans and walking the beaches with a dog, while I had left a lady pregnant, carrying my child, back in the city where I had been a pastor.

In His faithfulness, this process of continuing to draw me back to Himself, God used three men who had been colleagues with me in ministry during that season when everything seemed to be going so well. These men, Maury Davis, Randy Carter and Terry Bailey, continued to testify of the faithfulness of God.

Those 3 men would call me every week – every single week. They did not miss a week saying, "Dave, we love you, God loves you, He is waiting for you, pursuing you." I think that sometimes God shows His faithfulness to us most powerfully through relationships.

God uses, in our own insanity with sin, those who know how to restore a brother gently. Because they are faithful when we are being unfaithful. They also are being faithful to God, and continue to paint the picture of faithfulness. But even in their kindness, I pushed those guys back, shoved them away.

Randy Carter called me one Thursday night in 2007 and said, "Hey, Dave, my wife and I are coming down to see you. God loves you and we love you, and we just want to come and see you." I replied to Randy (and I apologize for the words, but this is what I said), "Screw yourself, Randy," and added a few other choice words.

Randy didn't flinch. Instead, he said, " Dave, don't forever ruin the ability of God to use you in ministry." I responded, "What are you talking about?" He said, "You are really close to jumping off the cliff of bitterness, and if you would jump off that cliff of bitterness you will be like every other pastor who has ever failed and gotten bitter. God can never restore through bitterness until you understand and know that you are bitter and you need to repent. I love you, and I love you enough to tell you."

He said, "In fact, if you will do that – me and Maury and Terry – we won't have to work at restoring you, and it will be okay. Just go out there and keep doing what you are doing in construction. The love of God is there, the calling of God is there, His faithfulness. My wife and I have a timeshare that we have reserved, and we are coming out there next week, so we expect to see you and we are going to see you."

I will never forget hanging up the phone after that conversation. Feeling broken and humbled, I fell on my face and said, "God, I have been so unfaithful, and I have screwed a lot of things up. I got a lot of stuff happening here. Please forgive me – I don't want to be bitter." My prayer didn't change the fact that I still had someone pregnant that I was not married to. It did not change the fact that I was in a mess. What did change, however, was that I understood that I was not a Christian because I was being paid to be one. I knew I was a Christian simply because I loved Jesus at that point more than anything else.

At that point I began to draw from what I knew about God's love and what I had learned in the Scriptures about the faithfulness of God. Despite everything, He was faithful and waiting for me to turn around and run to him. What an amazing thought – He was there waiting for me.

I started going to church again, Myrtle Beach Community Church, because I knew that is what faithfulness was, my first step to getting to where I needed to be. Every time I went to church, it seemed the pastor was preaching directly to me. He was preaching to me about backslidden preachers that needed to come back to the Lord. He would talk about how God loves me and how He is faithful and can restore your calling. Every time I would go, I would think, "This dude is reading my mail!" (I had been a pastor from 1983 to 2006, and at one time people had said this about my preaching.) I thought, "Jesus, I love You, and I am so thankful that You are faithful enough to speak to me through this man of God that I do not even know."

I would sit in the congregation, and later would email the preacher and say, "I am a backslidden Assemblies of God preacher sitting in your audience, and I have returned to the Lord, and you are messing me over, man. You are preaching to me every time I am here."

He would send a gracious note back and say, "I am grateful to be a testimony of the love and faithfulness of God. You are loved. You are welcome here." I emailed him several times.

Meanwhile, I still had the three men calling me every week saying, "Dave, we love you, man." God used these men to love me and reveal His love and faithfulness while I was in the middle of a mess. God used this pastor in Myrtle Beach, and He even used the three Guatemalans I worked with. You talk about amazing!

These three Guatemalans had come all the way from Guatemala to be in Myrtle Beach working for me as their project manager. They had found out that I was a former pastor, and every day as we started work they would say, "Pastor, what would you want us to do today?" "Pastor, we love you." I said, "Stop calling me a pastor. Don't call me a pastor again. I am done, guys. Now don't do it." They would reply, "Oh yes, you are a pastor. God loves you. God's got a calling on you, we can see the glory of God all over you. We are so glad you are our project manager."

I said "Shut up, Carlos, stop man, stop. Don't say that any more." Their reply would be, "No, we know you, Pastor. We want you to teach us scripture while we are working." The Lord spoke to me every day through these three illegal Guatemalans that were working under my leadership. I think God sent those three guys, walking all the way to me, just to let me know that He knew where I was.

So there I was, in the middle of a mess, and these guys were calling me pastor, exactly what I was pushing back from. I was messed up, not married, still having a lady nobody knew about. In my previous marriage I had prayed for a child. I had dedicated many, many children in our church. And I wanted kids.

The faithfulness of God was everywhere around me – He is faithful no matter what. Whenever you take the will and plan and the ways of God into your own hands, sin follows. The very thing I had dreamed about, I could not tell anybody about. The dream of my life had been having a child, but now I, a former pastor, had someone I was not married to, Christy, who was pregnant with that baby.

I was so ashamed in how that all had happened, I could not tell any one. Christy and I were the only ones who knew. I could not tell my brother, and could not tell my parents. Those working with me did not know. I was so scared. I knew I had taken the destiny of God on through my own sinfulness. Looking back at that, I know it had nothing to do with a previous marriage, but simply that Dave Deerman had pushed back the faithfulness and the hand of God due to selfishness and sin.

Yet in the midst of everything, God was still faithful. He loved me enough to send three Guatemalans. He loved me enough to have three former colleagues – who still believed we were "colleagues" – call me every day. The power of three illegal Guatemalans calling me "Pastor" that I worked with every day in a ditch, and the power of three former colleagues in ministry who were telling me every day, "Dave, God loves you." If you want to talk about the faithfulness of God – that is an amazing, very real example.

One day I called Pastor Maury and said, "Hey, there is something I have not told you." He asked what it was, and I told him my girl-friend was pregnant. He replied, "That is a problem, a real problem. She is living in the county where you were a pastor. That's a problem, man. I love you, Dave, but you have made a mess, a real mess."

I still had not told my family. Nobody knew but my girlfriend and me, but she was starting to show that she was with child and was in the city where I had been a pastor. You see, God wants to restore the picture of His faithfulness, yet Satan wants to destroy and humiliate you. As we walk in humility, we experience and know the faithfulness and power of God, but at the same time the devil can keep us in humiliation. Through sin he keeps us bound up, away from the grace, mercy and faithfulness of God. It has nothing to do with the Lord, but has everything to do with what we are serving.

Over the phone Maury said, "Dave, you have a real mess. Do you love her?" I replied, "Yes." Then Maury said, "You need to marry her as fast as you can, so that you do not have an unwed woman carrying your child in the city where you pastored." I asked, "Do we need counseling?" He said, "You have already blown counseling. If you love her, marry her, and marry her fast." At that point Maury Davis, my one-time colleague, became my pastor because he spoke something to me I needed to do, and I said to myself, "I am going to do what he tells me."

You see, we can experience the faithfulness of God through fellowship and friendship, as I did through three colleagues and three illegal Guatemalans, but also we experience the faithfulness of God when we follow spiritual authority. What happens is that all of a sudden, the favor of God restores as you put yourself in the right position.

I said, "Okay, pastor, I will do it." That was a Wednesday. I called my girlfriend, Christy, and said, "I am buying you a plane ticket to fly there on Friday, and I want us to get married on Saturday." She said, "Are you kidding?" I said, "Will you marry me?" She answered, "I guess I should." So we got married on that Saturday.

We had to deal with a court date later, because of my new wife's ex-husband did not want her to leave Dickson and take the children. You see, we became a blended family since she had already had five children and the one she was carrying was mine. God can help with the blended family situation, but it is a hard, hard thing.

So still adjusting to the newness of married life, we had to come back to court. And when we appeared in court there were a lot of people looking forward to witnessing my demise, my having been a pastor in the city and now with the word out on the street that this lady was pregnant with Pastor Dave's child.

We walked into that courtroom through a gauntlet of people waiting with baited breath to hear what would be found out. You know what? We lost that battle, yet because of God's faithfulness, He protected us against ourselves.

I had been working in the housing industry in Myrtle Beach, but because of my new wife's children we had to move back to Dickson, even though I did not have a job there or anything else. When I moved back to Tennessee was right before the housing crunch hit across the nation. I had taken a new wife, and she brought her five children into the marriage and we had a baby on the way – right in the middle of the housing crunch.

So we went to Nashville and started going to Cornerstone Church, where Maury Davis was the pastor. We placed ourselves in his hands, under Pastor Maury's authority. There were a lot of repercussions yet to come – my sense of personal and moral failure, and a lot of financial failure as well. But the whole time, Pastor Maury and the other two guys were continuing to love me – Pastor Maury more directly since we were in his church. And I sincerely submitted to his authority.

It is amazing how, through all of that, God continued to be faithful. Our baby was born in November of 2007, and I call her my daughter of mercy every time I see her. To be honest, the body of Christ became pretty wicked and difficult toward us. When they first found out about the baby, we were told many mean, insensitive things – that it would be crippled, retarded, would die, that it was cursed, illegitimate. So I will never forget when she was born, watching as this baby came out of her mother. I was looking to make sure she had all of her fingers and toes, and as she came out I exclaimed, "Oh, God, this is my daughter of mercy. You have been so merciful to me."

Attending Cornerstone, listening to sermons, the Lord was dealing with my heart. The first year at Cornerstone I could not even stand up and worship; I would just sit down and cover up. I would say, "God, please don't strike me. I am so sorry."

Pastor Maury's preaching of the Word brought conviction to me. He was walking with my wife, Christy, and me, encouraging us. Then he approached me about teaching a class. I told him no, and sent him a long letter about why I would not do that. He said, "Okay, I am going to turn you over to the Holy Spirit. He will deal with you. I am tired of messing with your hard head."

Within 30 days I was sufficiently convicted and Maury helped me start. A one-time refugee from the Lord, I began teaching the class.

In that process I found myself being happy and serving at work, and just loving the Lord. I really thought I had disqualified myself for pastoral ministry and had given myself to the assumption that I was going to serve the Lord with all my heart in the local church, work in the business world, and do the best I could to love and minister to others.

I was not looking to be responsible for people. I just loved my kids, loved my wife, and really loved Jesus. God was taking care of us. Then the Lord began to deal with me about being in the pastoral ministry again, and I said, "Lord, I can't do that, I can't do that." But in February of 2010, He was dealing with me strongly. I said, "Lord, you have been faithful to me. I want to obey you and I love you, and if going back into ministry is what I am supposed to do, You will have to open the door, because I am not doing it." You know, I had five calls within the next seven days from churches about executive jobs they wanted to fill. Not from Cornerstone, just random churches. I said, "Wow, Lord, this is crazy!" Talk about the faithfulness of God!

Following such encouraging calls, I said, "Okay, Lord, I will serve you in ministry, but You will have to open the door – show me the right door – because I am not going to say anything to anybody. I'll just trust you with that. You lead my path."

At that time I did not know Christy was pregnant with our second child together, our seventh for the family. There were five girls and one boy. I had never asked the Lord for a boy because my dream had always been for a girl. But now I prayed, "Lord, please just let it be a boy, but Lord, I love you so much it does not matter. I am excited to have this child." So we went to the doctor and sure enough, we learned it was going to be a boy. Now I have a daughter of mercy and a son of obedience. I look at my son and say, "Because I said yes to God, I have a son."

I did not get right back into ministry, even though I still had calls coming. I had a young man I had mentored call me, and he started working on me to come to work. So I called Pastor Maury and another friend and said, "You guys are the ones I want to be my sounding boards on this." Pastor Maury said, "Yes, Dave, I think it is time for you to get back on the bike and ride." I told him, "Okay, if you bless it, I will." When I talked with the other friend, he felt it was the Lord's timing as well. So I went to work with the young man I had mentored. Then in 2011, I went to work at Cornerstone Church and served Pastor Maury there.

The Lord began to deal with me in 2012 while I was serving my pastor. That was my whole goal, to serve my pastor. But the Lord was impressing on me the idea of planting a church. I said, "Lord, I can serve as an associate, but what I have done in my past has disqualified me from leading my own church." I was wrestling with this in 2012, and I began to tell my wife, "I've got to talk to Pastor Maury." She said, "No, you cannot do that now. Dave, listen, we are safe at Cornerstone Church. Leave that alone." But I said, "I can't leave it alone."

In August of 2012, I went to church on a Saturday night and called my wife and said, "I've got to talk with Pastor Maury. I am not being faithful to him, because my heart is somewhere else about planting a church. I can't do this – the Lord is dealing with me." She said, "Dave, just be quiet through the weekend. He has got to preach Saturday and Sunday."

I had attached myself to Maury Davis because I wanted to have a mentor that had a growing church. We had become good friends through those years. I had never imagined how God would use these two men, whom I had met many years before, to be the hand of provision in my season of unfaithfulness and in my time of coming back to the faithfulness of God.

There is a phrase I have coined that I live by today, and I think it is very important. I think it is part of the faithfulness that we demonstrate and experience as we obey God. It is that we should always be looking to see God's faithfulness at work, "for every hand you shake could be the hand of provision for your future destiny that God will flow through." We should never take for granted relationships with people we have met. We should never kick people when they are on their way down because they may one day wind up being above us.

Consider the story of Joseph. So these two men, whom I had met so many years before, God had used as His provision for me as I was coming out of one of worst seasons of my life.

That was my thinking as August of 2012 arrived and I was serving Pastor Maury at Cornerstone as his executive pastor. I was praying, "God, I know You're calling me, but You have got to speak to my pastor." So I will never forget that Monday in August when I received a call from Pastor Davis's assistant and she said, "Pastor would like to see you today at 3 o'clock." I simply said, "I am there."

At 5:30 that morning, driving to my office at Cornerstone, I had said, "God, You have got to speak to my pastor. You have to confirm – given where I have come from – You have got to confirm in me what You are putting in me and it has got to come through my pastor. He is the one that is my employer and mentor." After I receive the call from Maury's assistant, I called my wife and told her, "Here it comes!" She said, "Dave, please don't say that." But I replied, "Now I know the Lord wants us to plant a church."

When I walked into pastor's office, since we had been friends for a very long time, I could see he was under a strain. I could tell by his face. Anybody who knows Maury Davis knows that is not him – he is always confident. But I could tell by the expression on his face that a difficult conversation was about to take place.

Maury said, "Dave, you are miserable here." I said, "You don't know the half of it." He said, "Well, you don't have to say it like that." Then I replied, "No, I am." Then he said, "I think you are miserable here because God wants to plant a church with you." I responded, "Pastor, would you please stand up? I want to hug you." He said, "Don't come over here now if you are mad." I said, "No, I am not mad. I need to hug you." He said, "Are you serious?"

I explained, "Pastor, I asked the Lord at 5:30 this morning on my way to the office to please speak to my pastor. I need to plant a church" Again he said, "Are you serious?" I said, "I have been dealing with this for six months." Maury replied, "So that's what has been wrong with you." I said, "Yes, I have been constrained because I don't believe in myself enough that I am supposed to pastor again, and I needed God to speak to you. I needed that confirmation through the one in authority over me."

There again is the faithfulness of God. In His faithfulness he even knows our weaknesses and acts in spite of them. So Pastor Maury told me, "I want to plant a church – and I want plant a church in Bowling Green (a video campus), and I want you to be pastor and I am going to release that to you." That is how I wound up in Bowling Green, Kentucky, planting a church in January 2013.

So we have started here. We do not know what's going to happen, but God has been faithful. The real testimony of faithfulness of God is that we are still here after 18 months, and still have resources in the bank to pay next week's bills. So I want to tell you without question, God is faithful. God is faithful when we have been faithful – and God is faithful when we have totally pushed back His faithfulness.

To me this faithfulness has been the grace, power, love and peace of the Spirit of God, ever-present and available for our access. Even when we run from it, it is still accessible when we turn and come back to Him.

Bringing It Home

Being a friend and having a friend are both blessings from God. Proverbs 17:17 tells us, "A friend loves at all times." There is a reason the Bible speaks about the importance of relationships. God has not intended that we walk this journey from the cradle to the grave alone. First we have a friend in Jesus. Secondly, we are expected to build relationships. There are times when we will need a friend, as well as times when we need to be a friend.

The Scriptures highlight relationships through "one-another" phrases: love one another, encourage one another, forgive one another, comfort one another, and so forth. God is always faithful. We are assured, "If you are faithless, he will remain faithful" (2 Timothy 2:13).

Does it comfort you to know, to have the confidence, that God is faithful when we are unfaithful? In what ways is that meaningful for you?

Reflecting on a time when you were unfaithful to God, as we all have been, how did God stay with you during that time? In what ways did you experience His faithfulness, and how did it impact your own desire to be faithful to Him?

29

NEVER GIVING UP, NEVER GIVING UP

By Terry Bailey

T   *he Rev. Terry Bailey serves as the Superintendent of the Tennessee District Assemblies of God. A "pastor's pastor," Terry leads by example. A model of faithfulness and persistence, his determination is fueled by his love for God and His people. Although he has had to deal with a number of major disappointments in his life, Terry never gives up. In this story, he explains what he has learned in striving to overcome some of life's bumpy experiences.*

꧁

Sometimes in talking with non-believers, they raise the objection, "How could a 'loving God' allow the terrible things that we see happening around the world?" I would counter by observing that we often see God most clearly and fully while we are going through some of these terrible things. That certainly has been the case in my life.

The year 1968 was a turning point in my life. While attending a youth camp that summer, at the age of 14, I made a total commitment of my life to Jesus Christ. Even though I had received Christ when I was six years old in my home church, it wasn't until I was 14 that I decided to be all-in, totally committed to the Lord.

That fall I was baptized in water and also received the baptism of the Holy Spirit. The next summer our family in 1969 moved to Nashville, Tennessee and we began to attend Calvary Assembly of God, where Glenn Burks became my pastor. Today, 45 years later, he is still my pastor.

Two qualities about my pastor that influenced me and shaped my spiritual formation were his emphasis on prayer and the faithfulness of God. Brother Burks was an incredible influence in my life as a teenager, especially because our home life was dysfunctional. "Home" was a very difficult place because my dad was physically abusive, to my mom and to us children. As you might imagine, it became a very trying experience. My pastor provided much-needed encouragement and support for me during that time.

As I entered my junior year of high school, I sensed the Lord calling me to preach. So I went to Brother Burks and told him that I felt called to preach. He told me if that was the case, I needed to go to Bible school. That became one of my first major experiences with the faithfulness of God because I knew Mom and Dad didn't have the money to send me to Bible school.

I really had to believe and trust that the Lord was going to provide because at that time I had been planning to be a football coach. My intent was to go to the University of Tennessee and become trained to coach football. However, I decided that if God was calling me to pastoral ministry, I needed to give up football so I could work more hours to save toward enrolling in Bible school. At the same time I decided that instead of tithing 10 percent of my earnings, I'd double my tithes to 20 percent. Then I made, what for me at that time, was a huge commitment to Speed the Light, a missions program in the Assemblies of God. I made a $100 commitment to Speed the Light and just did what I felt I needed to do. By the time I went to Southeastern Bible College in Lakeland, Florida, in the fall of 1972, the Lord had provided me with two scholarships. He had made a way for me to enroll, and in fact continued to make a way for me all the way through Bible school.

At Southeastern I met my wife, Susan. She was not a student on campus, but we met at the school. We dated, got married, and God began teaching us about Himself right there. As most students know, in Bible school, you don't have any money. We were flat broke most of the time. I'd sack groceries at Publix, work at a hardware store, or find something else to do just to work part-time. Susan was working full-time, helping to put me through school.

There were weeks we didn't have anything, but that didn't deter our desire to give to the Lord who had been so faithful to us. I remember being in church one Sunday night and we both felt prompted to give what we had in the offering that night. We gave it all, and the very next week money came to us from an unknown source, along with food that came from a totally unexpected source. For us, this just proved God's faithfulness. It showed that if we do what were supposed to do, if we take that one step, God will take more than one step on our behalf – because he is a faithful God and can do no less.

I remember after graduating from Southeastern Bible College I was ready to get going, to start my preaching ministry, but the problem was, we couldn't find anywhere to go. Finally a door opened up in Kentucky for us to become a youth pastor with Ernest Driver. That first youth pastoring role wasn't a full-time position, so I also was driving a school bus, selling insurance and doing other work on the side. But again God proved Himself faithful.

We encountered a very difficult season in our lives during 2003, when Susan dropped into a deep depression. Her mom had battled with depression her entire life. It's now eleven years later, but looking back now, I realize I probably was contributing to some of that because I was working hard, many long hours. At times I concentrated too much on my work and ministry, and didn't focus on Susan as I should have. A lot of times we as pastors are able to deal with a lot of stuff and sometimes the stress seems to roll off of us. But much of the time it rolls onto our wives and it doesn't roll off of them as easily.

When Susan went into a deep depression in 2003, I frankly wasn't sure if we were going to make it as a couple. It was a tough time, difficult to find the help we needed. I recall being on the fourth day of a fast, and I remember it like it was yesterday. I was praying and fasting specifically for Susan. On the fourth day, after much prayerful agonizing, I just felt a release in my spirit. Whatever it was, it was broken, and from that day forward she started getting better.

Our District Superintendent at that time was Eddie Turner, and he went to visit her in the hospital, giving her some wise, godly counsel about speaking the Word. Even though you're in the ministry and you know the Word, it's good to hear that. As Susan began to apply what Eddie said, I believe spiritually her depression was broken, and she began to heal.

A couple of years later, she was diagnosed with melanoma, a result of a mole. We began to have PET scans and many different tests, and the doctors basically gave us a very grim report. They felt Susan's cancer had gone into the lymph nodes and had already moved into her pelvic area. But there was a scripture verse the Lord dropped into my heart, saying, "you shall not die, but live and proclaim the works of the Lord" (Psalm 118:17), and the Lord healed her and touched her body.

After she had gone into surgery and went into the recovery room, her doctor came to us and said, "Look, I'm more surprised than you are." Then he said, "As far as I can tell – I have already sent the report out to the pathologists – but from what I can tell, she's okay, she's going to be fine." That was an amazing time when God proved Himself faithful to us once again.

There's a time that comes to mind when we were in a major building program. It was ending up costing us a lot more money than I ever dreamed possible. As I was praying about that, seeking from the Lord how things were going to work out in this building program, someone came by anonymously and gave our church a check for $100,000 for our building project. Amazing, yes. But

God is faithful – always. You've just got to pray things through; you've got to listen to the promptings of the Holy Spirit, because He will prove Himself faithful to you.

Another couple things I want to mention concern my parents and my brother. My dad spent the first half of his life building on what I call "the sand of life," and only spent a portion of the second half of his life building on the Rock. My dad was physically abusive to us, his kids, but my sister, Barbara, and I were able to leave and go on to Bible school. My other sister, Wanda, tells me things got a lot worse for her and my brother, John, after we left home.

It basically ended up that Wanda dated Paul and they got married, so she left home, leaving just Momma and John. My mom is probably one of the most godly women I have ever known, especially seeing how she would stay faithful to God and trust in the Lord, no matter how difficult things were getting at home. I would hear her, over and over again, just humming the tune to "'Tis So Sweet to Trust in Jesus." As a nurse, she had to work many Sundays, but made sure us kids were in church. What a blessing it was to have a mother who knew about the faithfulness of God.

My little brother, John, was quite a bit younger than my sisters and me, 12 years my junior. We were very close when he was growing up, but we were total opposites. I'm all sports-minded and John was mechanically minded. He liked hands-on stuff, and I was more about, "Hey, let's go play ball." I think things at home stayed pretty rough for him and my mom for a long time, and John ended up going into the Army and served in Desert Storm. He worked on tanks and things, and they were in the front lines going into Baghdad. During that time he was exposed to chemical warfare. Whether it was the wartime experiences, the chemicals, or other factors, when he came back from Desert Storm, he was not the same person. We could tell his personality was different, the way he processed life became much more complicated. His marriage failed, and he got involved with another woman and then that marriage failed.

John was dealing with what we now commonly call post-traumatic stress disorder (PTSD), and he got into a situation in which he made some terrible choices. His life became complicated and difficult, sending John into a spiral downward. He couldn't seem to come out of it. One day he took the life of a young woman, a tragic event for everyone, and he ended up being incarcerated for the murder of that young lady. The victim actually was the mother of a child that was in the home where John was living with another woman. In January of 2014, he was convicted of first-degree murder and will spend life in prison.

Strange as it may seem, I am grateful my mom is now dealing with Alzheimer's. The only blessing I see with Alzheimer's is that she has no knowledge of my brother's situation, but again, no matter whether it's Alzheimer's or a family member in prison, God is faithful. God just proves himself over and over to be God, and that He will be glorified and magnified in the earth. Even though we human beings may make some wrong choices, sometimes very bad choices, God will remain faithful. We must walk in obedience to Him, we've got to walk close to Him and be totally committed to Him, and as we do that we find that He will be faithful, always faithful.

For each of us, faithfulness means keeping the faith and never giving up, never giving up. The Word says, "Faithful is He who has promised, who will bring it to pass" (1 Thessalonians 5:24). With every birth of a vision will come the death of the vision, but in that time of waiting, in that time of preparation, God will develop us and help us because He's molding and shaping our lives, if we'll just stay on the Potter's wheel and let the Potter shape us.

To use an old sports analogy, we've got to be faithful – we've got to be willing to stay in the game with God, because God will determine the final score. But again, for us, faithfulness means keeping on even when we don't want to keep on. We just have to hang onto Him – because we know He's faithful.

Bringing It Home

Even with disappointments, challenges, setbacks and failures, we still march forward in Christ. Paul writes, "Forgetting what is behind.... I press on toward the goal to win the prize for which God has called me heavenward in Christ Jesus" (Philippians 3:14-15). The Scripture also says, "The one who calls you is faithful and he will do it" (1 Thessalonians 5:24).

What disappointments, failures or setbacks have you faced while striving to move forward in Christ? How have you dealt with them?

What comfort do you have in knowing, having confident assurance, that God will be with you until the end – no matter what?

30

GOD SPELLED BACKWARD IS 'DOG' - A REAL ANSWER TO PRAYER

By Esther Myrl Lee

*E*sther Myrl Lee, "Sister Lee," as she is commonly known to her friends *and acquaintances, is the wife of the former pastor and evangelist, Charles O. Lee. She stood with Pastor Lee through more than 65 years of ministry assignments. She is known for her compassion for what we commonly refer to as the "lost and hurting." She has a generous heart, always giving of herself to others in many ways. Her three children are Jimmy Ray Lee, a ministry leader; Sammy Lee, a pastor, and Ruth Workman, retired from Tennessee Valley Authority (TVA), where she was manager of community and employee relations.*

The book of Numbers tells us about an unusual moment when God used a simple donkey to communicate his message. Apparently the Lord uses other animals to carry out his work – even dogs.

Lilly Campbell was a hard-working mother and housewife who was faithful to God, truly a godly woman. To help support her family, she would wash and iron clothes for people. This was commonly referred to at the time as "taking in washing and ironing." Lilly knew what it was to work hard and trust God for her provisions.

My husband, Pastor Charles Lee, and I became acquainted with Lilly and her family when they were attending our country church in Mt. Zion, Tennessee. Next to the small, white-framed building where our congregation would assemble was a beautiful garden owned by neighbors who also attended the church. To help Lilly, knowing her financial resources were very limited, the neighbor would invite her to gather vegetables from the garden.

Lilly was picking vegetables one day when she became very alarmed because she noticed that the $20 bill she had in her shirt pocket was missing. To some people this might not have been a matter of much concern, but for Lilly this was all of the money she had earned that week from her washing and ironing. It was to help buy the week's groceries for her family.

She immediately stopped what she was doing and rushed to our Lee family house, which was on the other side of the church building. My husband and I rushed with Lilly to the garden to help her in locating the $20 bill. We looked everywhere, but couldn't find it.

Since the search was unsuccessful, Pastor Lee said, "Let's pray that God will show us the location of the money." So he stopped and prayed a simple, right-to-the-point prayer. A short time later, the neighbor's dog walked up to Lilly with the $20 bill in his mouth and laid it at her feet. God used a dog to answer an urgent, heartfelt request.

As the Scriptures assure us, "The prayer of a righteous man is powerful and effective" (James 5:16).

Bringing It Home

Just as God cares for his people, the Bible tells us He also cares for animals. Proverbs 12:10 says, "A righteous man cares for the needs of his animal." God has also been known to use animals to accomplish His will, as He used the donkey in speaking to Balaam, a very reluctant prophet: "When the donkey saw the angel of the LORD, she laid down under Balaam, and he was angry and beat her with his staff. Then the Lord opened the donkey's mouth, and she said to Balaam, 'What have I done to you to make you beat me these three times?'" (Numbers 22:27-28). For more detail surrounding this episode, which was probably humorous to anyone except Balaam, see Numbers 22:21-26 and verses 29-41.

Think of a time when God used an unusual way to answer a prayer in your life. What were the circumstances, and what did He do?

What is your favorite account of an animal or a bird mentioned in the Bible? Why does this story stand out for you?

31

HOW DO YOU LIVE THE CHRISTIAN LIFE?

By Robert J. Tamasy

*R*obert *J. Tamasy is a veteran journalist – a former newspaper and magazine editor, and author, co-author and editor of more than 20 books, many about faith and the workplace. Currently vice president of communications for Leaders Legacy, Inc., his latest book is* Business At Its Best: Timeless Wisdom from Proverbs for Today's Workplace.

"How do you live the Christian life?" This question was posed to me by John, a businessman in a suburb of Washington, D.C., whom I was preparing to interview for a magazine article. Since I had recently been hired to be the editor for what was then known as Christian Business Men's Committee (CBMC) and was still a young believer, my first thought was, "Is this a trick question? Are they trying to find out if I really belong here?"

But seeing John was waiting for my answer, I responded, "Well, you have to go to church, read the Bible, pray…." When I finished my list of "to-do's," he smiled and shook his head slightly. Then he said, "You *can't* live the Christian life. There's only one person who has successfully lived the Christian life – and that's Jesus Christ."

After pausing a moment to let that statement sink in, John quickly changed the subject and never brought it up again. But I never forgot his question – and his response. Three years later, in October 1984, I was attending a CBMC weekend event in Minneapolis, Minnesota and it "happened" that I was invited to be an overnight guest in the home of a couple named Loren and Betty.

I quickly learned that Loren had devoted much of his life to studying and teaching what he called "the real you from God's perspective." Over that weekend he and I spent nearly 10 hours discussing this topic, exploring what the Bible says about who we truly are in Christ, rather than what we might think or feel that we are.

This turned out to be one of God's "divine appointments" for me, an example of His perfect and faithful timing. Even though I had been in vocational ministry for several years, not only editing a well-respected magazine but also engaged in discipling a number of men one-on-one, I arrived in Minneapolis feeling defeated. I'd been dealing with anger, anxiety, and some family conflict, and even though I constantly prayed for God's help, victory over these trials seemed beyond my grasp.

In memorizing Bible verses with a discipleship group I had joined, I had encountered two passages that apparently didn't apply to me. One was Galatians 2:20, which states, "I have been crucified with Christ, and it is no longer I who live but Christ who lives in me. And the life that I now live, I live by faith in God, who loved me and gave Himself up for me." As I studied and meditated on this verse I thought, "This can't be true – at least not for me. If Jesus lives in me, as this verse says, how could He allow me to harbor such anger and fear?"

The other verse was 2 Corinthians 5:17, which expresses a similar idea: "If anyone is in Christ, he is a new creation; old things have passed away, behold the new has come." Again I thought, "Well, that can't be me. I don't feel like a new creation – I feel and act like the same knucklehead I've always been."

Greatly discouraged, I even wondered whether I was truly one of God's children, or whether I was fooling myself and others.

But as Loren and I met that weekend, discussing those verses and other passages, particularly from Romans, I realized my problem was a faulty understanding of who I really am from God's point of view and the person He was (and is) molding and shaping me to become.

I realized the Lord had already given me all I needed for living a godly life (2 Peter 1:3), but was not appropriating all He had graciously provided. As John had pointed out years earlier during my trip to D.C., I was endeavoring to live the Christian life in my own strength, a spiritual impossibility.

Over this weekend one other passage came to life for me. At a conference weeks before, the speaker had talked about gaining a deeper understanding of the Bible. He explained one way to master a book of the Bible was to read it over and over, and suggested starting with 1 John, since its five short chapters can easily be read in less than 15 minutes.

I had started doing this, but found myself repeatedly stumbling over 1 John 2:7-8, which states, "Dear friends, I am not writing you a new command but an old one, which you have had since the beginning. This old command is the message you have heard. Yet I am writing you a new command; its truth is seen in him and you, because the darkness is passing and the true light is already shining through."

Being a writer, each time I came across these verses I paused, thinking, "This doesn't make sense. Come on, John (the apostle), is it old or is it new?" The passage seemed to contradict itself, one verse saying one thing and the next verse said something very different. But before the weekend came to a close, God opened my eyes, providing understanding I never had before.

The context for this passage concerns demonstrating love toward one another, but through these verses the Lord seemed to be saying, "Bob, the command is both old and new. I've given all of mankind my standards and commands, and if anyone could successfully keep each one, from the moment they were born to the moment they died, they would be perfect and I would have to accept them no questions asked.

"But of course, as you've discovered, no one can keep my commandments perfectly – even for a day, much less for a lifetime. The new command, however, is that you *can* live the life I desire – but only through Jesus Christ and His Spirit that lives in you."

Tears came to my eyes as the truth of this filled my heart. I had been striving, and failing miserably, to live for God when all along He had been saying, "You can't do it, Bob. In fact, I never asked you to do it. But I can do it – in you and through you. So you can cease striving – know that I am God."

Scripture passages that Loren and I had been discussing – like "We were therefore buried with him through baptism into death in order that, just as Christ was raised from the dead through the glory of the Father, we too may live a new life" (Romans 6:4), and "In the same way, count yourselves dead to sin but alive to God in Christ Jesus" (Romans 6:11) – suddenly made sense. And I knew they applied to me as much as to any other follower of Christ; praise the Lord, I was not exempt.

This isn't to say I've attained anything close to perfection. Far from it. Old habits die hard, even after more than 30 years. But now I realize that when I get into the flesh again, thinking or speaking or acting in ways contrary to God's laws and desires, it's because I've started striving again instead of dying to self and letting Him live through me.

What has been the result, this recognition that "I can't – but God can"? For one thing, the Lord has fulfilled His promise to do "immeasurably more than all we ask or imagine, according to his power that is at work within us" (Ephesians 3:20) in my marriage and family, my career as a writer and editor, and in my one-to-one ministry of discipling and mentoring other men.

Ten years ago I was diagnosed with an aortic aneurysm that made my aorta more than twice as big as it's supposed to be. Not a good thing. After a routine arteriogram I suddenly was being scheduled for open-heart surgery to correct that, along with several arterial blockages.

I didn't fear death, assured that on the basis of Jesus' atoning sacrifice for me that I had the assurance of going to Heaven when I died. But at the age of 58, with our youngest daughter preparing for marriage and a grandson due to be born midway through the next year, I wasn't ready yet to say good-bye to this life.

Crying out to the Lord and seeking His comfort, I turned to the Psalms as I often had in the past. Two days after being told about my impending surgery, God led me to Psalm 41:3 which said, "The LORD will sustain him on his sickbed and restore him from his bed of illness." Wow! It was like God saying, "Calm down, son. I've got this. No problem."

And true to the assurance He gave me through this verse, the surgery was successful, without complications, and I've done my part by maintaining a regular physical exercise regimen ever since.

I could list so many other examples of God's faithfulness to me, but it's important to note that just as I can't live the Christian life apart from the power of Christ in me through His Spirit, neither can I be faithful to Him without His enabling grace. Proverbs 20:6 states, "Many a man claims to have unfailing love, but a faithful man who can find?" Because the fact is, even when our intentions are good, we fail miserably at being faithful to God, our spouses, even our employers. But God, ever faithful, can and will equip us to be faithful if we're willing to die to self and recognize we're alive spiritually in Christ.

One definition of faithfulness is "adhering strictly to the person, cause, or idea to which one is bound; dutiful and loyal; worthy of trust or credence; consistently reliable." I don't know about you, but there are many times I find this difficult to do. But as Colossians 1:27 tells us, the key is "Christ in you, the hope of glory," and I believe this includes the capacity – through Him – to be faithful to the God who is so faithful to us.

Bringing It Home

When Bob Tamasy meets with men to help them grow spiritually by digging into the Scriptures, he always makes certain at some point to remind them of the assurance from both Deuteronomy 31:8 and Hebrews 13:5, where God declares, "I will never leave you nor forsake you."

He says among the many wonderful attributes of God, without question one of his favorites – and one of the most important in terms of our walk with the Lord on a day-to-day basis – is His faithfulness. And because He is always so faithful to us, we can be faithful to Him – through His power.

Before reading this chapter, if someone were to have asked you, "How do you live the Christian life?" how would you have responded?

Do you agree with the idea that some express that the Christian life isn't difficult – it's impossible? Why or why not? What, in your view, does that even mean – the Christian life is *impossible?*

Understanding that to live as God desires – being faithful to serve and honor Him and obey His laws – is possible only through the power of Jesus Christ, how does that underscore God's faithfulness to us?

32

SOMETIMES GOD'S
FAITHFULNESS IS A SHOE-IN

By Dr. Jimmy Ray Lee

When I was a teenager, a homeless man knocked on our door one day and my father went to answer the door. The homeless man was without shoes and asked Daddy if he had an extra pair of shoes that he could give to him. Daddy told him to wait and that he would go to check his shoes.

As my father looked at the shoes in his closet, he reasoned with himself, "I will give him this pair because they are already worn-out and I don't need them." Then he thought, "Perhaps I should give him the pair that hurts my feet." But then the Lord impressed on his heart, "Why don't you give him the new pair of Florsheims you have just purchased?" So Daddy gave the man the new pair of shoes, and he went away thankful and very happy.

After that experience, my father never wanted for good shoes. He had been faithful to share some of his shoes with someone who needed them – brand-new shoes, in fact – and the Lord was faithful to make sure Daddy never lacked for shoes in his own life. Since for most of his life he was a preacher for small churches and an itinerant evangelist, he couldn't just say, "Well, I'll work a little longer or a little harder to earn some money for shoes." He had to trust God – even for new shoes.

And God never failed him. It seemed that many times over the years, people would either give him expensive shoes as a gift, or he would find an unbelievable bargain somewhere. One time he paid $5.00 for a new pair of Johnson and Murphys. The storeowner told Daddy, "These expensive shoes were special-ordered a year ago, but the person who ordered them never returned to claim them. So, they are yours for five dollars."

Shoes were important to him because Daddy loved to walk. He once walked from his country church to town and back – eight miles each way. As a result, he was not only spiritually fit he was physically fit. He also demonstrated how much shoes meant to him by always having a fresh shine on them. He loved the gospel, and he also loved a good pair of shoes.

Bringing It Home

A comfortable pair of shoes for walking is a blessing. God is also interested in the steps we take with our shoes – the paths our feet follow. The scripture says, "Your word is a lamp to my feet and a light for my path" (Psalm 119:105). God provides guidance directly ("lamp to my feet") and generally ("light for my path").

Isaiah talks about the beauty of feet that bring good news. "How beautiful on the mountains are the feet of those who bring good news, who proclaim peace, who bring good tidings, who proclaim salvation, who say to Zion, 'Your God reigns!'" (Isaiah 52:7). He's not writing about the physical appearance of feet, because some are bruised, or gnarled, or just worn through years of use. But when feet bring an ambassador of the Good News of Jesus Christ, those are among the most beautiful feet in the world!

Describe Psalm 119:105 in your own words. In this context, does someone you know have "beautiful feet"? Do you?

What does it mean to you to "walk with God?" What is that like in your experience? How easy do you find it to walk faithfully with God from day to day?

33

UNEXPECTED, LIFE-CHANGING ENCOUNTERS WITH GOD

By Jerry and Aleta Nichols

*A*leta Nichols is the Director of the Living Free ministry at James River Church in Ozark, Missouri. Her husband, Jerry, is involved in Living Free and was involved in the Kids Across America camp ministry for many years. Drawing from their own experiences, Aleta and Jerry have had a very effective ministry through Living Free for many years. The Lord has brought about a dramatic change in their lives, rescuing them from the depths of sin to new life through His bountiful grace. In this chapter, they share in telling their story.

(Aleta) What comes to my mind immediately is the fact that I was adopted, and that my adoptive parents were killed when I was a young girl of 18. I never felt like I belonged to anybody until I gave my heart to the Lord. When that happened, I realized I had a family – the people of God. That was an awakening moment for me. Two scriptures come to my mind as I think about this. The first is John 15:16, "You did not choose me but I chose you that you should go bear fruit and that your fruit should remain." Realizing I was chosen by God to be

who I am was a big thing for me. And the other passage is Psalm 139, which says He knew everything about me even though I did not come into the world in the best of circumstances because my mother was not married. She wasn't a Christian, she wasn't godly, but God had a plan and He has been faithful to show it to me ever since I have given my life to Him.

When I realized how much God cared about me, I came out of a lifestyle that was totally ungodly. After my adoptive parents had died in a plane crash when I was 18, I felt like nobody loved me, that nobody cared about me except for Jerry, whom I had known for only three months. Together we were like two lost souls. My extended adoptive family at that time pretty much disowned me. They said they did not have to be nice to me anymore since their mom and dad had died; they had been nice to me only because of Mom and Dad. So after their death I spent the better part of 10 years trying to kill myself with drugs and alcohol, just trying to find something to soothe myself from the terrible feeling that no one cared. I was very disconnected emotionally from everybody.

(Jerry) I helped Aleta do drugs and alcohol. We were out for a good time; we lived in Pennsylvania and were always partying. It was in the 1960s, during the Vietnam War, and all my friends were in the service. I had been the only one with a 1-Y draft status. My family did not want me in service, so I went to college and my friends sent all of their drugs back to us. We were happy to try them all out. My brother was arrested, and law enforcement authorities were coming after us, so Aleta and I decided to leave Pennsylvania and went on a journey to Florida. There our drug culture got worse.

I was a working drug addict and ended up doing drugs every day for about 13 years. We did not know the Lord and never sought Him.

(Aleta) My thinking was we had only known each other for three months before we married, and I felt Jerry only married me because my parents died. It took a week for the bodies to be transported back, and Jerry went home with me for a week and saw the dynamics of how my family acted. I remained convinced for many years that

Jerry only married me because I did not have anybody else and he felt sorry for me. Well, I did not have anywhere else to go, so it was very easy for me to go with him. I did not realize he really loved me. I don't think he really thought about it, but I definitely thought about it. It was real easy for us to get into drugs because we both were totally lost kids looking for a good time and did not know any better. The way I dealt with the rejection from my family was by running away from it.

God came into the picture when we moved to Arizona. We married in 1968 and I came to the Lord in 1976. Between those years I had two babies. They were still little, and I think having kids makes you think about your family – in my case, what I missed and didn't have. I was not close to anyone and did not have anybody. Jerry, being the oldest of seven kids, was very connected to his family, but none of them really understood me and did not know what to do with me. Socially I was a mess. I never could get my emotions together. When you think nobody loves you, you don't love yourself. And I did not love myself.

I felt like because I had been adopted, and because my adoptive parents were killed, God could not possibly love me. Why would He let the only two people who loved and cared about me be killed? So when I had the kids, it kind of made me think they were the only thing in my life that was truly mine since I thought Jerry did not really love me, that he just put up with me. I was not sure of his love until after I came to the Lord.

In reality, I think the driving force for us in coming to the Lord was that our marriage was such a mess. Jerry went out a lot, drank a lot, and did a lot of other stuff. So I found myself thinking, "He doesn't really love me because he goes and does whatever he wants to do." My thought was, "God, if you really exist, I dare You to show Yourself to me. I dare You to show me You really care for me." That is when I got involved with a lot of people and went to Austin, Texas. I was in a "new age" meeting one night when they said, "We are going to start praying." I did not know anything but the Lord's Prayer.

I started praying, and at that moment I had a supernatural visitation, an appearance, right in the middle of this kind of a service where they were praying, "Our Father." I actually did see a huge, white figure with no face. I became extremely frightened, standing there with one other lady. When this happened I just went to the floor. I could not believe what I was sensing, but found myself saying again, "God, if You exist, I dare You to show Yourself to me."

When I went to the floor, a voice spoke to me and said, "You don't have to be afraid. I am here for you. I accept you and I love you." At first I thought this whole experience was my imagination, but I knew one thing for certain: When I came up off of that floor, I was not the same person. To this day, I believe God actually chose to reveal Himself to me directly.

Afterward, the reason I knew this was true is that the lady who went with me to the meeting told me that I had fallen to the floor – that it was just like something hit me and I instantly went down to the floor. She did not touch me, but said when I got up that I was not hurt. When I got up I was a totally different person, and she could see that. My demeanor and everything about me was different. I truly had a born-again experience, even though I now know this is not how it happens for everyone. This event occurred three years before Jerry came to the Lord. He did not know that something had happened to me.

(*Jerry*) That was because the neighbor who went with Aleta to the meeting was afraid to tell me that something had happened to Aleta.

(*Aleta*) After that experience I spent two years just trying to learn about God. The lady that went to the meeting with me told me I needed a Bible, so she bought me a King James Bible and had my name engraved on the front of it. She told me just to read what was written in red because those were the words that Jesus said, and if He said it, then I could know it was true. So I started reading Matthew, Mark, Luke and John. I did not know anything about the Bible, but by the time I got to chapters 15 and 16 in the gospel of John, I realized that God had picked me. He had specifically chosen me to be

His child. I could understand this because that was what my adopted parents had said to me since my brothers weren't adopted. So I understood that whole concept, being adopted by God.

That was during a time when things had become really bad between Jerry and I. Our marriage wasn't good. He was not happy with me, and I was not happy with him. He worked all the time, and when he was not working he was partying and drinking. When I came back from the trip to Texas, I could not force myself to do drugs anymore because I had started reading the Bible. I got so interested in God that for six months I did not read anything else but Matthew, Mark, Luke and John. Jerry was gone most of the time, so I spent days just reading and wrote down what I was trying to understand, partly because I found the King James Version was difficult to read. Since I could not do the drugs anymore, that made it even harder for our marriage – it made Jerry mad that I was no longer partaking in our accustomed lifestyle. He really struggled with that.

(*Jerry*) It was a real bummer. My parties were not any good anymore. Nobody wanted to come because we would pass a joint and Aleta would pretend to take a hit on it, but everybody was getting stoned except her.

(*Aleta*) Up to that point, I had never set foot in church.

(*Jerry*) When I became a Christian, it was partly because, as they say, curiosity got the cat. Aleta started to go to a United Pentecostal Church, a full holiness church, and I went with her to the church to find out what was going on. She was not coming home until late, and I thought she was having an affair. I thought nobody goes out and stays out like that – she must be up to no good.

I went with her to church on a Sunday morning and felt like I got pinned up against the wall. There was an evangelist that had come to the church, so they invited me back for the Sunday evening service. They started that service about 6, but I was still feeling stuck on the back wall. They had an altar call, and I don't remember raising my hand or walking down front, but I do remember kneeling at the altar and crying to the Lord because I thought the world was coming to an end, that everybody else was leaving and I was going to be alone. I did not want to be alone, and I wanted to have what they had. I did not realize there was something else.

At that altar I cried and I cried. I pulled my cigarette pack out of my pocket – at the time I was smoking three packs a day – and besides the cigarettes I had three or four joints of marijuana in my pocket. I threw them on the altar and said, "Lord, I am giving it all to You, and no more drinking."

Aleta and I both left that service, got in our vehicle, and I drove in the wrong direction for about 10 or 15 miles before I realized I was going wrong. We turned around and when we got home, I thought, "I have never been this high before." I had been at that altar from 9 o'clock at night until midnight, and the people in the church were all laying hands on me and praying for me. All I could think was, "Something has really happened to me."

At the time, my brother and I were running a towing business together. We towed for the city, the highway patrol and the sheriff's department, and had an auto repair shop. We worked together all the time. When 10 o'clock came, we would stop and smoke a joint, and then at noon we would do it again. Then somewhere around 3 or 4 o'clock we would go get a drink, and that is how our days would go.

After that Sunday night service, I did not do any of the smoking or drinking anymore. My brother and I started having words with each other, so we started to split. I saw he was treating our customers differently than I would want them to be treated. I felt I could no longer take it, so I left work, got into the car, looked in the mirror and said, "Lord, if you will take the desire for drugs and alcohol away from me, I will not put another cigarette to my lips." I went home and stayed home for three weeks.

Aleta and I had a little bit of money and I wanted to bring it to the Lord because that church was going through a building program. So I got a lunch bucket, put a couple of ingots of silver in it, and took it over to the church and gave them to the pastor. I told him to use the silver to start the church building program.

(Aleta) We began to see God use us to touch other people's lives. The church put us right to work on their greeting committee. This helped connect us with them and their ministry. But as far as reaching people, I feel it was at James River where God started to use us in a powerful way. As bad as it was, He used our background to help prepare us for ministry at James River Church.

Key elements to ministry are loving God and loving people. First of all, I could see that God loved me so much He saved me from myself. I often see people who are like we were, people very much like me that have had similar things happen to them so they can relate to me and my own experiences.

But I knew right away, "Okay, God, You love me but this is not just something that happens in one person's life. If You can do this with me, You can do it with other people." I realized early on that if I could get past this drug and alcohol thing, get my life changed and become somebody who could walk right, then surely I could help somebody else do that. So I began to have an idea that maybe I could be a speaker in hospitals, go and visit people who were there. I thought of that but did not know how it was going to work out. I thought maybe I should go back to school and get a social worker degree, but I had kids, so there was no way I could do it.

When we came to James River, we learned the pastor wanted to start a recovery ministry for people struggling with abortion, grief, divorce, and addictions. He felt each would be important in starting the ministry, which would be called Living Free. So right away Jerry and I talked about it and felt we would help in the addictions area. We told the pastor who would be over the ministry that we would like to come and help in the area of greeting. Our point of reference was that we had already been greeting there at James River since we had been going there. That was the thing we knew how to do, since that is what we started out doing from the time we first came to the Lord. We did not know anything else, but knew we could stand at the door and welcome people in.

So on the first night we showed up with about 10 or 12 other people, but the couple that was to be the leaders did not show up and we did not have the keys to open the doors. The next week the couple again never showed up. There were no leaders, but people were coming and bringing in food, getting ready to meet. I had gone downstairs to pray and Jerry was to speak to the group, but he got sick because he felt so nervous. He spent the entire evening running back and forth to the bathroom throwing up. This was our initiation into the ministry. After this rough beginning, we started using a specific study book and then developed some curriculum on our own.

(Jerry) Finally I told the pastor we were out of curriculum to take the group through and asked if he wanted to preview a book for us to use, or let me go ahead and use one with the group and then let him know how it went. He decided at that point we should have a pastor over us. That was fine with us. Our driving force was to see people changed like we were and then discipled.

(Aleta) There is a place for a person being prayed for, and there is a miraculous transformation in a person's life when the lights go on like what happened for me when I read John 15:16, "You did not choose Me, I chose you." The first time I read that I thought, "Oh, that is phenomenal." When the Word of God came to life to me, it had transforming power. Then all of our drug friends and people who were involved in our lifestyle just disappeared. I had no idea what happened to them, but the next thing I knew we were being integrated into a different kind of lifestyle with a different kind of people. Since then our desire has always been to watch people get that lifelong, life-changing experience.

Over the years we have seen thousands of people come to the Lord. It has got to be in the thousands. There are some people we will always remember. Recently there was this guy that came into Living Free who gave his testimony at Easter. He worked at Walmart for 18 years, and a lady who worked with him would witness to him. She would tell him about God. He suffered terribly with depression and had experienced awful setbacks and hardships in his life – disappointments with his wife, his family was such a mess, and even issues with his horse.

The lady at Walmart just kept telling him about the Bible and our church, James River, and that there was a program there. The lady went out and bought him a Bible, and he came to the Living Free program at our church. There he was, a Catholic with deep roots in Catholicism, and very suspect of the church and our program because he believed all of what he had been taught in his church.

This guy was on all kinds of medications for anxiety and depression. He would take all his medications before he came to the meetings because he was so anxious he could not bear to come. Still, he did come and we put him at a specific table with a specific facilitator, and the group began to love him and minister to him. They invited him to sit by them at church. So one day he came to church, again taking all of his medicines because he was so anxious, but he went forward during the service and got saved.

Today he is not on any medications and is on fire for God. He speaks about God and has something new that God has shown him every week at church. He has grown in the Lord by leaps and bounds, and that is what we see from people who truly believe that there is a possibility they don't have to be like this for the rest of their lives.

(*Jerry*) Another one is a gentleman who used to drive by and see alcohol recovery on the church marquee. He was an air conditioning and heating guy who had his own business and had been an alcoholic for more than 20 years. He had been through AA and other programs, but had never gotten clean. He got tired of just looking at the marquee so he decided to drive up to the church. But he had been drinking a little bit, so he decided he could not go in because he had been drinking. The next week he drove by and pulled in. He walked in the front door, looked around, and thought to himself, "This place is too big. I am not going on."

So he did not come that week either, but the next week he came and told himself, "I have got to get to the meeting." He came upstairs and introduced himself to me and I sat with him. He was with us and went through Living Free for about six months and got clean, but never went to church. Neither him nor his wife. Then I invited him to a Wednesday night service, and he and his wife came and sat through it. Afterward, Aleta and I invited them into the Living Free office and were able to lead them both to the Lord.

This is how we would define faithfulness. We made a pact with each other and with the Lord. The agreement is that even if only one person comes to our Living Free group, we will be there. We have made the decision that we are going to do this no matter what. We are going to be faithful no matter what – and our faithfulness has never been to people. Our faithfulness has always been, "I am going to be faithful to You, God, because You have been faithful to me." All we ask for in return is that the Lord will show us some fruit from our faithfulness – show us so we can be sparked on, encouraged.

(Aleta) There are times when we get discouraged even now, when things are hard and we don't know if we are going to see anybody changed. We just want to see that there is fruit. People that come to James River's Living Free groups fill out prayer cards every week. I take those prayer cards home every Wednesday night, and usually I don't go to sleep until 3 a.m. because I pray over each one. The group members know that. They know I am going into prayer before God. And I see a lot of answered prayers.

This is what I would say to those reading this story and needing help. Step one is that you know there really is Someone who cares for you. Step two is, don't be afraid to surrender yourself to Him. Step three is simple: just show up and let God do His work.

Bringing It Home

With God, nothing is impossible. Nothing is too hard for God, as Jerry and Aleta have seen in their own lives and the lives of people they have met over the years. When we are without faith, God is still faithful. "If we are faithless, he will remain faithful" (2 Timothy 2:13). The Scriptures also tell us, "But where sin increased, grace increased all the more" (Romans 5:20). So we never need to be concerned about running out of God's grace.

In Jerry and Aleta's story, how do you see God's grace in action – both in their lives and through their lives?

What part of their story do you find yourself relating to the most? Is there anything that you can't relate to? If so, what is that – and why do you think that might be the case?

34

PROFOUNDLY INFLUENCED BY BILLY GRAHAM

By Tex Reardon

*T*exas *"Tex" Reardon has served in many capacities with the Billy Graham Evangelistic Association (BGEA). He has served as crusade director for Billy Graham Crusades, personal assistant to Dr. Graham, Director of Associate Evangelist Ministries, and Assistant Director for Amsterdam 2000. He also served as director of Franklin Graham Ministries and executive director of Ruth Graham & Friends ministry. Tex is known as a man of faithfulness and integrity.*

Over the years I have had multiple opportunities to witness God's hand moving in a powerful way. Back in the early '80s, the Billy Graham Association started a telephone counseling ministry. Four times a year there would be a series of two or three telecasts of Mr. Graham's Crusades. BGEA established telephone counseling centers all over the country to respond to people who called in after watching one of the programs, wanting to talk with someone about making a profession of faith.

I supervised the center in Dallas and went there four times a year to train additional local people to answer the phones as well as providing help to the callers and to share Christ with them. We were doing a telecast and answering calls from around the Southeast one particular night. A gentleman from Second Baptist Church in Houston, Texas called in, just to thank us. The phones rotated so the calls would randomly go to the first available phone. His call was answered by one of the more experienced counselors.

The caller told the counselor that he did not have a problem that he wanted to talk about. He said he went to church faithfully and just wanted to thank us for what we are doing because he was sure there were people watching the telecast who needed to get started in their spiritual life and get themselves right with God. He said he just wanted the counselors to know there were people in the audience praying for them and asked for that message to be relayed to the rest of the counselors.

The counselor told the man his call was appreciated and then asked, "Before you go, is there anything I can pray for, for you?" The gentleman hesitated for a minute and then answered, "Well, yes, there is. I am going in for surgery tomorrow. I have a great doctor, but it's a very new procedure. I understand only four people have had this surgery." He went on to say he was not scared, that his affairs were in order and he was ready to meet the Lord if that was what happened. But as with anything else when you don't know what is going on, you can't help feeling a little bit apprehensive.

The counselor said that was understandable and assured him, "We will certainly not only pray for you before we hang up tonight, but I will bring your story before the other counselors when we get together to debrief and have all of the 50-plus people here pray for you." The counselor also asked what hospital the gentleman would be going to and the doctor's name. "We would like to include him in our prayers," the counselor explained. So the caller gave him the doctor's name.

The counselor then asked if the caller's surgery was a specific type of procedure, which he went on to describe, and the gentleman replied, "Yes, that is exactly what it is!" The counselor calmly but excitedly replied, "If you have a few minutes, sir, you are speaking to one of the four people who had that surgery. I will be glad to help you and give you as much information as I can."

When I look back at it, how amazing is that? Here was a random situation when a telephone call came in and happened to come to the only person out of 50 people answering phones at the center who could particularly relate. Not only that, but that counselor was one of only four people in the entire world that had undergone the same procedure! As they say, "what are the odds"?

You can see how God works to manage things and put the right people in the right places at the right time. It gives me chills to think about how much He loves and cares for us and how sometimes these things we think are insignificant are actually events God has orchestrated to give us the encouragement or support we need at that moment – and He has been working ahead of us all the while.

Working with the Billy Graham Evangelistic Association for so many years has greatly influenced me in terms of understanding what faithfulness is and what it looks like. When I started with the Graham Association, I had been very active in my home church and had gone through all the leadership positions and served in a capacity of teaching Evangelism Explosion, so I had an interest in evangelism. I started working with Dr. Graham and as I got to know him, I was really impressed with the fact that this was a man who, whether I saw him in private or in front of 60,000 or 70,000 people, was the same man. There was a genuine faithfulness and a devotion that he did not deviate from.

Dr. Graham encouraged us to read one chapter of Proverbs and five Psalms every day. This would result in having read the entire book of Proverbs and the entire book of Psalms each month in addition to our regular Bible readings. He did more than recommend it; he did it himself and spent much time in prayer before making decisions. He had such insight. He could recognize things that a lot of people would miss. Through the years working with this great evangelist, I saw a tremendously insightful person, which I think was one of God's blessing to Dr. Graham.

Dr. Graham's faithfulness and support for the people around him was a great influence. I saw how he relied solely on God's Word. He is one of the most humble people I have ever met. And he was always a person that one would do well to pattern their life after, just from the way he handled things. He called his wife, Ruth, whenever he was on the road, sometimes several times a day. He always called her at night before retiring to bed. I don't recall that he ever went through a day, none that I know of, when he and Ruth did not pray together regardless of where they were.

When I witness how God blessed Dr. Graham's ministry efforts and the faithfulness he has had to the Lord and to his calling, I can't help but realize that this is what God desires for all of us. It is not about how good we are. It is not how great we are. God wants us to be available. It is not our abilities particularly that He is looking at. It is our availability. The importance of making oneself available to Him has influenced my life and my wife's life. It has just been an absolute blessing to have been part of Dr. Graham's life, the man and the ministry he has had.

Bringing It Home

The Bible says, "For he guards the lives of his faithful ones" (Psalm 97:10). We can be confident of God's love and guidance. The Scripture also says, "For the LORD is good and His love endures forever; His faithfulness continues through all generations" (Psalm 100:5). Reading his story, we can see that God has guided Tex's life – and that should provide encouragement for us as well.

In what ways have you seen God guard your life?

What does it mean to you that His "faithfulness continues through all generations"?

35

'YOU'VE BEEN FAITHFUL, HAVEN'T YOU?'

By Skip Steffner

John (Skip) Steffner, Jr. is chairman of the board for Chattanooga Armature Works, a family business widely known for its integrity and support of Christian ministries and causes. Skip and his family have a unique business and gospel witness. A prayer meeting led by five generations in the family conducted at the same time and in the same place for more than 60 years, focused on the same, unchanging gospel, reflects the model of consistency of Skip and his family.

One of the simplest descriptions of prayer is talking to God, and listening so we can hear Him talking to us. So it seems that a key element to faithfulness as followers of Jesus Christ is consistent involvement in prayer – and for me, prayer has proved to be an indispensable part of my walk with Him.

I was seven years old when Billy Graham brought one of his crusades to Chattanooga in 1953, and leading up to it people were organizing prayer meetings at churches all over the city. A building was being constructed to house the crusade because they didn't know if it was going to be a week, two weeks or three weeks, and one of the companies that they came around to for help with funding was our family company, Chattanooga Armature Works. At the time we were a half-mile from the fieldhouse being built for the crusade, and there was much excitement about it. Our company jumped on the bandwagon in the sense of holding prayer meetings to prepare the city and people's hearts for the event.

To the best of my recollection, these prayer meetings were held always on a Wednesday. We began to gather our employees and would have a prayer time for the upcoming crusade and the people who would come to know Christ through this; also that they might be followed up personally and followed up in prayer. My grandfather was still alive then; he passed away in 1958. He, my dad and my uncle, the three of them operated the company and were very supportive of this.

Evidently the prayer time really worked because the Billy Graham crusade in Chattanooga was a huge success. We decided to continue the prayer meetings and lift up the people whose lives had been touched. Even though we didn't have a list of their names, we knew the Lord knew who they were, so all we had to do was pray for these people that had taken Him on as their Lord and Savior – and that's what we did. Then, somewhere along the way my dad decided if the prayer meetings had been good to do while Billy Graham was here, it was probably a great idea to just keep them going.

By the time my granddad passed away five years later, I was 12 and had gotten into the habit of hanging around our company. I remember we always had the Wednesday prayer meetings then, and each week they featured a different pastor from churches all around Chattanooga. Some of them were people that my dad or my uncle knew personally. After we'd used up all of the pastors they were acquainted with, they proceeded to invite other people they had met because of the Billy Graham crusade, asking them to come on Wednesdays and share.

Through the years we've had a number of ministers that worked at our company, and we probably have had at least a dozen people go into vocational ministry after coming to work at Chattanooga Armature works. I'm sure some of them, because of these weekly prayer meetings, began to understand the calling that the Lord had given them to go into the ministry.

By 1971 I had gotten out of the Navy, and my dad said, "Hey, how about you find preachers to come preach on Wednesdays" – that's the way we always referred to it, "come preach on Wednesdays." Today, more than 40 years later, when people hear my name and get a phone call, if they're a preacher they probably already know what I'm calling about. They'll hear me ask, "Can you come speak at our prayer meeting at Chattanooga Armature?"

We've been doing this weekly prayer meeting now for more than 60 years in all, and I've been directly involved in them for more than 40 years! Even after more than 60 years, it's always been a joy to hear people say they will come. I've never had anyone flat-out say no. They may say, "I can't come this week" or "I can't come yet," but I've never had any pastor, or really any Christian friend, turn down a chance to come and share. Some people have said, "You know this is going to make me famous." I would respond, "Why is that?" They would reply, "I'm the third preacher from our church that's been asked to come, and I wondered why you didn't call until now." My response would be, "If I didn't call you, it's only because I didn't know you." So we've had quite a variety of people come.

At our meetings, more often than not I will introduce people by saying, "He's not here because he's Catholic, (or because he's Presbyterian, or Episcopalian, or whatever denomination). He's here because he knows Jesus Christ." Sometimes I'll say, "I'm not interested in hearing what you're doing over at your place or your building, or any of that. Just tell us about what Jesus is doing in your life," and our guests always seem so relaxed and so comfortable to do that. And it continues this way today; we line up people usually about a month ahead. We've had families come. We've had columnist Nell Mohney – I think it was on her 90th birthday that she came and spoke at our prayer meeting. She commented, "I love being out in a factory."

As we did from the start, we meet every week in the break room at Chattanooga Armature Works. It is a time for prayer, to pray. The first thing we do when we meet is greet everybody. Probably in the 1940's or 50's, our company had an old pump organ, and then we obtained some songbooks, bought in the 50's. I've still got them, but we don't have a pump organ guy, so we don't sing much anymore.

Sometimes I'll make this statement: "One of the greatest times of the week is when the new speaker shows up," because we all know that if he doesn't show up, we're going to have to have an alternative. But regardless, we begin with, "Are there any prayer requests?" Without fail we have a time for sharing prayer requests, and everybody in the room usually has some. One of our customs is to say, "Do we have any unspoken requests?" and virtually every hand will go up. Of course, we are limited in time, and some things are very personal, so we just include unspoken requests with the others, since God knows what they are.

The meeting starts, as it always has, at 12 noon, and it ends about 12:30. Since our lunchtime at the Armature works is quarter till 12 to quarter after, we have a deal where we give our staff 15 minutes and they give us 15 minutes of their time. When people would ask, "How many people come?" I used to tell people, "Well, it's about like a real church – about half of the people who could come actually do." A lot of people are very faithful to this meeting. In fact, we've had a number of people through the years that come to this meeting that have never set foot in a church building.

We had a fellow who had been with us for over 30 years, and he had come to virtually every possible meeting if he was in town and not out on a job. Through all those years, many, many times invitations were given to receive Christ, but this fellow Glen would never raise his hand. I would sneak and peak to see if he had raised his hand, but he never did.

He had been retired and gone away from us for about five or six years, and one day unexpectedly he came walking into my office and stood there. Before he spoke, Glen had tears in his eyes, and I was afraid something had happened to his wife. I asked, "What's going on?" and he said, "I was sitting at home this last week, and my brother called me about nine o'clock, and said 'Glen you got to get over here. I've just been to a revival and I've heard somebody you've got to hear.'" Glen said, "I went the next night with my brother, and when the invitation was given, I went forward and gave my life to Christ." When I heard that, I was the one that started crying. He said, "The next night I got Holly to go with me (that's his wife), and Holly got saved!"

At the company we were all so excited about this wonderful news. You sometimes hear people say, "You plant seeds and you plant seeds, and it may bloom in somebody else's pot, but I don't care." So we really never know the final results of having this prayer meeting every week, now for more than 60 years steady, but we do know it's a good thing, and we know it's something the Lord wants. If we ever feel like we need to give this meeting up or stop doing it, we just remember that this is something the Lord wants.

We have seen a lot of the results from the meetings, but that's not important. To be faithful to do it, just to have it each week, is as important possibly as the results are. Because it's not a result-oriented meeting. We aren't trying to get anybody to sign up for anything, and I think we would all feel guilty in a way if we did. We have never just not met. There have been reasons we couldn't meet – holidays, severe weather, unexpected things that have kept us away. But even if a speaker fails to show up, we either turn to someone in our group to speak, or just share with each other as a group.

Some time ago I met a friend, Kay Arthur, whom I hadn't seen in 30 years. She looked at me and said, "You've been faithful, haven't you?" and I thought, what an interesting thing to say to somebody. I think of faithfulness as just being true to that night so many years ago, the special night for me that I met Jesus Christ the first time and remembering the enthusiasm that I had then. I remember thinking I could conquer the world, and I just try to be in that conquer-the-world mood all the time. I understand that faithfulness is not, "Well, I've gotten everything right now for 20, 30, or 40 years." Faithfulness is just keeping on doing what you know the Lord wants you to keep on doing.

When my long-time friend told me, "You've been faithful, haven't you?" my thought was, I hope I hear those words when I get to heaven. I would just love to have the Lord look at me and see the smile on my face and say, "You've been faithful, haven't you?"

I'd love to think that we don't do this meeting out of habit. If you do anything simply out of habit, you'll eventually break the habit. But if you're doing it in honor of something, you just don't forget that.

I don't think that anyone in the 1950's, when we started this, ever imagined it would go any further than maybe through the next year. It has never been made an imperative; no one had to be there at any one of the meetings. It was always open to anyone. But we would always make it known, making an announcement over the PA system, and didn't mind if visitors might be there and hear it. If something at the company were being scheduled, I would always tell people, "I could do it at any time, except I can't do it on noon on Wednesdays. I'm already taken."

Bringing It Home

Consistency in prayer is a powerful force. Communion with God should be frequent, not rare. Paul writes that we are to, "pray continually" (1 Thessalonians 5:17). Jesus exhorted us, "always pray and not give up" (Luke 18:1). And as we pray, calling out to the Lord and looking for His answers, we have this assurance: "Your (God's) faithfulness continues through all generations" (Psalm 119:90).

Who or what would be at the top of your prayer list most often? Why has this been a priority for you?

How would you describe your frequency – or rarity – of prayer? Why do you think this is? If you pray often, is there anything you would change? And if your prayer life is less frequent than you would like it to be, what steps might you take to change that?

36

THE WHOLE TRUTH... AND NOTHING BUT THE TRUTH

By Judge Clarence Shattuck

C *larence Shattuck is a General Sessions Court Judge in Hamilton County, Tennessee. For more than 32 years he has presided over cases ranging from simple traffic offenses to first-degree murder cases. In a time when government officials commonly avoid being associated with matters of faith, at least in the public eye, Judge Shattuck is unapologetic about his faith in Jesus Christ – because of how he has seen God's faithfulness in times of tragedy and in times of joy, and times when justice is at stake.*

"The LORD giveth and the LORD taketh away. Blessed be the name of the LORD." This passage (Job 1:21) is often quoted, but several experiences over the years literally brought these words to life for me. Sometimes you have to have something taken away before you can really appreciate what God has given.

I started practicing law in 1960, and my wife, Ruth, and I got married in 1961. We had joined a church and became very active. I had a good practice, we soon had a son, Clarence, and life seemed to be going good.

We wanted to expand our family, but because Ruth had suffered a bad accident, we delayed having another child. So it wasn't until seven years later that we had our daughter, Lisa. She was born in October 1969 – then, on May 1971, she passed away due to a freak home accident.

It was a Saturday afternoon, May 1, and Clarence and I had been over at the shopping center. When we arrived back home, my son stayed outside. Just as I walked in the door, the phone rang. Ruth answered and it was my aunt. After they talked a few minutes, my wife asked me to go upstairs and get Lisa. The baby had been napping, and it was time to give her a bottle.

So I went to pick her up, but I walked into her room, Lisa was hanging between her baby bed and the windowsill. Her little chin had gotten caught between the opening in the bed and the sill, and her head had flopped back. I immediately jerked out the bed and she fell to the floor. I knew she was gone, but we tried everything before rushing her to the hospital, where they pronounced her dead. How do you describe such a traumatic time? There are no words.

I remember during our time there at the hospital, desperately hoping something could be done for Lisa, three verses came to me. One was the 23rd Psalm, "The LORD is my Shepherd, I shall not want…. Though I walk through the valley of the shadow of death…." Another was the verse I've already mentioned from Job, "The LORD giveth and the LORD taketh away. Blessed be the name of the LORD." And finally, the Lord's Prayer came to my mind. These verses did not take away the grief, but gave me an overwhelming sense of peace, the peace the apostle Paul talks about that passes all understanding (Philippians 4:7).

Even though we were grieving and had never gone through anything like this before, there it was – the supernatural, unexplainable peace of God. This was one of the significant moments in my life when I knew there was a God in heaven, a God that answers our prayers, a God that is with us at all times. This was an extremely painful, traumatic experience, but we got through it.

Because of Ruth's earlier difficulties, we did not want to take a chance on another child, so we applied for adoption. We went through Family Children's Services. Typically they do not approve for a couple that has lost a child to adopt a child of the same sex. We had lost a daughter, so they were not going to approve us for adopting a daughter, but we talked with them and went through a lot of testing and interviews. Finally they did approve us for a daughter. After we got the approval for a daughter, we had to wait. As the Lord would have it, we got pregnant and called off the adoption. It became clear to us that as the Bible says, our ways are not His ways, our thoughts are not His thoughts. We were thinking we did not want to have another biological child so we would adopt one. But the Lord had a different plan and we learned we were going to have another son.

Everything went well during Ruth's pregnancy, and the time came for her to deliver. Well, my wife delivers quickly. With our first son, I was only at the hospital 54 minutes. I had just barely gotten her checked in before he was born. With our daughter that we lost, Lisa, we were at the hospital 19 minutes before Ruth delivered.

So we figured things would move quickly when this baby was ready to be born. With this one Ruth woke me up at 3 in the morning and said, "We have got to go." We had made plans to drop Clarence off at my aunt's house on the way to the hospital, but Ruth said we did not have time to go by there. So we went rushing out straight to the hospital.

About a mile from the hospital, she said, "I can't hold it any longer." I reached over and felt her and could feel the head coming down, but I knew we were close to the hospital, so I did not stop. As soon as we got there, I parked at the emergency room entrance, jumped out and ran into the hospital. The nurse at check-in said, "What can I do for you?" I replied frantically, "My wife is having a baby! My wife is having a baby!" She just stared at me with a look that said, "Not another hysterical father!" I said, "Look, I mean she is actually having it!" and I ran back out to the car, with the nurse saying, "I'll be right out."

When I got back to the car my wife had already delivered and the baby was lying in the seat. Ruth told me to pick him up. I did, but didn't see any breath at all or any movement. I remember so distinctly the thought going through my mind, "Please Lord, not another one." I had been the one that found Lisa and picked her up and held her in my hands. So there I was with our newborn son in my hands, praying, "Please Lord, not another one." Instinctively, I turned him upside down and started spanking him – I guess because I had seen someone do that on television. He immediately started crying. Ruth said I did not quit spanking him until the nurse came out and cut the cord.

The two incidents were so similar that once again the verse came to me, "The LORD giveth and the LORD taketh away. Blessed be the name of the LORD." I had experienced Lisa literally die in my hands, and I then I had seen our newborn son, whom we named Paul, come to life in my hands.

There is no question in my mind that the Lord was involved in these two events. Not that I think He took Lisa from us, but it was just one of those things of the rains falling on the good and the bad (Matthew 5:45). Events like these occur, and I knew God's presence was in both events. I could see the parallels between the two situations. In both cases we were frantically trying to get to the hospital and Ruth was crying and wailing in each situation. In fact, we laugh now as I tell the story of trying to get to the hospital for Paul to be born. I say I did not need a siren to get me there. I just had to roll down the window and my wife's screaming was loud enough.

We later had a third son, but Ruth was put in the hospital before labor started that time. That was a quick delivery also. I calculated that if we had left the house the minute she had her first labor pain, we would have been halfway to the hospital when he arrived.

After Lisa's death, both Ruth and I drew closer to the Lord. I have had some friends that had a similar situation and turned away from the Lord when it happened, but for us the tragedy drew us closer. We had so many people come and share with us and support us that we became more intense in our study and reading of the Bible.

For a time I thought the Lord was leading me into pastoral ministry, so I talked to at least four or five pastors in various denominations. Every one of them told me the same thing, that if the Lord was calling me into the ordained ministry, He would keep after me and I would know for sure. At the same time, they suggested, "You may be able to do the Lord's work and have a better ministry exactly where you are." Every one of them said I would come in contact with people that would never walk in their doors. As it turned out, that was the way it worked and I took it as a clear word from the Lord.

Dealing with my clients and handling the type of cases I have, I found myself taking a different approach. Most of my cases were about families and marriage relationships. I was associated with Judge Payne at that time and we handled a lot of domestic matters, lots of divorce cases.

There were a couple of instances that remain vivid in my mind from that time. One couple came in that had decided they wanted a divorce because the woman had gotten into an affair with the guy she was riding back and forth to work with. She had decided she loved him and wanted a divorce from her husband. However, he did not really want a divorce; he wanted to keep their marriage together because he said he really loved her.

I talked to them and counseled with them. I learned she taught a young kids' Sunday school class. I asked if she knew what the Bible says about adultery. "It says it is a sin," I told her. "There is no question that you have sinned, but the Lord is forgiving. All we have to do, according to the Scripture, is confess our sins and He will forgive us."

She stayed with her decision to file for divorce because their pastor had told them that if they could not make a go of their marriage, they should divorce and start a new life. That was one of the things that had prompted them to come to my office. So I took down all their information for filing an agreed divorce, told them it would take two or three days to get the paperwork completed, then I would give them a call.

Two days later I received a call from the husband. He said, "Don't do any more work on those papers. Just send me a bill for what I owe you." I asked, "What happened?" He said as they were going home from our meeting, his wife started crying and they started talking. "We have been talking for two days," he said. I asked him what had changed. He answered, "You will not believe this, but you were the first one to tell her that what she had done was a sin and that she needed to ask for forgiveness. Her own pastor had not said it was a sin. So after our meeting with you, she got to thinking about that and now we want you to drop the divorce. We are reconciling."

Another instance involved a man and woman caught up in a somewhat similar situation with adultery that came to see me. I talked with them along the lines of working toward reconciliation. They walked out, but called back a few days later and did become reconciled. When I asked what happened, the wife replied, "When we first walked out the door, my husband said, 'I don't want any damn preacher being my lawyer.'" But before long they got to considering what we had talked about and then decided to reconcile.

Reflecting on those two incidents, I know the Lord was in them both, and that served as confirmation that the Lord had me where He wanted me.

I have been a judge for more than 30 years now and have never had anyone run against me. I had one of my very politically oriented colleagues, who is now deceased, say to me, "Clarence, your appointment and your serving was providential."

There are challenges to being a judge – as there are for being any public servant. But over and over I have seen the faithfulness of God. I think the biggest challenge that just about any judge has is trying to discern the truth. Pontius Pilate reflected on that dilemma whenever he had Jesus Christ standing before him. Truth itself, in the person of Jesus, was standing in front of him and still Pilate asked that question, "What is truth?" So many times that situation comes up because we have one person saying one thing and another person saying something else, and I have to make the decision about what is truth. So many times I say in my spirit, "Lord, help me. Give me discernment."

Sometimes this discernment can come through cross-examination. Sometimes it can come through another witness. When one party says it is black, while the other party says it is white, it is hard but you have to make that determination.

I had one fellow come up before me who had been in court numerous times, but this time he had been involved in the Transformation Project (a pre- and post-prison release ministry) while in the workhouse (a correctional facility) and wanted to be released to finish their program. While he was standing before me, he kept looking toward the back of the courtroom, so I asked him who he was looking at in the back. He said his fiancé was there. I asked her to come up, because I like to hear from everyone involved. When she came up, it was obvious she was pregnant.

During the hearing I decided I was going to let him complete the Transformation Project, so I told them that they needed to get married. I said, "You don't want this baby to come and not have his daddy's name on the birth certificate. You need to get married if you love each other like you have told me." After the hearing they started going to Transformation meetings and after counseling from the leaders of the program, they did decide to get married. Transformation helped them to put on a very nice wedding, and the couple asked me to do their ceremony, so I did.

There have been so many cases where I have been able to counsel people. Of course, there is always the matter of the state-church relationship, but many times I had the opportunity to witness to people because if they bring it up or say they are Christians, that gives me an opportunity to witness to them on that particular situation.

I have had many thousands of people come before me since I have been on the bench. There are now five Sessions Court judges. Over the years we have had 40,000 to 58,000 cases a year. That includes cases ranging from simple traffic cases all the way to first-degree murder cases. If you divide that number (40,000) by five, that would mean 8,000 cases a year on the criminal side. Then on the civil side we have 15,000 per year. So that is 3,000 that would come up in front of me. If you multiply that by 32 years, you will come up with quite a number of people.

Sitting on the bench, I have found you can feel sympathy and sometimes empathy for people as you are in the process of searching for the truth. That is one way I know the Lord has to be helping me.

Recently I went to a visitation at a funeral home and ran into a guy there who told me, "I was in your court about four years ago with dear friends of mine. You were a godsend to them." I said, "I don't remember, tell me." He told me about a young boy, the son of the couple he was there with, who had gotten into trouble. He had committed a burglary by breaking into a church. I had worked with the family and helped get the boy into the Teen Challenge program, the man told me, but to tell you the truth, I didn't remember that specific case. But it doesn't matter.

I have come to realize, in so many different ways, that the Lord is faithful. He is faithful to us even unto death, as the Scripture says, and that is what we need to try to do as well. We need to realize that at all times He is faithful, and we need to return that faithfulness. As Hebrews 11:1 says, "faith is the substance of things hoped for, the evidence of things not seen." So many times things have come up and later on down the road we find God saying to us, "Yes, you tried to do the right thing." And that's what does matter.

Many times of late people have told me their life has changed since the time they stood in front of me. To what extent I have had something to do with it as an individual, I do not know. Maybe it was just because I was the one on the bench at the time, but I really believe the Lord puts people in certain positions. This is why we have to pray for them as Paul told Timothy, "pray for those that are in positions of leadership." I believe the Lord can use us even if we are not fully committed and faithful to Him, because He has used pagan people to bring about His purposes. Think of what He can do with a faithful person.

About a year ago, one Saturday morning Ruth said to me, "Why don't you go over to McDonald's and get us something for breakfast?" I said, "That is a good idea. I think I will." So I drove to McDonald's and went through the drive-thru. I drove up to the window to pay and the young lady there did a double-take and asked if I was Judge Shattuck. I answered that yes, I was, and she said, "You were my judge back when I was bad, and I haven't been in trouble since I was in front of you." Those words alone were worth the trip to McDonald's!

Bringing It Home

God's faithfulness is based on truth. The Bible tells us, "Righteousness and justice are the foundation of your throne; love and faithfulness go before you" (Psalm 89:14). God will never betray His faithfulness. Isaiah provides comforting words – "No weapon forged against you will prevail. . . . This is the heritage of the servants of the LORD" (Isaiah 54:17).

When you think about truth, what comes to your mind?

Why do you think is it important to have God-fearing people in the judicial system? Can you see how, as Judge Shattuck stated, this can be "ministry"?

37

GOD'S TIME ISN'T OUR TIME

By Dr. Jimmy Ray Lee

I t's often said that God is rarely early, never late – and always on time. In our human impatience, this can be somewhat disconcerting, but because His timing is always right we can generally know for certain that it was God in action. I learned this many years ago, during the early years of my ministry to the Lord and His people.

We were blessed in Nashville, Tennessee during the first few months of the Teen Challenge ministry in that city to have the late Ambassador Joe Rodgers organize a benefit concert that featured singers and songwriters Bill and Gloria Gaither and entertainer Pat Boone. Proceeds from this event were to benefit Teen Challenge, as well as several other Nashville ministries. Each ministry sold tickets for the event, which was staged at the Grand Ole Opry House.

The Teen Challenge staff and board worked hard to sell tickets and we sold the most tickets among the ministries. Even though the concert was a huge success, and we knew we would be benefiting financially about a month later, we found ourselves confronting an immediate financial challenge. We needed funds to pay our bills until the contributions from the concert would be distributed.

Over a period of three weeks, we saw God meet this need in special and unexpected ways. The first week we could pay all of our bills and staff salaries, except there was not money for my own salary. Then I went to the mailbox on the day paychecks were to be issued and found checks that provided sufficient finances to cover my salary as well.

The second week turned out to be an exact rerun of the week before. We had all the needed funds on hand for bills and staff compensation – except for my own. But God graciously, faithfully, and in a very timely manner saw fit to have enough funds that came through the mail to meet my weekly pay as well.

The third week we again faced the same challenge, except this time when I went to the mailbox there was no money to pay my salary. I returned to the office very disappointed, not knowing what to do. A short time later, however, I received an unexpected phone call from a gentleman who was unaware of this special need. He had called to tell me that he had a gift for the ministry. That same day I went to his place of business, where he gave me a check for the ministry. Wouldn't you know it? His gift to Teen Challenge met the exact need of our deficit.

This series of events – and how the Lord chose to meet our needs – served as an important benchmark in my walk of faith and growth as a ministry leader. Even though I knew God had called my family to start the Nashville Teen Challenge program, my faith had been wearing thin. Trusting the Lord from week to week – literally, from paycheck to paycheck – wasn't easy. But God again proved himself faithful, affirming both His call on our lives and His promise to provide for our needs. "The one who calls you is faithful and he will do it" (1 Thessalonians 5:24).

Bringing It Home

It's important to remember God is in control of time. Always. As the apostle Peter writes, "with the Lord a day is like a thousand years, and a thousand years are like a day" (2 Peter 3:8). Jesus was born "when the time had fully come (the right time)" (Galatians 4:4). The Scriptures also tell us He will "appear a second time, not to bear sin, but to bring Salvation to those who are waiting for him" (Hebrews 9:28).

As we live this life in anticipation of our Savior's return to earth, it's good to know what David declares in Psalm 31:15 "My times are in your hands."

Have you ever experienced a significant "timing situation" where you could see the Lord at work, whether the moment His intervention occurred or at a later time when you were able to view how the situation unfolded in retrospect? Describe the circumstances and what God did.

What comfort do you receive from David's words in Psalm 31:15, his declaration to God, "My times are in Your hands"?

38

PROVIDING HOPE FOR THE HOPELESS

By Tim McLauchlin

Since October of 2009, Tim McLauchlin has served as the Executive Director of Teen Challenge – Upper Cumberland in Livingston, Tennessee. Tim is not a stranger to what life can be like when the future seems dim and without hope, and God has used his experiences to enable him to lead a fruitful ministry that seeks to provide hope for the hopeless and helpless.

There's a saying, "When God guides, He provides." This might sound like a cliché, but it's true – when the Lord calls you to do something, without question He will give the resources necessary for you to fulfill your calling. Even if sometimes you have no idea of what He's going to do, or how, or when, or even why. I'm living proof of this.

After struggling with drugs and alcohol for many years, God radically delivered me from my addictions. Afterward I felt God calling me to vocational ministry, but I ran from it. Then in 2001, I went to my pastor and we began to talk about what I felt God was saying to me. He took me to Phoenix, Arizona to Tommy Barnett's church for a ministry leader's conference it was hosting. While we were there, the

Lord specifically spoke to me about helping people who were strug-gling with drug and alcohol addictions.

I sensed the Lord telling me that I was going to be giving hope to the hopeless. "You're going to tell people what I have done in your life, and they are going to find freedom from addiction, as you have found," He said, speaking to my heart. I remember writing all this down on a napkin and feeling that God had really spoken to me. So I returned from Phoenix with this plan in mind. Of course, upon my return to Cookeville I realized there would be a lot more involved than a simple plan.

For one thing, I had been in the car business there for about six years and was making lots of money, working as the general man-ager of a local car dealership. Leaving that kind of financial security would be difficult. However, I felt if I were to be obedient to God's call, I could not continue in that role.

Being a young Christian, very zealous but not very educated and still getting grounded in my faith, when I got back from Phoenix I walked into my boss's office – the owner of the car dealership – handed him my keys, and simply said, "I have to quit." He replied, "You've got to be nuts!" I told him, "Well, that may be true, but God has called me to ministry." He did not understand what that meant and frankly, I did not know that I knew what it meant either.

What happened next was a friend of mine who learned that God had called me to a ministry of offering hope to the hopeless gave us a 1,000-square foot building in downtown Cookeville. He said, "I will give it to you, and you just pay the utilities and use it for whatever you want." We did not have a clue on what we should do, but we gave it a name, calling it the Cookeville Dream Center, and I started going out and doing street ministry.

During the evenings I walked around alleyways and stood outside of the bars, just meeting people, sharing my testimony and telling them about Jesus. We started Bible studies at the building. I found out about a national ministry called Teen Challenge and read David Wilkerson's book about the beginnings of this ministry, *The Cross and the Switchblade.* As men and women that I was ministering to got saved, we would send them to Teen Challenge centers.

After about seven months, my wife, Sheridan, called me and said we needed to sit down and have a talk. At that time we had two children in diapers, a mortgage, I had walked away from a lucrative career in the car business, and was engaged in this ministry without having a clue about what I was doing. My wife said, "We need to talk, because we are broke." I replied, "Honey, we are not broke." She explained she had paid all the bills and bought groceries, and we had only $150 left in the savings account we had spent years building. We had also cashed in my 401k and had spent all of that.

Feeling puzzled, I asked, "How can that be? We had tons of money saved." Sheridan reminded me that I had paid for bus tickets, paid intake fees, and had run the ministry and paid utility bills for the building, and all the while we had no income. In about seven months we had gone through $20,000, and she wanted to know what we were going to do. I remember just looking at her and saying, "All I know is I heard what God said, and all I know to do is to pray."

So we knelt down by our couch and I prayed, "Lord, Your Word says that You will supply all of my needs according to Your riches in glory. I don't know where I have missed You, but I am sorry and I need to take care of my family. Amen." My wife stared at me and said, "Is that it?" and I replied, "Honey, that is all I've got."

We went to bed without knowing what was going to happen or how the Lord would answer my prayer. We got up the next morning, and I was sitting at the table eating breakfast when the phone rang. Sheridan answered it, and within seconds she had a look on her face that was unusual. She asked the caller to hold on and handed the phone to me. The lady on the other end said the guy who was my former boss at the car dealership wanted to meet with me for lunch. I agreed to meet him and we scheduled the place and time.

When I arrived, my former boss asked how the ministry was going. I responded, "It is going good." He said, "You are lying." Then I admitted to him it was rough because I did not know anything about raising funds, I just wanted to help people get saved. Then he said, "Why don't you come back to the car business?" I replied, "I can't come back to the car business, because God has called me into the ministry."

He suggested I could return to the business and have every Wednesday off so I could preach wherever I wanted to; since the dealership is closed on Sunday, I could preach on Sundays. "As long as the dealership is going good, if you need to be gone, just let me know in advance and you can be gone for a little while" he told me. Then he added, "We could make this work, because you need to take care of your family."

I told him I needed to pray about it, and he wanted to know how long that would take. I kind of dropped my head and replied, "You know I need to take care of my family, so I will come back to the car business." He said, "I hoped you would say that. God woke me up in the middle of the night and told me to call you, and God told me to give you this." He handed me a check for $6,000 and said he would see me at the dealership the next day. So I went back into the car business for two-and-one-half years until the Lord opened the door for me to get on staff at Trinity Assembly.

Trinity Assembly had wanted to get a program like Teen Challenge going in the area for several years, but had not been able to get it off the ground. So in 2007, Pastor Campbell came to me and said, "When I hired you, you said that you felt like the Lord had spoken to you." Then he asked what it was God had said to me. I told him that it was to help those who were addicted. Pastor Campbell began to weep and said the church had always wanted this, and he believed the Lord had spoken to him that this was the time to get it launched.

We found four families in the church who agreed with us about establishing this kind of program, so we started visiting Teen Challenge centers and praying. For two years we met and would travel to Teen Challenge centers, getting their information, sorting through it, and then praying and fasting just to see what God wanted us to do.

We had everything ready to start the ministry (501c3 non-profit status, articles of incorporation and bylaws) in December of 2008. We just needed a place. In January of 2009, I told my pastor and the board I was going to spend time in prayer and fasting to see where it was that God wanted us to go.

My wife asked how long I planned to fast. I said, "I have no idea. I love to eat, but it will last until God tells us where He wants us to be," I told her. I had been fasting for about two weeks and as I was standing in church one Sunday morning worshipping the Lord, I said to Him, "God, I don't know what You are wanting to do and where You are wanting to do it, but I will go and do whatever You tell me to do." Very clearly I heard these three words: "Gainesboro, crisis, hope." I wrote those words down, stuck the paper in my Bible, and stayed through the rest of the church service.

When I got home I asked my wife to fix me some soup. She asked if I was done fasting, and I told her I believed that God had spoken to me. She asked what He said, so I showed her the piece of paper with the three words on it. She asked what I thought it meant, and I told her I thought we needed to look in Gainesboro (a small town with one red light) for some land to open a crisis center, as that is what we had been talking about for over two years. Hope was a word the Lord had given me in 2001 at Tommy Barnett's church in Arizona. We are to give hope to the hopeless, according to Psalm 10:17 (NLT). It says, "Lord, you hear the cries of the hopeless. Surely you will answer them." So I knew we had heard from the Lord.

Tuesdays were my day off each week at Trinity, so every Tuesday morning I would go down to Gainesboro and drive around. I started contacting real estate agents and talking to people that I knew had rental places, trying to find some property or something. The second time I went down, I was going to look at a house and drove by a building that was made of lime green and brown block. I remember driving by and thinking, "Oh my gosh! That thing is ugly." I went on to the house I was going to see, but after looking at it I knew it was not the one. As I was heading back I passed by that ugly building again and my attention was drawn to it. So I stopped, got out and looked in through some of the windows. I kind of laughed at what I saw, got back into my car and left.

The next week I was on my way to Celina, which is on the other side of Gainesboro. My wife was with me and as we drove by I told her to look at that building. She asked what I thought about it, and I told her I just wanted her to see it because it was so ugly. She agreed it was ugly and we drove on to Celina.

The next week – the third week I traveled to Gainesboro – a board member and I went together to look at some more land. We looked at the land, but knew that was not it. So we are coming back through Gainesboro, and I told him to look at that ugly building. He said, "You know, it might have some potential." I replied, "Man, you are crazy," and we drove on.

Week four came and once more we drove down to Gainesboro. I had not heard anything else from God, but I knew Gainesboro was where He wanted us. I drove into the parking lot of the ugly building and looked in through the windows. You could see into the rafters. The building was block walls, concrete floor and no ceiling. It used to be an old muffler shop that had been closed down, and the building had been sitting vacant for about two years. Looking in I remembered thinking, "Lord, I don't know why you've got me here, but this building needs to be condemned." Then I heard the Spirit of the Lord say to me, "That's what they say about My children."

I began to weep and then heard another voice – a human voice – say, "Can I help you?" I turned around and saw that a guy had pulled up in a pickup truck. I told him who I was, and he told me he was the guy that owned the building. We went inside and I began to share my heart with him. He asked if I could come back next week and talk with his two sons, "because I am trying to give my business over to them and I want them to hear what you are talking about."

I came back the next week and shared with the two sons what God had been saying to me. As I was sharing about why we wanted the building, tears began to roll down one of the son's cheeks. He said,

"What you are wanting to do in this community is what we need. This town has no hope." When he said those words, I asked, "What did you say?" He said again, "This town has no hope." Then he sent me to the local Chamber of Commerce to talk with a lady there. I told her all about what I and the church were wanting to do, and she sat there and cried, and also said, "This town has no hope." I had not told her what the first person had said to me. I just thought to myself, "Well, there is number 2."

The lady asked me to go and see her preacher. I got his name and the church location, but thought, "This will never work." However, I felt God was saying, "Go." So I drove across town and introduced myself, and told the preacher what we were wanting to do. Like the man and woman before, he began to cry and said, "I'm not against you. We are on the same side. This town needs that kind of hope."

I went back to Gainesboro a couple of weeks later to talk to the owners of the building and we began to negotiate. We agreed to lease the building from them, but there was extensive remodeling that was needed, so they asked me to show them what I thought had to be done. One of my board members was a builder, so he and I went to the building and discussed plans for the renovation. In a couple of weeks he had drawn up the blueprints for every wall and door, and we went back to the owners and showed them what we needed.

The owner looked at it, asked me some questions about it and said, "Okay, this is what you want?" I said, "Yes." He said, "We can do this." I said that was great and asked for an estimate for what it would cost so I could start raising the funds to get it built. He looked at me and asked, "You are going to help people with drug and alcohol addiction, right?" I told him I was, and he replied, "Okay we can do this."

I told him I appreciated that, but insisted that I needed to know how much it would cost us so I could raise the money required for the project. He looked at me again and said, "You aren't too smart, are you preacher?" I said, "Maybe not. Am I missing something? He replied, "If you do what you say you are going to do, and you are going to help people around here that are on drugs and alcohol, we are going to do this. It will not cost you anything."

They ended up remodeling the entire 6,000-square foot building. They built two offices, a conference room, chapel, classroom space, dorm room, and kitchen, redid the plumbing and wiring, added drywalls and paint, drop ceiling, lighting, and four new heating and air units – everything we specifically needed. I talked to a couple of builders who said the owners probably spent $150,000, if not more, on the building. It did not cost us a dime. It took the owners about six and one-half to seven months to complete the project.

We made it both residential and non-residential. When we first opened up in that facility, it was just me and one lady that worked there. She lived in the apartment above our building and would come down and work. We had six beds and were strictly a crisis center. Ladies would come in and stay three or four weeks, and then we would drive them to another Teen Challenge facility. We grew from six to eight beds, and eventually we reached a point where we began to look for land. It was three years after moving into that "ugly building" that we were able to buy 49 acres for the program we have now.

We had moved into that original building in October 5, 2009. Two weeks after that, we were conducting our very first fund-raising banquet here in Cookeville. I had never done a banquet before, so I did not know what we were going to do. But we had a great turnout, with 200-225 people at the banquet. I simply explained what we were going to do, and we raised about $25,000 that night.

When we initially opened up, after buying some furniture we had about $5,000 in the bank. Following our first banquet and the $25,000 it brought in, after paying our rent and utilities we had enough money to stay open about six months. After that, we did not know what we were going to do.

Leading up to the banquet, we had announced in the newspaper the dinner would be on Thursday, and then there would be an open house at the facility for people to walk through the following

Saturday from 9 a.m. to noon. We wanted people to come and see what we were planning to do before we actually brought students in.

For our open house we had a display table with brochures at the door, along with coffee and cookies in the kitchen area. People came in and walked through for a couple of hours, then by 12 o'clock no one had been through for about 30 minutes. So I looked at my wife and some board members and told them I was going to the other end of the building to start turning off the lights, locking the doors, and taking down the display table so we could get ready to leave.

I left them there talking, and as I was walking to the back of the building I looked out the window and saw an old black car pull in the parking lot. A guy and his wife got out of the car. He was about six-foot-four, skinny, with long black hair hanging down his back, a long beard that was braided, wearing a black leather jacket, black pants, and motorcycle boots. His wife was decked out in leather also.

They came walking in and asked if this was the Teen Challenge place. I told him it was, and he asked if I was Tim McLauchlin, the guy in the paper. I told him I was. Then he asked in a gruff voice what I was intending to do there. So I told him we were going to help people struggling with drug and alcohol addiction. He asked how. I told him we were a ministry and were going to talk to people about Jesus Christ and the plan God has for them as He explains in the Bible. As I shared the vision we had, he just stood there and looked at me, no smile or any other expression. Then he wanted to know if I was going to give them a tour.

We started walking through and I began pointing and telling him everything about the building. He was not saying a word, just following me. We walked into the kitchen area where my wife, kids and a couple of board members are standing. Seeing us walking down, they all started to scatter, but I was thinking, "Don't leave me with this guy."

Standing there in the kitchen, as I finished telling them about what we intended to do, he asked how we planned to fund the program. I told him we were going to do that through partnerships with

FAITHFUL, NO MATTER WHAT

churches and private donors, people who believed in what we were doing and wanted to make contributions.

The man then wanted to know where the money would go, and I told him it would stay right there in Gainesboro. He said, "The money that comes in to help run this thing to help people get off drugs and alcohol stays right here in Gainesboro?" I said, "Yes, it will." He asked, "You are not going to send it off to one of those other centers off in Texas or something?" I said, "Sir, the money stays right here."

The man turned and looked at his wife, then said, "Give it to me." She handed him a checkbook and he asked to borrow my pen. As he began to write the check, I could not see what he was writing but his wife could, and I noticed that she turned her head over to the side with a funny look. I thought that could be bad or very good. Then he handed me my pen back and said, "God has blessed me and I want to be a blessing to you because I like what you are doing."

I took the pen and the check, and as I was putting my pen in my pocket I looked at the check briefly and saw a 1 and some 0's. I though it was $1,000, so I said, "Thank you so much." Then I looked back down and focused on the check and saw he had written it for $10,000. He told me, "Like I said, God has blessed me and I am going to be praying for you." When he was getting ready to leave, I asked him for his name, address and phone number. He said, "You do not need that information. Don't you worry about that."

He left the center and I was just standing there in shock. My wife and the board members came back and asked, "Who was that guy?" I said, "I don't know, but this is what he gave me." We all just stood there rejoicing, then we prayed and thanked God for what He had done.

The address on the check the man had given me was a bank address. So when we went to the bank on Monday, I told them that I did not want to be a person that doubts, but asked if the check was good. They assured me it was a good check. I asked who the guy was, but they said the reason he used their address was so that no one will know. I tried to locate him by asking people in the community and looking him up in phone book, but could not find him. I have never seen the guy since. I don't know his name or anything about him, but that is how we got our start in this ministry – a tall, lanky guy in a black leather jacket gave us $10,000.

My personal definition of faithfulness has everything to do with what God has done in my life. I never met my real father, and my stepdad died when I was young, so my experience with an earthly father was not good. I ended up in a life of addiction and moved from Detroit to down South. I always go back to Jeremiah, chapter 1, where the Lord says, "I knew you before you were born and I anointed you." My grandmother (my stepdad's mother) told me years later that she used to pray for me. She said when I was two years old she would lay hands on me and pray. All through my time of addiction, she always told me, "Go back to God. He has a plan for you," but I ran hard from God.

In 2004, when Pastor Campbell offered us the job at the church, I went to my grandmother and said, "Nanny, you are never going to believe this, but I am starting in the ministry." She reached over and grabbed my hand and said, "Son, I always told you God has a plan for your life." She died about six months after that, but she got to see me go into the ministry.

Even when I was not faithful to God, He was always faithful to His promise to me. What my grandmother had prayed for and all of her personal sacrifices for me were honored by God. He honored her faithfulness, and all I want to do is to continue being faithful to Him.

Bringing It Home

Dr. Thomas Idiculla has said, "Man can live without food for 40 days. Man can live without water for three days. Man can live without oxygen for only a few minutes. But man cannot live without hope – not even for a few seconds." Jesus Christ brings hope to a hopeless life. Apostle Paul assures us, "And hope does not disappoint us, because God has poured out his love into our hearts by the Holy Spirit.... You see, at the right time, when we were still powerless, Christ died for the ungodly" (Romans 5:5-6).

Have there ever been times in your life when you experienced hopelessness? What was that like for you? What do you think kept you going, even when the future looked bleak and without hope?

If you were to describe your life now, which word – "hope" or "hopeless" – would be a more accurate description of how you feel? What role does hope play in your life right now? Do you wish you could become more hopeful? Why or why not?

39

WHEN YOUR PRAYERS FALL A LITTLE SHORT

By Mike Chapman

Sometimes when God is getting ready to do a big thing, He utilizes little things to get things started. Like using a simple announcement to announce He is up to something really special.

When I came to City Church in 1976, the congregation I'm leading right now, it was a little church of about 50 to 55 people in Chattanooga, Tennessee. At 25, my wife, Trudy, and I were both young, and I had been told by some other preachers, "Oh, no one ever does anything good at that church, and you'll probably leave the ministry if you go there. It will be discouraging and disappointing." I thought people like that were supposed to encourage you, but I was being discouraged. I told Trudy, "Let's go and give it our best shot, and let's see what God will do."

One of the things I discovered when I came to the church – the congregation was called Lee Highway Church of God then, before we renamed it City Church of Chattanooga – was it was a virtual secret in the area. When I went around the community and met somebody, I would introduce myself and tell them I was the pastor of Lee Highway Church of God. Not more than a block away, people would say, "Where's that at?" I began thinking, "These people don't even know our church exists!"

Going back to our church, I said, "I know one thing – people are not going to go to a church they've never heard of. We somehow have to establish our presence." So I came up with this idea – a young, rash idea, and told our people I wanted to send an announcement to everyone in our area. We would send it to 2,000 homes, stating we were there to be of service and would be honored if we could serve them in any way.

I wanted to do the announcement in a professional manner, even though I look back at it now and realize how unprofessional it was. When I proposed this idea to the congregation, the members all looked at me as if to say, "We can't do that, we don't have enough money." I replied, "Maybe not, but I believe God wants us to do this." By this time I had been pastoring them about a year. "We've got to let people know we are here," I said.

This was toward the end of 1976, and I had already begun calculating the cost of sending out the announcements, including printing, postage and everything else. I told the congregation we would have volunteers to help us in typing address labels, using the city directory and drawing a circle around our church to establish our target for the mailing. We didn't try to get pre-printed labels from any company. In fact, we didn't even know those things existed back then. All we knew was we were going to mail an announcement to people, informing them we are here to serve. Factoring in all of the costs, I had come to the conclusion it was going to cost 400 dollars.

When I said 400 dollars, everybody looked at me, about 50 people (and that included children and babies), and they were all thinking, "We don't have 400 dollars!" I responded, "Well, maybe God will help us." Then I said, "Let's take up a special offering." I remember we had some naysayers that were saying, "This will never work. We will never get that much money." So I went to the local Christian bookstore and bought some little envelopes that were popular back in the day. All each envelope said on it was "Love Offering" and it had a big red heart in the middle.

We began to announce the special offering and I explained to our members, "What you put in this envelope is for the special project.

Your regular offering goes in the offering plate." That Sunday I was praying, "Oh, God, please let us get 400 dollars. Just please, Jesus, let us get 400 dollars." I told the ushers and the treasurers, "If you would, would you take all the envelopes that come in those special red heart envelopes, keep them separate, and leave them in my office? I want to count those myself. The rest of the offering, you can count." So when church was over and everybody was gone, I went to my office and there was this little bag on my desk with those envelopes. I began to open them one by one.

There was two dollars in one, in another there was 50 dollars. In some there were coins. As I was counting, I kept feeling better. The total got to 300 hundred dollars and there were still some more envelopes to open, so as I opened them I kept thinking, "Praise God, we're going to reach the 400-dollar goal!" When I got through counting it all, we had 398 dollars, which to me sounded like 400. I decided, "I'll put in two more dollars, praise Jesus!"

I thought, "Hallelujah, nobody's going to believe it we actually got 400 dollars!" Remember, I was 25 years old then, about 37 years ago. I turned off the office light, secured the 398 dollars in a locked drawer I had, and went out to get into my car. Everybody was gone. My car was an old Chevy Monte Carlo; I can see it in my mind to this day – white with a maroon vinyl top on it. As I got behind the steering wheel of my car, I saw there was an envelope with a red heart under my windshield wiper. I got back out of the car to retrieve the envelope. There was no name on it, but when I opened it up, there was two dollars in it.

Amazed at God's faithfulness, how He had met our financial need for mailing out the announcement – and without my help to reach the 400-dollar goal – I had myself a wonderful shouting time. I just jumped up and down in the parking lot, saying, "Praise be to Jesus!"

To this day I don't know who left that envelope under my windshield wiper; no one has ever come forward to acknowledge this. I even said, "Whoever you were, I'd love to hug you." When I look back on this very simple but clear miracle of God, I saw our congregation change at that moment. I saw them start to think, "Well, you know what, maybe we can do something for God. Maybe if we trust God a little more, if we go out on a limb and trust Him, He will be faithful."

From that moment, people got excited. We were able to take a layout to a printer and get the announcement printed, but we still had to stick all the labels on. We didn't even have a bulk mail permit. I had to go and get that before we could do the mailing. We were stuffing envelopes, and ladies were there with typewriters typing labels from a city directory and then sticking them on the envelopes.

That proved to be a major turning point, the moment that everyone knew God was going to do something in this church. It was the breakthrough we needed, because at that point, one man in the church even told me, "You know, I call our church sometimes the 'tobacco road church,' after the old novel, *Tobacco Road.*" I said, "What do you mean?" He replied, "You see, they were always talking about something they were going to do, but they never got around to doing it." Then he added, "Now I think we are actually going to do something." So that truly was a turning point that the people clearly saw. It was an important lesson for them – and for me as a young pastor – that if we will take a step of faith, God will meet the need.

So it was a two-dollar miracle, but it made a phenomenal point and spoke two million dollars' worth of encouragement to us, an unquestionable demonstration that God is with us, and He is faithful.

And I can say that to any young person out there, as well as any pastor. God comes along in the big things and the little things, but it's those little surprises that really stand out. I like to think of it as in the book of Ruth, where Boaz told his workers to purposely leave some handfuls of grain for Ruth. In essence Boaz said, "Hey, leave the stuff that accidentally falls, but also throw some down on purpose to encourage her."

I think sometimes those little things are like those two dollars in the envelope under my windshield wiper. God was saying, "Hey, Mike, here's a little handful on purpose. I'm with you." That's what it was, just two dollars. I could have gone home and said, "Honey, give me two more dollars to put in this." But instead, it was God saying, "No, I'm going to show you. I'm going to put it in."

Bringing It Home

As Pastor Chapman pointed out, in the book of Ruth, Boaz instructed his workers to leave handfuls of grain in the field for Ruth on purpose (Ruth 2:15-16). God, as we trust Him and as that illustration demonstrates, always provides enough for us. David writes, "The LORD is my shepherd, I shall not be in want" (Psalm 23:1). And Paul affirms that, writing, "And my God will meet all your needs according to His glorious riches in Christ Jesus" (Philippians 4:19).

Describe a time when God unexpectedly met a personal need of yours. How did it make you feel when you saw how the Lord had faithfully met that need, in a way you could never have anticipated?

What are the greatest needs you are asking God to meet for today? Do you believe He is faithful enough – and sufficient enough – to meet them?

40

GOING TO THE MOUNTAINS FOR A TRUE, MOUNTAINTOP EXPERIENCE

By Roger Helle

There's a saying that "you can't go home again." But sometimes you can, even when "home" happens to be the site of a traumatic wartime experience. And sometimes God can use that return visit for a wonderful healing encounter.

When my wife, Shirley, and I started making missions trips to Vietnam back in 1989, the government was very skeptical. They watched us. We were under surveillance a lot of the times but would take the returning veterans and tour the country to expose them to what Vietnam looked like now and the vision we had for seeing God touching the people of Vietnam with a ministry of reconciliation. It was particularly meaningful for older Christians like me who may have seen movies like, "The Green Berets."

There was an ethnic group in Vietnam called Montagnards. They were mountain people and during the war they fought many times alongside the Americans, especially with our Special Forces. They trained the Montagnards, who were incredible jungle fighters and for the most part fought with us rather than against us.

After America lost its resolve to support the conflict in Vietnam, we pulled out and the country fell to the Communists. Most people know history shows that hundreds of thousands of people died in Vietnam, and that as many as two million in Cambodia and tens of thousands of Hmong mountain people were ethnically cleansed in Laos.

When we started touring the country, we would go back up to the area of the demilitarized zone that existed between North Vietnam and South Vietnam during the war. No border exists there now, but there was an area, including a village called Khe Sanh, where the Marines fought during the Tet Offensive in 1968 – 6,000 Marines in fierce combat for 55 days, holding off thousands of North Vietnamese regulars.

The Montagnards, a tribal people, lived in that mountainous region. When the fighting got more intense they pulled out to other areas, moving away from where the heaviest fighting was. After the war was over, they started returning into the mountainous areas. They loved to strip farm and they lived in shacks. Huts were built on stilts to keep them off the floor of the jungle because of snakes, wild boars and tigers at that time.

One particular tribe we would go visit a couple times a year. They were called the Bru tribe, one of twelve ethnic groups in Vietnam. When we would go there, an organization in Bangkok, Thailand provided Bibles in the Bru dialect we could take to them. These Bibles were illegal to take into the country, but we would smuggle them in and go up to near Khe Sanh and visit these villages. We would hand out these Bibles in their language, and as best we could, also take them rice, medicine and clothing because they were very poor. The government was very discriminatory in its attitude and actions toward them. So we would try to give them a little bit of encouragement, along with helping to provide for some of their essential needs.

Twice a year during a six-year span we went to a polio orphanage in Saigon. The first time my family went with me, due to the extremely hot weather – we endured 120-degree temperatures there the whole trip – we didn't find enough bottled water for traveling. We needed that so I could take my wife, Shirley, and kids to visit the mountain area villages. I really wanted them to see this area because it was where I had fought a couple years before the Tet Offensive, but they couldn't go with me at that time. My son, Josh, was twelve years old and my daughter, Jamie, was nine.

Ten years later, in 1999, Shirley and I were making another trip to Vietnam, and both of our kids said they would like to go back. And I said, "Do you mean it?" and they said, "Yeah." So we agreed we would take them back. So our whole family went back and by this time things had changed in Vietnam. In the cities, getting bottled water was not a problem, so I was able to take my family to the mountain region.

In the countryside, however, things were pretty much the same. We were on our way to the Khe Sahn area to visit the group of Montagnard villages we had been traveling to for ten years. On the way we had to stop in a town, probably the little village of Khe Sahn where I had been as a young Marine, to pick up our local guide. We had been going there long enough to know there were supposed to be secret policemen that would tag along to make sure we didn't do anything we were not supposed to be doing.

Just before we got into town, one of the members of a team from six months earlier was telling me that the last time they were there was right after the village chief's brother-in-law had been hoeing a garden. He had hit a grenade hidden just below the surface of the ground that exploded, going off in his face, causing extreme injury.

When the team got to the village, the village chief was very distressed and took them to his brother-in-law's hut. They climbed up into the hut, where they found the man lying on a straw mat, all he had for a bed. The brother-in-law was a bloody mess with multiple wounds from head to toe. They went about trying to stop the bleeding; he had lost a tremendous amount of blood and was likely beginning to suffer from infection.

The village chief said, "Would you pray for him?" So the team gathered around and prayed for the man, that God would heal him and have mercy on him. The team leader told me that after they walked out, the team members just shook their heads because they felt certain this guy was going to die. There was nothing more they could do. They couldn't call a helicopter, an ambulance, or offer any other kind of emergency aid because there was nothing nearby. So they left lamenting the man's condition, concluding that the village chief's brother-in-law was not going to live much longer.

We arrived back at the town six months later. I was the team leader and when the guide, a member of the secret police, got into our vehicle he came to Shirley and me and kept saying, very softly to us, "I see miracle, I see miracle." That was about the extent of his English. We are looking at him as if to ask, "Okay, what does that mean?" I did not associate what he was saying with what I had just been told to me about the village chief's brother-in-law. So we got off the bus and were walking down the trail to the village. When the villagers saw us coming, it was a big deal. We couldn't have called ahead because there were no phones there.

A surprise visit by a team like ours was always a big deal, but this time it seemed bigger than usual. I noticed several things, one being that the women who usually didn't wear much were all fully clothed. They still were wearing their traditional garb, but this time they had tops on, too. There seemed to be more pandemonium than normal, and the village chief was just blabbering away to the guide, who also was serving as our interpreter. We were just standing there, watching all of this, and the chief was yelling, giving instructions or something. A huge crowd had gathered, several hundred people standing around us.

All of a sudden the crowd parted and a young man walked out and stood next to the village chief, with a big smile on his face and everything. The leader of the team from six months earlier was standing next to me. He suddenly grabbed my hand and said, "Roger! That's him!" I replied, "Jim, who?" "That's who?" he answered, "The village chief's brother-in-law! That's him! That's the guy right there!" And we were standing there, just looking at him, totally amazed.

During my time in the Vietnam War I had a grenade go off at my feet. I've still got scars from head to toe to prove it, and until I get my new body in Heaven, they're there as a reminder of my own experience. But as I looked at this man standing by the village chief, I could see he had no physical evidence, none at all, that he had been injured in any way. God had totally and miraculously healed him.

Asking about this later, it was unclear whether it had happened a day later, two days later, or exactly when, but one morning this brother-in-law who had had the unfortunate encounter with a grenade simply got up, totally healed. What the villagers were especially excited about was that there had been a few people in that network of villages who had professed faith in Christ. But when the chief's brother-in-law was healed by the power of God, all those villagers saw a physical manifestation of the power of the living God.

Once Jesus had told His followers, "O ye of little faith." Well, the team that prayed a prayer didn't have a lot of it either. They had prayed for the man, but didn't even think God was going to answer it. The point is, they did pray – and because of their faithfulness to pray that prayer for God's healing and mercy, He healed that man.

Until that time the Montagnards had been pretty much believers in animism, spiritualists, praying to the spirits of ancestors and animals, and things like that. But when they saw the power of the living God that brought physical healing, to save this man's life and totally heal his body, the whole network of hundreds of Montagnard villagers came to know Jesus Christ as their Lord and Savior.

As you can imagine, as exciting as it was, we desired to confirm this story after we left. We were just in awe of what we had heard and what they said God had done. We had been going there for 10 years, but until then had seen minimal results. We could identify with how missionaries feel that spend years before they see a convert.

So we went back to the Imperial City of Hue and were meeting with a group of medical nuns. They were doctors and nurses, and would go out and treat the Montagnards. We had stopped to give them some money for medications they could use when they went out to treat the villagers.

One Vietnamese nun could speak English fairly well. As we were negotiating this new project, she said to me, "Have you heard about the Montagnards up by Khe Sahn?" And I thought to myself, "Okay, yes I have." But curious to find out what she was going to say, I just replied, "No, tell me about it?" Then she relayed the same story, that she knew some Americans had come to the village and prayed for an injured man there. She didn't realize we were from the same group, but explained she knew a family member of the village chief had been seriously hurt and dying, and then somebody prayed for him and God healed him. And, she added, she had learned now all the Montagnards in that whole region were serving Jesus Christ because they had witnessed that miracle.

Hearing the nun's account confirmed for us that it was not just a story the villagers had made up. We rejoiced at such a wonderful story of God's healing power and mercy. But more than that, the lesson for all of us was that for 10 years we had been faithful to do what we could do, despite working within the limits of a very restrictive government. We were sowing Bibles and the Word of God into that village and others, not knowing what the Lord would do. The team, when they prayed, had not had a lot of faith, but pray they did. And in response to their faithfulness, such as it was, God had said, "Okay, you did what you could do. Now I'll do what you cannot." He healed the man, and then the fruit just exploded in that whole region.

The ever-faithful God acted in an incredible way in response to the faithfulness of a small group of people with just a mustard seed worth of faith.

Bringing It Home

In the gospels we see numerous accounts of Jesus performing miracles and various healings, both physical and emotional. Such visible ministry can give a strong witness for our Lord and Savior. John 9, for example, records Jesus healing a blind man who was born without sight. There were those who were skeptical of this healing. But the skeptics' doubts were addressed. "We know he is our son," the man's parents answered, "and we know he was born blind. But how can he see now, or who opened his eyes, we don't know. Ask him. He is of age; he will speak for himself...." The son then replied, speaking of Jesus, "whether he is a sinner or not, I don't know. One thing I do know. I was blind but now I see" (John 9:20-25).

How does reading the stories of Jesus' various miracles and healing affect your walk with God? Do you think, "Well, that was then. This is now"? Or do they encourage you to trust Him more, regardless of what challenges you are facing?

In what ways have you experienced an emotional and/or physical healing from the Lord? What was that like – and what has that meant for your relationship with God today?

41

FAITHFULNESS IN SMALL THINGS THAT PROVE TO BE BIG THINGS

By Kevin Tyler

*K**evin Tyler is a veteran missionary, having served more than 30 years in various roles with Teen Challenge, mostly in Europe. He served ten years in Germany with Europe Teen Challenge, later serving for 20 years in Ukraine, working as academic dean, country coordinator, and as pastor at the International Church. He and his wife, Eunice, helped to build the church and start a medical ministry. Kevin's next assignment was director of Eurasia Teen Challenge, and today he is chief operating officer with Global Teen Challenge in Columbus, Georgia.*

When Jesus exhorted in Matthew 19:14, "Let the little children come to me, and do not hinder them, for the kingdom of heaven belongs to such as these," one of His assurances was that we can trust Him to take care of our children and meet their needs. My wife, Eunice, had this truth reinforced in a very unexpected way years ago when God was leading our family to Ukraine.

We had been serving as missionaries in Germany when the Soviet Union broke up, introducing new freedoms to the nation's various republics. With doors opened for presenting the Gospel in these new-ly independent nations for the first time in decades, a call went out for missionaries to go. Eunice and I felt God was speaking to us, that this was what we were supposed to do. We had come home at our normal time to itinerate, visiting with our U.S. supporters, and said we were willing to go. However, when we learned our destination would be Ukraine, we had serious concerns.

Ukraine was a difficult place to live in at the time, and the Chernobyl nuclear disaster had happened about fifty miles from Kiev, the city where we would live. As we prepared to leave, we felt a lot of fear and apprehension, mostly because our daughters were six and seven years old, and we did not know where they would go to school. In Germany they had been going to a Department of Defense school and kindergarten, but now we did not know where they would go. I did find one international school in Kiev, but the price was atrocious and we knew we could not afford that. Facing so much uncertainty, we felt much apprehension, especially about the children's needs.

We attended a church meeting with a lot of people there. Burdened down by our concerns, Eunice and I went over to a corner by ourselves, just praying together, when it seemed the Lord was speaking directly to both of us. What He said was simple, yet profound: "I love your children more than you do." This gave us such great reassurance that God would watch out for our girls, we actually ended up leaving for Ukraine early.

I went over first to find housing and while in the process of doing this, received a call from my own pastor. He said, "Hey, we just had a missionary here and he was telling me about a contact he has in Ukraine. Maybe you should look him up." My pastor gave me the phone number of the person, so I called the number. I did not reach the contact person, but got a secretary who answered, "Hello, this is Saint Andrews." I soon learned this was a tiny little school the contact person and his wife had started.

When I succeeded in reaching the contact person, he gave me the name of a real estate person whom he thought could help me. The realtor did help me in finding a suitable place to live, and it turned out to be very close to the little school, and we ended up sending our girls there.

We later found out one of our daughters, Michelle, had a mild learning disability. As it happened – not a coincidence – the contact person's wife specialized in helping children with learning disabilities, and she was able to get our daughter off to a great start. How God provided for all of these details was just tremendous, and the schooling our girls got in Ukraine was wonderful. Later, when Michelle was ready to go back to the United States, she went through Southwestern University on scholarship and did very well. She now has a teaching degree.

This was one real example for us showing that God would take care of us and be faithful. The thing we were most concerned about, how we would educate our children, turned out to be a wonderful blessing – they received a better education than we would have ever dreamed of. We had been greatly worried and concerned, but all the time God was telling us He would take care of us. And He did. Over those first years in Ukraine, it was incredible the number of times we experienced God's faithfulness in providing for and protecting us, because it was kind of wild in the beginning.

I think of another story of how God manifested His faithfulness while we were getting ready to start Teen Challenge in Moldova, a very small, very poor country just southwest of Ukraine. A couple of rehab centers already established there wanted to become a part of Teen Challenge, so we did a seminar for leaders.

A couple we met worked at one of the centers, and the husband had just gone through the program. He had been a heroin addict for a number of years. Eunice and I found out they had been married for just a month, so we were teasing them a little and having a good time. At the end of the day they suggested, "Why don't you come to see our rehab center?" It was about 30 miles away. When we got there we discovered their rehab center consisted of one very, very small farmhouse. They had a small kitchen, a small living room, a bedroom in which they had crammed 10 beds for the rehab center, a tiny, rudimentary bathroom, and that was it. Then the couple led me outside and showed me they had some pigs and a little garden.

After we went back into the farmhouse-turned-rehab center, we were standing around in the kitchen because the custom is you must always have some tea and cookies. Then we went into the living room to pray. A missionary, Calvin Klaus, and an attorney friend of his had accompanied us on this visit, and we all were getting ready to pray when another couple, Pentecostal pastors, asked to join us. So there we were, three Ukrainian couples and three Americans, a truly cross-cultural prayer group.

As we prayed, Calvin leaned over to me and said, "I do not know what to do, but I sense the young couple has a need." Standing there I was thinking, "Okay, what do I do about this?" John the attorney had heard us talking and offered, "Hey, I ask questions for a living. Let me handle this." So John stepped in front of the couple and pointing to Calvin, said, "Calvin says you have a problem. What is it?"

Immediately the couple became scared, their eyes looked like saucers, and they were probably thinking, "What is God saying to them about us?" We still were in our prayer circle, with their pastor on one side and their director on the other.

Seeing their obvious discomfort, the only thing I could think to do was to create a diversion. So I looked at the pastor and said, "By the way, where do you guys live?" So he started saying, "Well, we live across the village by the church." I asked the other couple where they lived, and they pointed out the window and said, "That house across the road my parents left me, so we live over there."

Then to finish it out, I asked the newlywed couple that worked at the rehab farm where they lived. They replied, "Here." That was when it got interesting for me, because I had been through the house and knew there was no space for a couple to live. But then I stepped over and opened a door nearby. It was a tiny closet only big enough to handle a few coats. On the back of the closet there were nails that held the couple's belongings, and we quickly discovered they had been sleeping in the closet, on the floor.

Calvin and I both agreed, "No, this isn't right," and soon we figured out a way to get them into an apartment. A few months later I was back in America, speaking at a church in Oklahoma, and told that story to illustrate the kind of dedication demonstrated by some of the workers that work in this ministry.

After the service the church leaders gave me a check, but one of the deacons walked up and gave me $150 in cash. He said, "I want you to give this to that couple you told us about." I replied, "You know, it is not like they have a bank account. I cannot just transfer this." He said. "Well, give it to them when you see them." I responded, "Well, that may be a year or so," but he said, "Just put it in your wallet and give it to them when you see them."

So I folded up the money and put it in a little place in my wallet. Sure enough, it was about a year before I was back in Moldova, where we were conducting another training session. The husband was there, but his wife stayed home because she was expecting their first child. On Friday during the week of training I asked the young husband to come back to the pastor's office. After I handed him the money, he gave me a look I will never forget.

The young man said, "I have to tell you a story. Yesterday one of the students here at this meeting asked me to go and look at his re-hab center. Can you believe that it was worse than ours? I was walking around there and I had $35 in my pocket, and God told me to give that $35 to this brother. I started praying saying, 'But God, you know my wife is home expecting our first baby, and You know this $35 is all the money we have.' I prayed, then I said to myself, 'Well, that is stupid. God knows all of that.'"

At that point, he said, "I started praying, 'God, I will be happy to give this to the brother if you will give me another $35 first.' Then I thought, 'No, I do not think that is how faith works.' Finally, I just handed the brother the $35 and said, 'God bless you.'"

With a look of gratitude, he went on to tell me that all morning he had been listening to the teachers but was not hearing them because he kept thinking, "How do I go home now and tell my wife that I gave away all our money?" Then he said, "But look, now I have $150!"

But that's not the end of the story. About a year ago I got an email from the committee there in Moldova, telling me they had just asked that young man to be the national director of Teen Challenge in Moldova. Can you imagine? It was just a matter of him being faithful in the small things, even though $35 was not really small to him at the time. But he and his wife had shown themselves faithful to do whatever God had wanted them to do. Now God has promoted him, and I think he has a great future ahead of him.

There are many great exploits of faith we can read about in the Bible. But to me, our faithfulness is exhibited the most when we engage in the discipline of obedience day after day after day, in spite of the fact we might not see the results as yet. That is especially true for our work in Teen Challenge, because day after day we see people that we minister to who seem hopeless; but just by being faithful, ministering to them day after day, you start seeing change in their lives.

Bringing It Home

In nature, and in the spiritual realm, good things often start as small things. Kevin Tyler's story gives just a few examples of how this is true, but if we look at our lives and the world around us through the eyes of faith, we can see many more.

The prophet Zechariah asks the question, "Who despises the day of small things?" (Zechariah 4:10). Just because an effort or situation seems small, that does not mean it will remain small forever. Jesus presented a parable to illustrate: "The Kingdom of Heaven is like a mustard seed which a man took and planted in his field. Though it is the smallest of all your seeds, yet when it grows, it is the largest of garden plants and becomes a tree" (Matthew 13:31-32). At the conclusion of another parable, Jesus said, "Well done, good and faithful servant! You have been faithful with a few things; I will put you in charge of many things" (Matthew 25:21).

Can you name one small thing that God started in your life that turned out to be significant? What was it, and describe the circumstances that were involved.

What would it mean for you to hear Jesus say to you, "Well done, good and faithful servant"?

42

FAITHFUL IN LIFE, ALL ALONG THE JOURNEY - AND IN DEATH

By Ivan Vernon

*W*hile driving along an interstate highway, you might have un-knowingly passed Ivan Vernon, who spent countless hours driv-ing Greyhound buses for 42 years. When he went to be with the Lord on July 8, 2014, he was 93 years old, having lived a life full of wonderful adventures. Here's a bit of his story, which he shared in an interview not long before his passing. It's just the tip of the iceberg of a faith-filled life.

If you were to sum up my life in a few words, you might say it has been a journey from turkeys to Greyhounds, with a lot of stops in between.

I was born on December 15, 1920, on a Georgia cotton farm where I grew up along with seven other children (five boys and three girls in all) to a praying mother and daddy. My parents observed the Sabbath day like it was the most holy day. They would not let us use a ham-mer or make noise of any kind on a Sunday. At that time there was a blue law in Georgia, which meant all stores were closed on Sunday. You could not buy anything on Sunday, so groceries or anything you needed had to be bought on Saturday. There were no supermarkets or even electricity back then, so stores did not keep meats and other perishables. Fruits were in the store mostly during the Christmas holidays; most people were farmers and raised their own vegetables.

My wife, Sarah, and I just lacked a few weeks being married 70 years when she died. How could it last so long with the same woman? I would say the secret is in one word – forgiveness. If you forgive your partner like God forgives you, everything works out. None of us please each other all the time, and Sarah and I were always quick to forgive one another.

The first year we got married we farmed, raising cotton because that was the only cash crop there was at that time in the county. Then I went to Atlanta to find a job. It seemed God sent me to the right place at the right time, because jobs were hard to come by in 1940. I approached a manager with the Kroger Company. I asked him about a job driving a tractor-trailer. The manager asked, "Have you ever driven a tractor-trailer truck?" I said, "No sir, but I can drive one if I get a chance." He responded, "How do you know you can?" I replied, "I know I can." He said, "If you have got that much confidence in yourself, I will give you a chance. Show up at the warehouse in the morning."

I went up to the warehouse and there were four or five tractor-trailers in the parking lot. The assistant told me to get in one of the trucks and back it in. I pulled one out from between two others – I had never even been in a tractor-trailer before. I had to get out into the street and figure out the gears, then I backed it in just as straight as could be. The assistant asked his boss, "Did you see that?" The boss said, "No, I was talking to someone." So he asked me to do it again. I pulled the tractor-trailer back out and after having to straighten up one time, backed it in again. I know God helped me back that rig in. After watching me, the boss said to his assistant, "Make him a work card."

Then a year and a half later, another guy and I were hauling frozen turkeys. At that time they came in wooden crates that were wired together. There were eight frozen turkeys in a crate and they were hard to handle. I commented, "I wish these things were alive so we could herd them into the truck." The other guy said, "Why don't we get us a job with something that can load and unload itself?" I thought about it and said, "That is an idea. What about a Greyhound Bus? I am going tomorrow to turn in my application to drive for Greyhound."

That was in 1942. As I had resolved, I turned in my application at Greyhound the next morning, and 10 days later they called me in for an interview. At that time you had to be 25 to drive a commercial bus, so they were hesitant to hire me. However, one man said, "But look at his record. He has been driving for one and a half years with a perfect record." Then they said, "We have a school starting in Jacksonville, Florida in 10 days. Can you make it?" I replied, "Well, I would like to give Kroger a two-week notice, but I will give them a 10-day notice." So I went off of Kroger's payroll one day and onto Greyhound's the next day; I was on their payroll for more than four decades. I drove Greyhound buses for 42 years and never hurt anyone.

Much of my life was spent driving Greyhound buses, but nothing gave me more joy than being a father to our children. If I were to speak to parents raising children today, I would tell them to live the kind of life before their children that they want them to grow up and live. I smoked until I was 32, but I had two boys that I wanted to ask not to smoke, so I knew I needed to stop. One day I had lit a cigarette and then decided to put it out, but found myself later starting to light up again. So I took that pack of cigarettes and threw them out the window into a creek. When I got home I took the carton of cigarettes and package of tobacco that I had, dug a little ditch and buried them. And that was the last cigarette I ever had.

Prayer has meant everything in my life. I was raised by one of the most earnest praying women – my mother. I still feel the presence of her prayers. My parents never used profanity in front of us, and I never saw my parents argue. They may have argued, but we never heard them. My daddy read the Bible every night after supper. He would read but did not force you to listen – but if you asked him about something, he would read or quote the Bible. Often when we all sat down in the evening, he would tell us Bible stories. This was an influence on all of us children. I have tried to live the kind of life I was reared to live. Now my younger brother is a pastor and has been preaching 50-plus years.

Being faithful to God is so important. There's a principle that the more you give the more you get in return, because you can't out-give God and you can't outdo God. You do something faithful to God, like going to pray for some sick person, and God will reward you for that. Just be faithful to Him and read his Word.

Tommy, my second son, asked me one New Year's what my resolution was, and I said my resolution is to learn more about Jesus. He said, "I like that." I have some of the best children this country has every raised. They put a lot into church work and go to church regularly.

Just as He has in every area of life, God has helped us during the time of death. We lost a baby when it was five weeks old. It was a tragedy – the baby died in the hospital. I was in the military and had just come back from overseas on a 30-day recuperation leave before I left for the Pacific. The baby died of meningitis and they gave me another week extension on my furlough. During that last week of my furlough, the Japanese surrendered and the military called me and gave me an honorable discharge.

Our second son died when he was 50 years old. He and his two brothers had gone to Memphis for a conference. He had a twin-engine plane and had dropped the two brothers at an airport in Cleveland, Tennessee. While there, he called the airport in Sylva, N.C. to see how the weather was because it was drizzling rain in Cleveland. They said visibility was good and did not think he would have any trouble landing.

So we waited for him to call to tell us he had landed okay, but we never got a call. We started inquiring and found out he had not made it to the airport in Sylva. So that night we drove over to the airport in North Carolina from Chattanooga. The airport manager told us a freak cloud had come up after my son had called and it started freezing and snowing. The wings of my son's plane iced up and he did not clear the mountain at Clingman's Dome in the Smokies. The plane crashed and he was killed instantly.

During the storm it had snowed two or three inches. We had just had his plane painted white with a one and a half- inch red stripe all the way around it. It took two days to find the wreckage and another day to get a pack horse in to bring the body out. We had a week of terrible challenges. It was a tough time, but my son was a good Christian man and a hard worker, and I sensed the Lord was helping us during that time.

A few years ago I was fixing lunch one day and my daughter, Babs, who was on another part of our property here, called and said there was a helicopter above that looked like it was searching for a place to land. A while before, one of my friends from church had asked me if I had ever seen the property from the air, and I said no, I had not. He said, "One day I want to take you up to see it." So in a few minutes Babs called back and said the helicopter had landed. I left my lunch and went to where they were. It was my friend, as I had suspected, and he was ready to take me up for a ride.

I got in the helicopter and it would not crank at first. The pilot asked for a wrench to make a quick repair, and in a few minutes we were up in the air. We made a circle and banked to the left, but lost power and we fell into the top of a big oak tree. That tree broke half in two and we rode the upper part of it down. Otherwise the crash would have probably broken every bone in us.

Then the helicopter burst into flames when it hit the ground. I could not get my seatbelt unfastened because there was a heavy weight on my chest and both of my legs were hung up. The pilot was able to thrust his hand in between my chest and the heavy metal and unbuckle the seat belt. He crawled out and got me by the legs of my blue jeans and was pulling me out when the fuel tank exploded. There was burning fuel everywhere, and I was on fire all over. The pilot was able to drag me over to a nearby creek and put out the flames that were all over me. I still have a little trouble with the arm that was most badly burned, but the fact that I survived was a miracle.

Another story of God's faithfulness in my life was when a boat I was on sank at sea. My son, the one who was later killed in the airplane crash, had gone to south Florida to build condominiums. A company in Columbia, South Carolina had heard of his engineering experience – he had a degree in engineering and geology – and they wanted him to join them and develop an island. There were no roads or anything on the island. So my son sold his house and vehicles and bought a 96-foot schooner (a combination sailboat and diesel-powered boat), but it was an old woodcraft.

One day he called and wanted his mother and me to go sailing with him up the East Coast before they left and went to Florida. So he came up to Charleston, South Carolina, and we went over and met them. He had stocked the boat with food and beef, but wanted to go out about 60 miles to the ocean shelf because it was a good place to catch grouper and snapper. We went out there, but on the way my wife got so seasick she became dehydrated. So we just turned around and headed back.

About 2 in the morning we ran into a severe storm. Lightning struck the boat and burned two of the guy wires that held the mast up. Then the boat started to break up. My grandson had just plugged a CB radio up and began to place a Mayday call. However, the Coast Guard later said they had had so many false calls on CB radios that they usually ignored those types of calls.

My son sent up three flares and policemen on the beach saw the flares, so they called the Coast Guard. They sent two boats to rescue us, but the waves were so rough they could not get to us. They called the Savannah, Georgia office to dispatch a helicopter that came in with baskets to get us at daylight just as the boat was breaking into pieces. We did have a lifeboat in our boat, and our son had been trying to tie it off so we could get into it until the helicopter arrived, but the waves were so strong they swept my son off the boat. I threw him a round buoy on a small rope, but the rope snapped and he floated off into the dark. We thought we had lost him.

The helicopter arrived with a one-person basket, but I put three in there and they took them to a nearby island. When they came back I put three more in the basket, and all I had to hold onto was the mast. When they came a second time to pick me up, the operator told me he was also going to pick my son up. I said, "You mean he is still alive?" and he said, "Yes, a shrimp boat picked him up about half a mile from here."

At last the Coast Guard got us all to headquarters. They put the women in one room and the men in the other, because all we had left was what we were wearing. They helped us get dry clothes on, then let us watch the 6 o'clock news – we saw more on the news about our rescue than we did when it was actually happening. After seeing it on the news, the manager of a local hotel called and gave us a big suite. People started bringing clothes and food in like you would not believe, and restaurants sent big trays of food.

Jesus means everything to me. I would not want to even get off the bed without the presence of Jesus. You can feel the presence of Jesus with you all the time. When you pray to Him, you feel His presence. There is a song that says, "Without Him I could do nothing, without Him, I'd surely fail, without him I would be drifting like a ship without a sail." And that is so true. I experienced it!

Psalm 103 became so important to me. One time when I was reading through the Bible I read Psalm 103, and when I finished, I thought, "What did it say?" So I went back and read it again. It said, "Bless the LORD, O my soul: and all that is within me, bless his holy name. Bless the LORD, O my soul, and forget not all his benefits: who forgiveth all thy iniquities; who delivereth thy life from destruction... who satisfieth thy mouth with good things; so that thy youth is renewed like the eagle's."

God has been more faithful to us than we were to Him. You cannot be as faithful to God as He is to you. The more you give, the more you get. The more you praise Him, the closer He is to you. I believe Jesus likes for His name to be praised.

Bringing It Home

The Bible tells us it is commendable to give our life to Jesus when we are young. "Remember your Creator in the days of your youth" (Ecclesiastes 12:1). We can give Jesus our entire life, but regardless of what age we start walking with Him, God is always faithfully with us. "I was young and now I am old, yet I have never seen the righteous forsaken or their children begging bread" (Psalm 37:25).

What tugged at your heart the most as you read Mr. Vernon's story?

Why is it important to give your full life – or what is left of it – to Jesus?

CONTRIBUTING AUTHORS' BIBLIOGRAPHY

Boice, James Montgomery. *Psalms, Volume I.* Grand Rapids, Mich.: Baker Books, 1994.

Chapman, Mike. *A Passionate Pursuit of God.* Chattanooga, Tenn.: Turning Point Ministries, 2006.

Finto, Don. *Your People Shall Be My People.* Ventura, Calif.: Regal Books, 2001.

Graham, Ruth. *Fear Not Tomorrow, God is Already There.* Brentwood, Tenn.: Howard Books, 2009.

_____. *In Every Pew—Sits a Broken Heart.* Grand Rapids, Mich.: Zondervan, 2004.

Helle, Roger L. *A Time to Kill A Time to Heal.* Cleveland, Tenn.: Dereck Press, 2007.

Ketola, Kim. *Cradle My Heart.* Grand Rapids, Mich: Kregel Publications, 2012.

Lee, Jimmy Ray. *Free to Grow Facilitator's Guide.* Chattanooga, Tenn.: Turning Point Ministries, 2006.

_____. *Understanding the Times.* Chattanooga, Tenn.: Turning Point Ministries, 1997.

Jimmy Lee and Dan Strickland. *Living Free Coordinator's Guide.* Chattanooga, Tenn.: Turning Point Ministries, 2008.

Tamasy, Robert J. *Business at Its Best: Timeless Wisdom from Proverbs for Today's Workplace.* North Charleston, S.C.: CreateSpace Publishing, 2015.

Trask, Thomas E. *Ministry for a Lifetime.* Springfield, Mo.: Gospel Publishing House, 2001.

Wilkerson, Don. *The Cross Is Mighter Than the Switchblade.* Shippensburg, Pa.: Treasure House, 1996.

Webb-Witholt. *A Harvest of Joy.* Mustang, Okla.: Tate Publishing, 2013.

ABOUT THE EDITOR

Dr. Jimmy Ray Lee, who has compiled *Faithful, No Matter What* and wrote several of its chapters, is the founder and president emeritus of Turning Point Ministries, Inc. now known as Living Free. He is the author of *Understanding the Times* and several small group studies published by Turning Point Ministries. He is also the author of *Behind Our Sunday Smiles* and *Committed Couples* published by Baker Book House

Dr. Lee is the founder and honorary chairman of Project 714 (now known as STARS/Center for Youth Issues), a chemical prevention/intervention program for schools. He also founded an inner-city ministry called Ark Ministries that reached 600 to 700 young people weekly. He started the Chattanooga Teen Challenge and served as its president for three years. Jimmy served as Nashville Teen Challenge Executive Director during its formative years. Also, he is a past recipient of the Highland Sertoma Club's Service to Mankind Award.

The purpose of Living Free is to help individuals, families and communities dealing with life-challenging and life-controlling problems, to find freedom and wholeness in Christ. Over 3,000 churches have participated in Living Free with over 1,000,000 participants. Sixty-five countries outside the USA are at various levels of development of the ministry. The curriculum has been or is in the process of being translated into 22 foreign languages.

Dr. Lee has earned a Master of Divinity Degree and Doctor of Ministry Degree from Luther Rice Seminary. He serves on the boards of National Center for Youth Issues and Teen Challenge of the Mid-South.

Contact for information: Jimmy Ray Lee, D. Min
P.O. Box 22127
Chattanooga, TN 37422-2127
Phone: (423) 899-4770
email: jlee@livingfree.org

ABOUT THE BOOK PROJECT DIRECTOR

Robert J. Tamasy served as project director for this book, editing and assembling the entire manuscript with Jimmy Lee, and guiding the book through the publishing process.

He is vice president of communications for Leaders Legacy, Inc., a non-profit that focuses on executive coaching, mentoring and leadership development.

A former newspaper and magazine editor, Bob has written, co-authored and edited more than 20 books. His most recent is *Business At Its Best: Timeless Wisdom from Proverbs for Today's Workplace.*

Bob also writes and edits a weekly email workplace meditation, "Monday Manna," distributed by CBMC International, translated into more than 20 languages and sent around the world. And he writes a twice-a-week blog, "Just Thinking," about everyday topics from a biblical perspective. Its address is: bobtamasy.blogspot.com.